CLASSICS IN PSYCHOLOGY

CLASSICS IN PSYCHOLOGY

A NOTE ABOUT THE AUTHOR

MARGARET FLOY WASHBURN, perhaps the most eminent female psychologist of American origins, was born in New York City on July 25, 1871. She studied at Cornell University under E. B. Titchener in the 1890s and was one of the few women to receive the doctorate in psychology before the turn of the century. After leaving Cornell she taught at Wells College, Cornell, the University of Cincinnati and Vassar. Among her many honors were the Presidency of the American Psychological Association (1921), Vice-Presidency of the American Association for the Advancement of Science, and editorship of the *American Journal of Psychology*. She died in 1939.

Though Washburn published on many topics, she is best known for her dualistic psychophysiological view of the animal mind, and for her strongly argued view that all thought can be traced to bodily movement. These notions are propounded in *The Animal Mind* (1908) and in *Movement and Mental Imagery* (1916).

MOVEMENT
AND MENTAL IMAGERY

BY

MARGARET FLOY WASHBURN

ARNO PRESS
A New York Times Company
New York ★ 1973

Reprint Edition 1973 by Arno Press Inc.

Reprinted from a copy in
The Newark Public Library

Classics in Psychology
ISBN for complete set: 0-405-05130-1
See last pages of this volume for titles.

Manufactured in the United States of America

———————◆———————

Library of Congress Cataloging in Publication Data

Washburn, Margaret Floy, 1871-1939.
    Movement and mental imagery.

    (Classics in psychology)
    Reprint of the 1916 ed. published by Houghton Mifflin,
Boston, in series: Vassar semi-centennial series.
    Includes bibliographical references.
    1. Thought and thinking. 2. Movement, Psychology of.
I. Title. II. Series. III. Series: Vassar semi-
centennial series. [DNLM: BF38 W315m 1916F]
BF455.W317 1973   153.4'2   73-2996
ISBN 0-405-05168-9

MOVEMENT AND MENTAL IMAGERY

Vassar Semi-Centennial Series

MOVEMENT
AND MENTAL IMAGERY

OUTLINES OF A MOTOR THEORY OF THE COMPLEXER MENTAL PROCESSES

BY

MARGARET FLOY WASHBURN, Ph.D.

Professor of Psychology in Vassar College

BOSTON AND NEW YORK

HOUGHTON MIFFLIN COMPANY

The Riverside Press Cambridge

1916

PUBLISHED IN HONOR OF THE
FIFTIETH ANNIVERSARY
OF THE
OPENING OF VASSAR COLLEGE
1865–1915

PREFACE

THE first debt of gratitude which I have to acknowledge in completing this book is to the Trustees of Vassar College, who have authorized the publication of the series to which the book belongs, in commemoration of the fiftieth anniversary of the opening of the college. I wish that I had a better contribution to offer in honor of my *Alma Mater*. My second debt is to my colleague, Dr. Elizabeth L. Woods, who by generous sacrifice of time has read through the whole manuscript and suggested many improvements.

Although the problems considered in this essay are of a technical rather than a popular character, I have tried so to present them that a reader without psychological training could follow the discussion. No topic dealt with in the book is treated in anything like an exhaustive manner. It is only fair to say, however, that if all the reading which was done in direct connection with its composition were represented in the list of references at the end, that list would be three times as long as it is. I have not aimed at a thorough presentation of the literature of my subject, but simply at an outline development of my own views. The psychological reader will miss references to Kostyleff's *Le mécanisme cérébral de la pensée* (Paris, 1914). The omission is intentional. The book did not appear until the framework of my theory had been erected. I have felt that any adequate discussion of the theories of others would occupy space which might better be given to the consideration of the bearing of facts on my own views.

MARGARET FLOY WASHBURN.

CONTENTS

INTRODUCTION

From the point of view of scientific investigation no two subjects could present a stronger contrast than the two named in the title of this book. Movement is the ultimate fact of physical science. The measurement of the direction and velocity of movements is the most satisfactory achievement of science, and the scientist is contented with his explanation of any natural phenomenon when he has reduced it to movements and expressed their relations in a mathematical formula. On the other hand, nothing could be less attractive to the scientific investigator with such an aim than the domain of mental imagery, the world of imaginary objects. Mental images are not only removed from general observation and open to direct study only by the individual who experiences them, but even he has no satisfactory way of measuring them and reducing them to mathematics.

The movements of a living being are of all forms of movements the most complicated and difficult to study. Science is still a long way from showing that even the movements of an amœba, the simplest of animals, are merely combinations of the invisible movements which constitute physico-chemical processes. But at least the movements which an animal makes belong to the world of external observation; they have direction and velocity; they are movements, although very complex ones, and an investigator like Professor Loeb can entertain the confident hope that science will some day be able to show their relations to the movements of lifeless things.

It is not surprising, therefore, that since psychology undertook to call itself a science, there has existed a strong desire to connect the facts of the mind with the facts of bodily movement. There are even psychologists, who, impatient at the difficulties of showing the relation between mental phenomena

and the 'behavior' or movements of the organism, have decided to abandon the attempt, to make no effort at an investigation of the inner world of sensations, images, and thoughts,
and to confine all their energies to the study of how persons and
animals act, how they move. For making such a decision no
one can be blamed. A man has but one life, and if he prefers
to invest his mental capital in an enterprise that promises
quicker returns than are offered by the scientific study of the
inner life, the life of the mind, he is within his rights. But he
is ignoring a challenge, nevertheless: shall we say that here, in
the world of conscious experiences, as distinct from the world
of external movements, is a whole field of phenomena which
man must leave unworked because he can borrow no tools from
other fields? Perhaps it is the irritating consciousness of this
challenge that has led the most extreme 'behaviorist,' Professor Watson, actually to deny that there exists any mental
imagery. If we are all deluded in the belief that we possess
mental images, then evidently the behaviorist who refuses to
study them is wise; although even under such circumstances,
one might think, a scientific investigator would feel some
curiosity regarding the cause of so wide-spread a delusion.
Watson (147) seems to argue that because the facts regarding
mental imagery are very complicated, therefore there is no
such thing as a mental image, whereas the opposite inference
would be quite as natural. Because Fernald (35) and Angell (5)
have shown that the differences between individual minds
as regards the occurrence of mental imagery are less simple
than had been supposed, "the way," he says, "is paved for
the dismissal of the image from psychology." But we have
just as good reason for denying the existence of all conscious
processes whatever as we have for denying the existence of
mental images. An outsider, studying merely my bodily movements, would be quite as unable to explain why a certain vapor
should affect me with the peculiar experience of the smell of
kerosene, or why certain ether vibrations should make me see
red, when red does not look at all like a vibration, as he would

be to detect the existence of purely 'imaginary' smells and colors in my consciousness.

If, then, one persists in being curious about the "inner aspect" of behavior and in believing that a man's thoughts are as legitimate objects for scientific study as his movements; if on the other hand, one realizes that it is through his movements that man takes his place in the rest of the order of nature, then the proper outcome of this twofold interest is an attempt to show that the whole of the inner life is correlated with and dependent upon bodily movement. This attempt is everywhere visible in the psychological theories of the past twenty years. The excuse which the present essay would offer for its own existence is that while the facts of attention, perception, and emotion have had their relation to bodily movement fully discussed,[1] there still remain many phenomena connected with the complexer life of the mind, the revival of past experiences and the construction of new thoughts and ideas, whose connection with motor processes has not been satisfactorily traced. Thus McDougall (73) can challenge the believers in a parallelism between mental and physical processes to show that certain forms of memory can possibly be due to associations between movements. Even the relation of consciousness itself to movement is not yet clearly conceived.

Nothing could be less dogmatic than the spirit in which this sketch of a motor theory of mental processes is put forward. There are grave dangers attending the attempt to form a complex and self-consistent theory where an appeal to fact is not possible at every step; and one of the chief dangers is that of taking self-consistency as equivalent to truth, of thinking that a subordinate hypothesis, for instance, must be true because it fits nicely with the rest of the theory, even though the whole structure be hung up in the air. And yet in psychology especially, it seems to me, one may be permitted to push theory ahead of fact. For clearly the phenomena of the mind are

[1] See *e.g.*, Ribot (116, 117), Lange (66), Münsterberg (94, 95), James (57), Judd (60).

enormously complicated. When a psychologist records the results of an experimental research, he usually analyzes them only from the point of view that he had in making the research: it is so difficult to analyze them at all that he has no time to do more. Thus he may practically throw away as worthless for his purpose material that to another investigator would be highly important. Hence a person with a theory to test nearly always has to make his own experiments: he looks through the literature in vain, for the men who might easily have observed the phenomenon in which he is interested overlooked the data bearing upon it because their own interest was elsewhere. The result is that the theories which get tested by experiment are usually theories covering a relatively small field; no one person in a lifetime could establish by experiment a complete theory of the motor basis of all mental processes. Yet there is an advantage to be gained by the attempt to construct such a theory: its failures and shortcomings especially may be helpful. The hypotheses developed in this book are not only often impossible to test experimentally, but may even be contradicted by known facts which I have overlooked. And yet I think the labor of writing the book will not have been wholly wasted if here and there a suggestion or a warning is derived which is of use to psychological theory.

The points where I have departed most from what is generally recognized as orthodox psychological doctrine are perhaps the theory regarding the physiological basis of central excitation, and the attempt to utilize, as actual causal mechanisms, certain motor processes which have been neglected by psychological theory as mere incidental phenomena. The most important of these neglected motor processes are the slight actual muscular contractions which accompany all attentive consciousness and are the basis, I believe, of all associative activity. Another motor process to which I have assigned a leading function is the attitude of activity or strain characteristic of strong attention, which I believe actually constitutes the essence of a problem idea.

The first step, evidently, towards working out the hypothesis that all association is association between movements is to describe the association of movements. And therefore the first chapter will briefly survey the way in which movements are combined associatively.

MOVEMENT AND MENTAL IMAGERY

CHAPTER I

TYPES OF ASSOCIATION AMONG MOVEMENTS

In animals highly enough organized to have a nervous system, we find as the essential feature of that system arrangements whereby a stimulus, that is, some form of physical energy, may act upon the outer end of a nerve and start in it a process of nervous change, which is carried inward through the branch of a nerve cell or neurone affected, through the body of the nerve cell, outward along another long branch, then to the branch of another neurone across a point of contact called a 'synapse,' through the cell body and the outgoing branch of this second neurone, across another point of contact or synapse, and through a third neurone down to a muscle, which the nervous process, reaching it through a chain of at least three neurones, causes to contract. Thus the animal performs a movement in response to a stimulus. A great number of such pathways exist in any of the higher animals, either ready at birth to make the animal move in a particular way when a certain force acts upon it (as when a young bird not yet hatched from the egg, under the stimulus of the mother's alarm cry, checks the piping noise it has been making), or developing in the course of the animal's growth, but developing out of its innate equipment and not learned by experience (as when the bird, when its nesting-time comes, builds a nest without being taught).

So, because of innate pathways in the nervous system, an animal comes into the world ready to make, or to grow naturally to make, certain responses in the form of movements to the forces that act upon it from outside. These innate responses are called 'reflex movements,' and the nervous pathways by which they are made are often called 'reflex arcs.' But we cannot, of course, think of the nervous system as composed of an aggregation of disconnected reflex arcs. It is probable that every nerve cell with its branches, forming the unit called a 'neurone' has connections, directly or indirectly, with every other. This does not mean that the whole system is a physical continuity or network of nerve threads: rather, according to the best authorities, each cell with its branches is an independent entity, the tips of whose fibres lie in contact with the tips of other neurone fibres. From any neurone in the nervous system, probably, it would be possible to pass, across many or few contact points or synapses, to any other. Whether the nervous process will actually pass from one neurone to another in a quite different part of the nervous system, however, will depend upon two conditions of the greatest importance.

First, the points of contact between the fibres of different neurones — that is, the synapses — are apparently of such a nature that the nervous process can cross them in one direction but not in the opposite direction. If neurones A and B are in direct contact, and the nervous process can pass from A into B across the synapse, it will never be able to recross back to A. The synapse acts like a valve which allows passage in one direction only. Thus, in a given reflex arc, a nervous process may start from a sense organ and travel to a muscle, but it can never travel back from the muscle to the sense organ. This law has been called the 'principle of the irreversibility of synapses.'

Secondly, every synapse seems to offer a certain degree of resistance to the passage of the nervous process across it. Since every neurone is likely to be in contact with several others, the actual course of the nervous process out from a neurone will be over those synapses which offer the lowest degree of resistance. It will then be actually possible for the nervous process to travel from one neurone to another in a different part of the nervous system, only if the two are separated by synapses which allow the process to cross in that particular direction, and which offer resistances less than those of the synapses leading in other directions. The nervous process could not travel from a muscle back to a sense organ because the synapses cannot be traversed in that direction. It could not pass even from a sense organ to a particular muscle if the resistances at the intervening synapses happened to be higher than those along a different pathway.

The amount of resistance at a synapse depends upon a number of conditions. First, it is low along all innate reflex pathways. Being born to make a movement means, probably, being born with low resistances at the synapses along the nervous pathway leading from the sense organ to the muscles. Thus resistance may be innately low along a reflex arc. It seems, in the second place, to be innately lower along certain reflex arcs than along others. That is, if two different reflex movements are simultaneously excited, one may have an innate advantage over another. This is especially true of movements having great significance for the welfare of the individual animal or the species. The water scorpion responds to the action of light by a turning movement that is of military precision, but if the insect is feeding, it does not react to light at all. The feeding reflex is master of the light reflex (52). A reflex that thus gains the victory because of specially low congenital resistance at its synapses is called a 'prepotent reflex.' The reaction of withdrawal from injury is a striking example of a prepotent reflex: it nearly always has the right of way. The resistance, thirdly, may be greatly heightened at certain synapses by being lowered at others. That is, when the nervous process has a choice between two pathways which would lead to *opposed*, not merely to different, reactions, the probability that it will take one of them is not to be measured by subtracting the weaker resistances along one pathway from the stronger ones along the other. The fact that the nervous process starts along the line of the least resistance actually raises the resistances along the other line. While before one movement was actually begun the opposite one was to a certain extent possible, it is now less possible by virtue of a certain amount of inhibition. The resistances at synapses, then, may be actually raised if a pathway

leading to an antagonistic movement is in action. Such antagonistic movements, for instance, are those of extending and of
flexing the fingers, or of singing a low and a high note. Fourthly,
resistances at synapses are left, after the nervous process has
passed across them, lower than they were before, so that, for a
time at least, it is easier for the nervous process to take the same
pathway again. And every time a nervous process transverses
a synapse it reduces the resistance.

All these statements are perfectly familiar to every student
of psychology and of the physiology of the nervous system.
Keeping them clearly in mind, we may pass on to survey very
briefly the way in which reflex arcs are organized into systems.
It is evident that in an animal whose structure is at all complicated, even a comparatively simple movement like the stretch-
ing out of a paw involves the contraction of more than one
muscle and the operation, therefore, of more than a simple
reflex arc. Plainly, movements that an animal is born to make
must require not only that resistances shall be low at the
synapses along certain pathways in the nervous system, but
that these pathways shall be organized into combinations, such
that several pathways shall regularly be traversed together.
Certain muscles must not contract unless certain other ones
contract also: further, antagonistic muscles must be kept from
contracting; that is, their contraction must be inhibited. A
part of the inborn equipment for moving given to every animal
consists in such groupings of pathways that the proper combinations can be brought about. The groupings, it is natural to
assume, would be of two types: on the one hand, it would be
arranged that a number of neurones leading from different
points open to stimulation should converge into a 'final common path,' leading to the muscles, so that stimuli from these
points should be able to combine in the production of the same
movement. On the other hand, a neurone leading from a single
point stimulated should have connections with neurones leading to a number of different muscles, so that the movement

made in response to a single stimulus may be a complex one, involving the contraction of one system of muscles and the relaxation of others. For instance, a ray of light falling on a single point of the retina should be able to bring about the rather complicated movements of raising or lowering the eyes until it falls on the fovea. At this point we may note that the organization of movements into systems does not seem to call for any direct connection between one neurone leading from a point of stimulation and another neurone leading from a point of stimulation; between what we may call, for short, one sensory neurone and another. Sherrington says (126, pages 140, 141), "In the central nervous system of vertebrates, afferent neurones A and B, in their convergence toward and impingement upon another neurone Z, towards which they conduct, do not make any lateral connection directly one with the other — at least, there seems no clear evidence that they do." The significance of this fact will appear later.

But our concern is not primarily with the innate nervous organization of man or of animals. Rather, as psychologists we are interested in the changes which that organization undergoes in an individual's lifetime. The phenomena which we call 'psychic,' which we can observe only each of us for himself, as contrasted with the facts of outward behavior which hundreds of persons can observe at the same time, seem to be connected not with innate behavior so much as with the acquisition of new ways of acting. The relation of consciousness to movement will be considered in the next chapter. Without further discussion of this point, let us turn to the ways in which new forms of movement are acquired by the organism.

No simple new movement can ever be made. Just as we can get only the sensations we were born to get, so we can make only the simple movements we were born to make. Just as all the creations of imagination are only new combinations of old elements, so all the complicated movements we acquire in a lifetime — the skill of a mechanician, the fingering of a violinist — are new combinations of simple movements we were born to perform. We could learn to perform a new simple movement only if we could create a new muscle, and that no athletic training will do. The formation of new combinations, then, of movements that are themselves given to us by our inborn constitution, is what we have to study.

Every simple movement that we are ever capable of performing has some stimulus, or set of stimuli, which innately produces it. That is, not only are we born with a certain equipment of muscles, and of motor neurones which cause the contraction of these muscles, but these motor neurones are connected with sensory neurones, and the sensory neurones are connected with sense organs fitted for the reception of a certain definite stimulus that belongs to each reflex arc and will call forth each movement. The sole way in which experience can modify this state of affairs is that a stimulus may come to produce a movement which originally, innately, could be called forth only by a different stimulus. Is the case, now, reversible? Does every stimulus by which our sense organs can be affected have a certain definite movement that innately belongs to it? There must at least be a certain range of movements that it produces more naturally than any others. Every sensory neurone, capable of being acted on by an outside stimulus, is in contact with certain other neurones, and the resistances at the synapses between it and them, whether great or slight, at least are not impassably great, so that the movements to which these other neurones lead are innately susceptible of production by the stimulus in question. Every simple movement that we ever make we were born to make when a certain stimulus or set of stimuli acts upon us: to every stimulus for which we have a sense organ we were born to respond with a certain range of motor responses, if not with one single, definite, foreordained movement.

A study of the processes of learning in man and in lower animals indicates that their essential feature consists in the acquisition by a stimulus, A, of the power to cause a movement whose original stimulus, B, occurred together, or nearly together, with A. Further, it appears that *learning, thus understood, has two types*. In one type, the stimulus A, in acquiring the power to produce the reaction that originally belonged to stimulus B, *loses its own original reaction:* it simply substitutes for the movement originally belonging to it the movement originally pertaining to stimulus B. In the other type, the single stimulus A, while acquiring the power to produce B's motor response, *preserves also its own original response.*

There are plenty of examples of the first type of learning. A whistle is blown before a dog is fed: the original reaction of an uneducated puppy to the sound might be that of cowering in fear; his original response to the actual sight of food would be running towards it. The sound of the whistle loses its fear response and assumes the response that belonged to the sight of food; the puppy runs to the feeding-place at the blast of the whistle. The sound of a musical tone has originally no power over the salivary reflex in a dog, the normal stimulus for such a reflex being the sight or smell of food, but Pawlow's (105) experiments show that when the tone has often been sounded before the animal was fed, the flow of saliva comes to be increased by the tone stimulus even in the absence of the food stimulus. The speed with which a response thus attaches itself to a new stimulus seems to depend on the vital importance of the response; that is, on its prepotency. Harm or great benefit to the organism are themselves stimuli which innately call forth certain movements, of withdrawal or approach. These movements, especially that of withdrawal, are, in general, prepotent; that is, the resistances at the synapses concerned are congenitally low, and a very slight degree of stimulus energy is enough to set them off. Learning to check or inhibit a movement that brings harm is simply a case where stimulus A, originally producing, let us say, a movement towards the flame, being followed by stimulus B, let us say, pain, whose natural and innate response is that of withdrawal, quickly, indeed immediately, drops its own reaction and assumes the withdrawing response proper to pain. The next time, the sight of the flame produces the withdrawing response at once: there is no need to wait for the pain. Schaefer (120) found that the green frog learned to avoid disagreeable caterpillars in two or three trials: the sight of the caterpillar was a stimulus that had cast aside its original motor response of seizing and acquired the new response of avoiding.

The second type of learning is important where new combinations of movements are to be formed. In the type just described, the movements themselves are old, not only as regards their elementary components, but even in their combinations: the only new thing is their being made in response to the particular stimulus used. It is nothing new for a dog to run; not only the individual component muscular contractions, but the whole system of them, is innate. What is new is that he should run towards the sound of a whistle. But in the second type of learning, where stimulus A comes to produce the reaction of B in addition to its own congenital response, evidently a new compound movement is acquired. Now in the formation of a new combination of movements the essential thing is that there shall be no dropping out, in the learning process, of any movement that really belongs in the system. The first type of learning is characterized by the elimination of a movement or movements. The reaction of running away from the whistle needs to be dropped out and that of running towards it substituted. No combination of the two responses is the proper result. On the other hand, a good example of learning of the second type, the formation of a new movement combination, is the getting by heart of a series of nonsense syllables, so that the articulatory movements involved in pronouncing them shall be made smoothly and rapidly with no looking at the printed or written list on the reciter's part. Evidently in such a case it is far from desirable that any of the movements shall be eliminated. All of the syllables need to be pronounced: what is aimed at is not a short cut from the first to the last syllable in the series.

The most natural way of conceiving the arrangement by which such a system of mutually dependent movements is se-

cured is to suppose that a part, at least, of the stimulus for
every movement in the combination is furnished by the actual
performance of the other movements. The contraction of a
muscle does, as a matter of fact, stimulate certain 'sensory'
neurones; that is, neurones whose synapses allow the passage of
the nervous process away from rather than towards the outside
of the body; towards, rather than away from, the spinal cord
and the brain. Muscular contraction may itself stimulate reflex arcs, as may light, heat, touch or sound: the stimulus for
a movement may thus easily be the actual performance of another movement. The convenient term 'proprioceptive reflexes' has been used to mean reflexes whose stimulus is the
process of muscular contraction itself: reflexes whose stimulus is some force outside the body are called 'exteroceptive.'
Now, if it is an essential feature of our second type of learning that all the movements must be preserved, a very good
way of making sure that certain movements in the set should
not occur without the others would be to make the necessary
stimulus for their occurrence lie in the performance of the others.
If the necessary stimulus for pronouncing the last syllable of a
series were the muscular contractions produced in pronouncing
the next to the last syllable, then the proper sequence of movements would be insured. When a series of syllables is learned by
heart, or a series of finger movements in playing the piano, we
get evidence that the movements have reached this degree of
organization, for we can usually recall a given movement in the
series only by running the series through.

In this type of learning process, movements often occur
which do get eliminated. A baby learning to repeat a nursery
rhyme pronounces it month by month more correctly, dropping
out the unsuccessful articulatory movements and supplanting
them with others. A rat is taught to run through a complicated
labyrinth to the food at the centre. Undoubtedly a system of
movements is formed in such a case wherein each turning
movement forms a part of the stimulus for the next. But in
learning the maze path the wrong turnings get eliminated,

dropped out. Thus both types of learning are found side by side: the 'wrong' movements are eliminated and the 'right' ones organized into an interdependent system. We have seen that when one movement is dropped out in favor of another one, the latter is usually a prepotent movement; that is, one which the organism is congenitally more ready to make, whose synaptic resistances are congenitally low. The successful or right movements must then be prepotent over the wrong ones. If a movement of approach leads to actual harm, that of withdrawal will substitute itself, being a prepotent reflex *par excellence*. Thus, many unsuccessful movements will be dropped out because they become connected with a withdrawing tendency that is antagonistic and inhibitory to them. We need not, however, discuss further the unsolved problem as to just how benefit and harm, success and failure, operate to 'stamp in' and 'stamp out' various movements connected with them. Our concern is simply to make clear the difference between the type of learning which involves the elimination of movements and that which involves their preservation and organization into systems.

Let us use the term *movement system* to indicate *a combination of movements so linked together that the stimulus furnished by the actual performance of certain movements is required to bring about other movements*. A useful term for a stimulus furnished by the performance of a movement is 'kinæsthetic stimulus.' There are certain classes into which movement systems naturally fall.

In the first place, not all muscular contractions produce what we should ordinarily call movements. Holding up one's head, in its ordinary erect position, for several hours is not what one thinks of as a movement. Yet it involves the contraction of certain muscles: it is not merely an effect of gravity such as that which keeps a snow-man's head on his shoulders. The maintenance of bodily postures, as distinguished from the movements by which these postures are reached, is evidently due to the continued contraction of certain muscles and the relaxation of certain others. We may designate movement systems which involve prolonged states of contraction and relaxation of muscles as 'static movement systems'; those which involve actual translations in space, movements as we commonly understand the term, will be termed 'phasic movement systems.'

Secondly, it is clear that an important difference in phasic systems relates to whether the movements are successive or simultaneous. In static systems, on the other hand, evidently the muscular contractions take place simultaneously: if one were to succeed another, change of position would occur, instead of that steady maintenance of a condition which is involved in the notion of a static system. But the carrying out of a phasic system may require the simultaneous contraction of several muscles, or their successive contraction, or both. We may therefore conveniently divide phasic movement systems into 'simultaneous' and 'successive' systems.

Plainly, the main difference between simultaneous and successive systems lies in the degree of interdependence that exists among the various movements which form the system. Such movements as those of skating or riding a bicycle require the contraction of a number of muscles in different parts of the body at the same time. To secure the making of these movements together, when the movements are thoroughly learned, it is most natural to conceive that each component movement furnishes an essential part of the stimulus for *all* the other components: it would be useless or even dangerous for any one of the movements to occur without the rest. On the other hand, take again the reciting of a series of nonsense syllables as an example of a successive system. The movements of pronouncing the second syllable have as a part or the whole of their stimulus the movements of pronouncing the first syllable, but of course the pronouncing of the second syllable does not stimulate that of the first: the connection is not mutual. In a simultaneous phasic system, then, as in a static system, each muscular contraction furnishes part of the stimulus for every other muscular contraction. But in a successive phasic system the process is chain-like: the performance of a particular muscular contraction furnishes the stimulus for one other only, which accordingly follows it.

Let us now inquire into the possibility of various types of successive phasic systems. Does there exist a type (*a*) where the movements are linked in such an order that they cannot easily be reversed? Is there a type (*b*) where the order of the movements within the system is wholly indeterminate? Does a type (*c*) exist in which the order of the movements is fixed but reversible?

Examples of type *a*, irreversible systems, are easy to find. The pronunciation of a word of more than one syllable, say, the word 'syllable' itself, involves a system of movements that cannot be reversed. The writing of a word with pen or on the typewriter involves also a set of movements whose order is absolutely determined: the performance of a particular movement, required for writing the first letter of the word, gives the stimulus for the performance of only one other movement in the system, that required for writing the second letter. We have already used the recitation of a series of nonsense syllables as an illustration: it is evidently a case of an irreversible system of movements.

Is there, now, such a thing as a successive movement system in which the order of succession of the movements is not determined (type *b*)? Such systems, if they exist, might be called systems of indeterminate order. Given the performance of any one movement of such a system, it may furnish the stimulus, if the order be wholly indeterminate, for any other movement in the system; this in turn may produce any other movement; and so on. Would not such a system resolve itself into a simultaneous system? Would not, that is, the first movement to be performed excite *simultaneously* all the others, since it is by hypothesis capable of exciting them all?

There seems no reason why a system of indeterminate order should not always be a simultaneous system, provided that its various movements were compatible, and could actually be performed at the same time. But suppose they are incompatible. Let us take, for example, a musical chord. One listens to it, and analyzes it, with a tendency to sing the various notes. It is impossible to sing more than one note at a time. Our analysis, then, must pass from one note of the chord to another, but there is no determinate order of succession in which we do so. The movements cannot be simultaneous, for they are incompatible, but their order may be varied in all possible ways.

But this possibility of varying the order, in the case of the musical chord, is due to the fact that there are external stimuli, the tones, acting upon us, simultaneously and continuously, so that no matter which one is attended to first, the others will patiently wait their turn. In other words, the movements involved in analyzing the chord do not form a true movement system at all. For in a movement system no outside stimulus is necessary except for the initial movement: the others have as their sufficient stimulus the kinæsthetic, proprioceptive processes started by the actual performance of other movements in the system. Clearly, then, it is not possible for a true movement system to exist which is at the same time successive and indeterminate in the order of its succession. For a set of movements to present this character there must be a set of simultaneous and fairly persistent stimuli: now, if these stimuli were themselves produced by movements, as they must be in a true movement system, then the system would obviously be simultaneous and not successive.

Thirdly, do there exist successive movement systems whose movements exhibit an order that is determinate but reversible (type c)? In such a system, if the various movements that comprise it be represented by the letters a, b, c, d, and e, movement a may furnish the stimulus for the performance of one movement only, namely, b; b, however, may give the stimulus for either movement a or movement c; that is, the series, if it starts at b, may proceed either forward to c or back to a. If c is the first movement to be performed, it may furnish the stimulus either for *d*, in the forward direction, or for *b* in the backward direction. In like manner, *d* may call forth either *c* or *e;* *e*, of course, unless the system is to end, can excite only *d*, in the backward direction. Thus, each movement in the system, except two, *a* and *e*, has two possibilities of exciting other movements: *a* and *e*, on the other hand, have only one. Evidently the two movements whose possibilities of stimulation are thus restricted are not necessarily the first and last in time. A reversible series may begin anywhere. The first movement, in point of time, may be movement *b;* the second may be *a;* then the series may reverse itself and the third movement be *b* again, the fourth *c*, the fifth *d*, the sixth *e*, and the seventh and last *d* once more. Neither *a* nor *e* would be either the first or the last movement in point of time, in such a case. Yet nevertheless *a* and *e* occupy a peculiar position in the system, for each of them has only one possibility of exciting another movement, while all the other movements in the system have two possibilities. It is quite evident that the kind of sequence thus involved is what we mean by a spatial rather than a temporal sequence. In a linear spatial series of points it is possible to move in two directions from any point except the points at the extremities of the line; from these one can move in one direction only. On a surface it is possible to move in any direction from any point except points at the boundary lines of the surface, and from these the possibilities of movement are much less than they are from other points. Taking the retina as an example of a surface bounded by a curved line, the possibilities of moving from any point within the circumference are decidedly greater than the possibilities of moving from a point on the circumference. Do eye movements form an irreversible movement series, and does this constitute the spatial character of visual experience?

Clearly nothing like the type of process we have described as a reversible movement series occurs in the case of eye movements. The eyes are moved by antagonistic pairs of muscles: one muscle by its contraction moves the eye to the right, another to the left, a pair, contracting simultaneously, raise it, and another pair lower it. The extent of an eye movement in any direction is limited by the power of the proper muscle or pair of muscles to contract. Any eye movement short of the extreme movements in any direction is produced by a contraction of precisely the same muscles as are involved in an extreme movement, only of less energy. If, as is obviously true, the eye cannot move so as to fixate the end of a line without sweeping over the points between, this means, not that there is a certain fixed succession of distinct movements, but that a single movement cannot reach its maximum energy without passing through the intervening degrees. These increasing degrees of energy, however, are not separate movements, and do not constitute in any sense a movement system. Nor are the motor processes by which the contraction of the muscle moving the eye is checked at different points capable of forming a movement system: they are always the same checking or inhibiting process, consisting in the contraction of the same antagonistic muscles, whether the checking occurs after a movement of brief or of longer duration. No eye movements, so far as one can judge, combine according to the type of a reversible movement system.

Eye movements, however, as well as the movements of certain other pairs of antagonistic muscles, may form the basis of successive movement systems that serve the purpose of reversible systems. These are series of movements, each series irreversible in order, but the order being opposite in each. Take a very simple example. We see a blue spot to the left of our field of vision, a red spot in the middle, a green spot on the right. As our eyes move from one side of the field to the other, we get the sensations in the order, blue, red, green: we can then move our eyes back and get the order: green, red, blue; or we can start with red and get the order red, green, red, blue; but we cannot get from green to blue without passing through red. Now, suppose that we name the colors as we look at them. The articulatory movements will form two series: blue, red, green, and green, red, blue. Each of these is a fixed and irreversible series, but the two may be established with equal firmness and form equally strong systems. Such a possibility, that a set of stimuli shall establish with equal strength movement systems in which the sequence of movements is opposite in direction, is furnished us only by a spatial series of sensations: may we not say that furnishing this possibility constitutes a spatial series of sensations?

To sum up, then: the successive movement system is typically and regularly a system in which the order is determined and irreversible. A system of movements with indeterminate order is not a successive movement system at all, but a simultaneous system: a set of movements with reversible order, if the movements are really different movements and not merely different durations of the same movement, resolves itself into two successive movement systems, each with a determined and irreversible order of succession, the orders being opposite in the two systems.

Finally, there is still another way in which movements may be combined. Instead of forming a system, they may form what we shall call 'sets.' A set of movements comprises a number of movements whose only relation to each other is that they are all associated with one common movement. Thus, the various possible means of realizing a certain desire may be entirely different from and independent of each other, but they are all alike capable of being excited by the movements which constitute the desire. The various words which indicate one of two opposed qualities, such as 'hard,' 'high,' 'smooth,' have nothing in common with one another; but they are all alike associated with the word 'opposite.' We shall find several instances of the functioning of such sets of movements.

CHAPTER II

WHAT do we mean by 'consciousness'? Every one knows what is meant when it is said that a man is unconscious. He is neither awake, aware of the sights and sounds of the outer world, nor dreaming, aware of images that are the product of his own fancy. Consciousness is that which is present when we are either awake or dreaming, and which is absent when we are dreamlessly asleep. That we can define it in no more direct way than this need not disturb us; even the term 'behavior' must include in its definition terms that are no more adequately definable than consciousness is. Behavior involves movement, and movement is change of position in space; but when we try to define space, we find ourselves in just the same kind of situation as when we try to define consciousness: every one knows what we mean, but since both space and consciousness are ultimate notions, not to be classed with anything else, we cannot give them definition, for to define is to classify.

Consciousness, then, we shall take as meaning that which is present when we are awake or dreaming, and absent when we are dreamlessly asleep. The question which we are to discuss in this chapter is: what is the relation of consciousness to movement? Is there any such thing as consciousness that has no relation to bodily movement?

Much of our consciousness is directly related to bodily movement. The greater number of the movements which a person makes during the day are recognized by others as the expression of what is going on in his consciousness. If he frowns or laughs; if he speaks, eats, sits down, walks in a certain direction, we take it all as the outward sign of certain conscious experiences on his part; of emotions, ideas, desires. Yet, on the one hand, we realize that some of his movements have no accompaniment in his consciousness, and, on the other hand, we know, because he later tells us so, that at times when we can see no movement in him he is yet conscious of thoughts and mental images. On the one hand, we know that his heart muscle is in constant motion without his being conscious of the fact: here is movement without consciousness. On the other hand, we see him lying with eyes closed and muscles all relaxed, yet, when later accused of having been unconscious, he tells us of the train of thought that was passing through his mind: here is consciousness without visible movement. Shall we, then, say that there are three orders of phenomena here: movement without consciousness, movement with consciousness, and consciousness without movement? Or shall we try to unify these three orders, and declare that the apparently unconscious movement is really conscious, and the apparently non-motor consciousness is really motor, so that consciousness and movement always accompany each other? Or shall we adopt a middle ground, and say that movement is broader than consciousness; that while there may be unconscious movement, there can be no consciousness without a motor basis? Still another middle position is evidently theoretically possible, namely, to assert that consciousness is broader than movement, and that while all movement is conscious, there is such a thing as consciousness unrelated to movement.

This last possibility, however, suggests that we examine the kind of evidence which leads us to conclude that consciousness is present in a given person at a given time, and to compare it with the kind of evidence that leads us to conclude the presence of movement. Of the presence or absence of consciousness introspection is the final witness. And the testimony of introspection on this point cannot be gainsaid. It is true that if I tell you from introspection, on waking, that I have not been conscious of what has been happening about me, it may be argued that I have forgotten my previous state of consciousness in the shock of waking. But if it can be demonstrated that a certain movement is occurring in my body, and if I assure you that I am unconscious of that movement, there is no possible ground on which any one can urge that I am mistaken. When a bright light is brought near, the pupils of my eyes contract. An observer informs me that they do so, but I do not feel the movement. There certainly are, then, unconscious movements.

The kind of evidence on which we may assert the non-existence of movement is different. It is external observation, and its accuracy depends on the means of observation that are at hand. I look at a person lying apparently asleep. I see the rise and fall of his chest, and the throbbing of his pulse; can I, because I see no other evidence of movement in him, conclude that these are the only motor processes which are taking place? No; I know that there are other motor processes going on which are withdrawn from my observation, such as those connected with digestion: these, however, belong to the class of movements normally unaccompanied by consciousness. But suppose the man is really awake and thinking deeply: I cannot possibly be sure that there is not connected with every one of his thought processes a process of movement, which I am unable to observe simply because I lack the material means to observe and record it. The man himself can in many cases discover such motor processes by introspection; can detect that as he thinks, slight movements of his vocal organs occur, he says things to himself, there occur slight twitchings of his fingers, movements of his eyes, variations in his breathing rate. It would never be safe to assert positively, then, that consciousness occurs without any accompaniment of bodily movement, for movements may be of a nature such as to escape our present means of observation.

There are certainly movements unaccompanied by consciousness. On the other hand (a) all consciousness may be accompanied by bodily movement, or (b) there may be some conscious processes that really have no motor accompaniment. The evidence from observation is insufficient to decide between these two possibilities.

It is the aim of this book to assume one of the alternatives which we have just stated, and to see whether it can suffice as a working hypothesis. Can we construct a working theory out of the assumption that *all consciousness is related to movement?*

Starting with the assumption that consciousness is always related to bodily movements, and holding on introspective evidence that some bodily movements are unconscious, we may ask whether the movements on which consciousness depends are *free, unhampered movements,* or *checked, difficult movements?* This is a problem which has not yet been satisfactorily solved even by psychological theory. Let us see just what the difficulty is.

On the one hand, introspection suggests that the more smoothly and easily a movement occurs, the less consciousness accompanies it. The process of habit formation is the convincing instance of this. A beginner at riding the bicycle makes the movements of balancing himself with anxious attention and care; later they occur smoothly, accurately, and unconsciously. In current physiological theory the ease with which a movement is performed is held to be due to the low resistance offered at the synapses or meeting-points of neurones which the nervous process has to traverse: hence it has been suggested that consciousness accompanies a high degree of synaptic resistance, unconsciousness a low degree. As Montague (86) has put it: "Perceptions are presumed to arise synchronously with the redirection in the central nervous system of afferent currents into efferent channels. When this process of redirection is prolonged by reason of the many conflicts with the cerebral association currents, then the consciousness is prolonged, keen, and complex. When, on the other hand, by reason either of innate adjustments or of long practice, the journey through the central labyrinth is quick, smooth, and direct, then the consciousness, if present at all, is simple, faint, and brief" (page 128).

But, on the other hand, a difficulty arises in the way of asserting that consciousness is directly proportional to the amount of resistance at the synapses. And this difficulty is concerned with attention. One would certainly say that attention and consciousness cannot be governed by opposite laws. That which we attend to is that of which we are most conscious. Attention would seem to be the highest degree of consciousness. Now, attention to one object involves diminished consciousness of other objects. And apparently the motor responses which we should otherwise make to these other objects are often suppressed when attention is directed elsewhere. If we had been attending when the telephone bell rang, we should have risen to answer it, but this well-established response to the bell was suppressed because our attention was fixed on something we were reading. Such a suppression must have involved a very high degree of resistance along the getting-up-and-going-to-the-telephone pathways; yet this high resistance did not mean heightened consciousness of the sound of the bell. The exact contrary was the case. The recognition that complete checking of a motor response often occurs when the stimulus to that response is not attended to led Münsterberg (95) to formulate the statement that the vividness of a conscious process is greater, the freer the pathway to motor discharge is. This statement seems to be, and as a matter of fact is, a direct contradiction of the statement made above, that free motor discharge means lessened consciousness. His critics were not slow in quoting against Münsterberg's theory of free motor discharge as conditioning vivid consciousness, the facts of habit formation. His reply to the objection was to declare that habits are based on connections in the nervous system below the level of the brain cortex, and are therefore not subject to the conditions that prevail in the cortex. He said: "It is merely a specious argument against the Action Theory to urge that impressions become less vivid the more readily they pass over into movement, and are apparently wholly inhibited if the movement takes place entirely without resistance. If we were really forced to the anatomical view that mechanized reactions still pass through cortical centres, the Action Theory would be indeed untenable. . . . Such an anatomical interpretation is, however, clearly indefensible. The mechanization of the passage from centripetal to centrifugal excitation means the formation of subcortical connections, by means of which the disturbance coming from the periphery is conducted to an outgoing pathway before it reaches the psychophysical cortical apparatus at all. . . . As long as the stimulus really has to go to the cortex, it never, however frequently repeated, becomes unconscious" (page 541). This answer treats the difficulty in too cavalier a fashion. One naturally wonders at just what point in the formation of a habit the transference from cortical to subcortical connections, and the consequent complete reversal of the relations between the learning process and consciousness, occurs. Let us suppose that a series of movements has become mechanized, and has thus by hypothesis passed into the control of subcortical centres. Yet, as a matter of fact, no habit is ever so perfectly acquired that if an obstacle occurs in its free performance, attention is not drawn to it. Thereupon, according to the Action Theory of Münsterberg, cortical pathways are brought into play, and as soon as this occurs, the interrupted movement should cease to be attended to because it is interrupted. The very cause that shifted its performance from subcortical to cortical levels, and thus made attention possible, prevents it from getting attended to.

The difficulty, then, remains that one body of facts seems to suggest that consciousness is correlated with delayed and obstructed movement, while another body of facts suggests that stimuli which are not represented in consciousness often have their motor responses entirely suppressed.

It is possible, I think, to find a real solution of this difficulty, but in order to reach it, we shall have to make a careful survey of the ways in which bodily movements are interfered with or suppressed.

There are two ways in which muscles are related as regards their joint action. First, there are *non-antagonistic muscles*. These can be contracted at the same time without mutual interference. Their contraction may result from one and the same stimulus, and they are then said to be identically innervated: several muscles that have to coöperate in the performance of a change in the position of a limb are innervated in this way. Or their contraction may result from different stimuli: the movements of walking and talking, for example, may go on quite well together with no interference.

Secondly, we have *antagonistic muscles*. These are muscles each of which would move a limb in a direction opposite to that in which the other muscle would move the limb. Thus the muscle that lifts the forearm is antagonistic to that which lowers it. The contractions of these muscles are antagonistic movements, and the relation between antagonistic muscles is one of 'double reciprocal innervation.' That is, when one of them is excited, the other is proportionately inhibited. Yet it would be a mistake to suppose that the two muscles of an antagonistic pair can never be simultaneously contracted. They can be, under two conditions. On the one hand, they may be simultaneously contracted as the result of the action of equal stimuli, if the amount by which each stimulus excites one muscle is greater than the amount by which it inhibits the other muscle. There will then be left over for each muscle a surplus of excitation, equal in amount to the excitation of the other muscle, and the two antagonists will be simultaneously and equally contracted. Of course, no actual movement of the part of the body thus acted upon can result; what results is a fixed posture or attitude. A fixed position of the eyes may result from the simultaneous contraction of antagonistic eye muscles; or a fixed position of the forearm bent at an angle of forty-five degrees may result from the equal contraction of the muscles which raise and lower it. On the other hand, if one of the antagonists is more strongly excited than the other, even then the other may contract and exert a certain inhibitory influence on the contraction of the more strongly excited antagonist. The effect of this is movement in the direction of the stronger component, but movement that is slow and controlled, instead of being free and rapid. The arm may be slowly raised, for instance, under this combined influence of antagonistic muscles:

as Sherrington says, there is algebraic summation of the excitations and inhibitions (127).

Now while it is perfectly possible for antagonistic muscles to contract at the same time, as we have just seen, it is clearly impossible for a limb, or any part of the body, to be *actually moved in opposite directions at the same time*. It is not possible for the arm actually to move up and down at the same time; or for the hand to draw a circle from left to right and from right to left at the same time, or for the muscles of articulation to pronounce p and o at the same time, since the former involves closing and the latter opening the lips. The reason why such movements cannot be simultaneously performed is not merely because they involve antagonistic muscles, but because, if a member could be moved in two opposite directions at the same time, the muscle moving it in one direction would have to be at once more strongly and less strongly innervated than its antagonist: the thing is logically an impossibility. We shall use the term 'incompatible movements' to designate movements that cannot be performed together.

Let us now suppose that two stimuli, which we will call S and S', simultaneously act upon the body, and that the motor responses which belong to these stimuli are antagonistic. S will then excite the response M by an amount which we will call eM, and will inhibit M' by an amount which we will call iM'. In like manner, S' will excite M' by an amount which we will call eM', and inhibit M by an amount which we will call iM. The amount of actual excitation which M undergoes will clearly be equal to the difference $eM - iM$, and the amount which M' undergoes will be equal to the difference $eM' - iM'$; that is, each centre will have the amount of excitation it receives from its own stimulus diminished by the amount of inhibition it receives from the antagonistic stimulus. (1) Now, suppose that these residual innervations of M and M' are equal. Both motor discharges will occur, weakly or strongly according to the actual amount of excitation left after deducting the inhibitions: but no actual movement will take place. There will be

an attitude, involving balanced contraction of the two antagonists. (2) Suppose, on the other hand, that one excitation, that
in M, is, after deducting the inhibitory effect of S', stronger
than the excitation in M' left after deducting the inhibitory
effect of S. In this case there will also be contraction, weak or
strong, of both antagonists, but as a result of the greater
strength of excitation in M there will also be actual movement,
slight or strong, in the direction in which M moves the limb or
other part of the body concerned. The chief difference in the
actual nervous processes involved between case (1) and case
(2) will be that different sensory excitations will be produced by
the resulting attitude in one case and actual translation of
position of the limb in the other. If these kinæsthetic excitations are accompanied by consciousness, we should say that
'it feels different' to maintain a fixed position and actually to
move a part of the body through space.

Now may the truth with regard to the opposed positions,
that consciousness accompanies obstructed motor discharge
and that it accompanies free motor discharge, not lie between
them: namely, in the statement that consciousness accompanies
a certain ratio of excitation to inhibition in a motor discharge,
and that if the amount of excitation either sinks below a certain minimum or rises above a certain maximum, consciousness is lessened? This idea will be more fully expressed in the
next chapter. It is not necessary to speculate further as to the
exact nature of the event that constitutes consciousness. One
may hold that consciousness, while it accompanies a certain
ratio of excitation to inhibition, is itself a phenomenon of
wholly different nature from nervous phenomena; or one may
adopt some such suggestion as that of Montague (86), who
holds that consciousness is identical with the potential energy
into which a portion of the kinetic energy of the stimulus is
transformed when there is a check in the motor discharge. One
would have in the latter case to account for the fact that a
motor excitation that is too completely suppressed apparently
gives rise to no consciousness; but it might be argued that a

consciousness is occasioned which is so far split off and dissociated from the rest of consciousness as not to be introspectively discoverable. However, the consciousness in which we are interested is that which introspection can reach, and consciousness in this generally understood sense appears to accompany a motor discharge which is at once excited and inhibited, the amount of excitation being neither too slight nor too great.

The other parts of the hypothesis which will be developed in the next two chapters are as follows. The kind of consciousness which we call an 'image' or 'centrally excited sensation,' such as a remembered or imagined sensation, also depends on the simultaneous excitation and inhibition of a motor pathway. The 'association of ideas' depends on the fact that when the full motor response to a stimulus is prevented from occurring, a weakened type of response may take place which we shall call 'tentative movement.' These movements are actual slight contractions of the muscles which the larger movements would involve; they are sometimes discoverable by introspection and sometimes not; sometimes observable by external means and sometimes not. They may very likely depend on a special system of motor neurones. They enter into movement systems, both successive and simultaneous, just as do the larger movements corresponding to them.

CHAPTER III

In the last chapter we found reason for thinking that a stimulus produces an effect on consciousness when it initiates a motor response which is partly checked in its execution by a process of inhibition, through the influence of an antagonistic motor response. The conscious process that is thus directly occasioned by the action of an outside stimulus is called a 'sensation,' and may be further distinguished as a 'peripherally excited sensation,' to denote the difference between it and a centrally excited sensation or image. For we can get, as conscious experiences, sensations not only from outside stimuli, but by the processes which are commonly known as 'memory' and 'imagination.' Not only can I see red when red light is acting on my eyes, but I can call up a mental image of red, and even, with fair accuracy, images of a whole series of different shades and tones of red. I can not only hear the tones of a violin playing the "Prize Song" from the *Meistersinger* when the violinist is actually before me (or the phonograph is actually running), but I can sit here in my study, with no actual sound stimuli acting on my ears save the voices of the children across the street, and hear the tones of the violin through the entire air. The very important question now confronts us as to whether these images or centrally excited sensations are each one of them dependent on an incipient motor process, as the corresponding sensations would be if outside stimuli were acting.

A fact clear to any observation is that there often intervenes, between the giving of a stimulus and the making of a movement that an outsider can see, a long interval. A man is sitting in his business office. To him there enters an acquaintance and asks him to write a check for one hundred dollars. The man of business says nothing, and makes no visible movement for a considerable interval of time. His friend knows very well, however, that the request has been heard and is being pondered, and waits patiently. At the end of a certain period, the business man draws his check-book and his pen to him and carries out the request. He responds to the original stimulus by making the same movements which he might appropriately have made to it at once; but during the interval between stimulus and response, he will report from introspection, a train of processes has passed through his consciousness which had no outside stimulus; which belonged to the class of centrally rather than peripherally initiated conscious processes. He may have heard in memory the words of another friend urging the claims of the cause to which he is asked to give; he may have had a mental picture of some scene from his past.

Now, it would be quite possible to hold (a) that while these conscious processes are, taken all together, the whole series of them, caused by the delay in responding to the original outside stimulus, and thus conditioned by the initiation of the final motor response, the several and individual centrally excited processes, images, or thoughts, that filled up the interval were not, each of them, dependent on an initiated motor response of its own. On the other hand, I think a very good case can be made out for the hypothesis (b) that each of these centrally excited processes, thoughts, or images, is dependent on its own special motor response. If the first view (a) is maintained, we should suppose that the energy of the stimulus S, not finding full discharge into the motor pathways of the response, passes directly through a series of sensory centres and finally, by this indirect route, finds its way back into the motor outlet which by the direct route was not fully open. As the nervous process traverses each of the series of sensory centres, there occurs, it would be held, a centrally excited conscious process in quality like the sensation which the centre in question would mediate if it were excited by an external stimulus. To take a simple example: the words, 'I promised my wife to give this money,' may pass through the mind of the man who sits silently pondering between the request for the money and the writing of the check. According to hypothesis (a), the energy of the stimulus (the request for the money) passes directly through a series of auditory sensory centres, and the accompaniment in consciousness is the mental hearing of the words in question. The implication of this view is that every sensory centre may have its functioning accompanied by consciousness under two wholly unlike physiological conditions. The first condition is when the energy of an outside stimulus reaches the centre. As we have seen, it appears probable that in such a case consciousness results only when the motor response is partly but not fully produced; only when excitation is partly balanced by inhibition. The second condition is when energy travels to the sensory centre directly from another sensory centre. But if the mere passage of the nervous process from one sensory centre to another is sufficient to call up a conscious process; if, that is, the traversing of a sensory centre by a nervous process coming from another sensory centre and on its way to a third is sufficient to bring an 'image' into consciousness, why is not the passage of the nervous process through a sensory centre on its way to a *free* motor outlet sufficient to cause consciousness in the case of the peripherally excited process? Yet we have noted the probability that the traversing of a sensory pathway by the nervous process is unaccompanied by consciousness when the motor pathway is free. On hypothesis *a*, then, the conditions for consciousness produced by outside stimulation, on the one hand, and the conscious processes, 'centrally excited,' involved in memory and imagination, on the other hand, would be quite unlike: the former would demand not merely the traversing of a sensory centre by a nervous current, but the partial inhibition of a motor discharge: the latter would demand merely the passage of the nervous current through the sensory centre from another centre.

Other arguments against hypothesis *a* will present themselves later on. Hypothesis *b*, that each of the centrally excited processes which make up a train of images or thoughts has its own special motor response upon whose initiation it depends, may now be further developed.

Suppose that a certain motor pathway, *M*, has at various times in the past been excited by energy reaching it from two

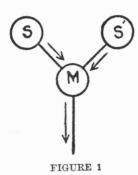

FIGURE 1

different sensory pathways, *S* and *S'*. And suppose that in a given case energy from *S* reaches it, the effect of which is partly compensated by an inhibition from some antagonistic centre. *M* will then be in the kind of incomplete excitation which according to the conclusion of our last chapter is accompanied by consciousness of the sensation *S*. But whatever reason there may be for thinking that a process, accompanied by con-

sciousness, is set up in *S* by the incipient excitation of *M*, would appear to hold also for the setting up of a process in *S'*, a centre which is not now receiving any excitation from outside, but which has formerly, under the influence of outside excitation, discharged into *M*. The very same process which, on our hypothesis, when added to the effect of an outside stimulus makes that effect conscious, will, when it occurs in a sensory centre that is not being externally excited, be accompanied by the type of consciousness that we call 'centrally excited,' the consciousness that occurs in mental images and thoughts. *Whenever a motor pathway is at the same time excited by a sensory pathway and partially inhibited by an antagonistic motor excitation, a process occurs in all sensory pathways connected with the motor pathway by low synaptic resistances, including the sensory pathway that is exciting the motor pathway in question. This process is accompanied by consciousness. When it occurs in a sensory pathway that is being excited by an outside stimulus, it gives rise to the type of consciousness that we call a peripherally excited sensation. When it occurs in a sensory pathway that has no out-*

side excitation, it gives rise to the type of consciousness that we call a centrally excited sensation or a mental image.[1]

How, under this hypothesis, can we explain the occurrence of a train of images or centrally excited processes, each one calling up the next? During the period between the getting of a stimulus to action and the carrying out of the action, a man's thoughts drift from one idea to another: he may in thirty seconds or so have a long train of conscious processes without any external stimulus. In the psychological laboratory, we ask students to take a certain word as a starting-point, and to introspect, without controlling, the images which follow one another through their minds.

On the theory which we are developing, such trains of centrally excited processes depend on the type of movement associations which we have called 'successive movement systems.' Take as an example the case of learning a series of nonsense syllables which are visually presented, printed or written, before one. For the sake of simplicity let us neglect the part played by auditory sensations, peripherally or centrally excited, and consider the process of pronouncing the syllables, as one looks at them, simply as a motor process whose stimulus is visual. In reading the series through we have a succession of visual stimuli, each followed by its proper motor response. Now, as the series is repeatedly read, each motor process comes to have two stimuli: the original visual one, the sight of the printed or written syllable, and also the kinæsthetic 'feel' of pronouncing the syllable just preceding. The more thoroughly the series is learned, the more the kinæsthetic stimulus becomes sufficient by itself, without the visual one, to set off the movement. When the series is thoroughly learned, one can say it 'without book,' that is, without any visual stimuli at all. If, however, in reciting a series of syllables without the copy before

[1] In an article (146) which I published a year or so ago I suggested that the nervous basis of the centrally excited sensation might be a discharge of the nervous energies stored up in a sensory centre, induced by the excitation, from some other source, of a motor pathway into which that centre had formerly discharged. I still think this a possible hypothesis.

one, there is a delay; if some inhibition arises, then one may recall the look of the missing syllable, more or less accurately; that is, delay in the discharge of a motor centre produces, in the sensory centre which formerly discharged into it, that process upon which there is based consciousness of the sensation, centrally excited, which would be peripherally excited if an actual stimulus were acting on the sensory centre and its motor response were delayed.

This is what happens, we may suppose, when the series of syllables is actually being recited; that is, when the movements of articulation are being fully performed. If a hitch comes in the recitation, a mental image of the look of the syllables may be recalled. What, now, takes place when the series is not recited aloud, or even whispered, but merely 'run through' mentally? The thoughts or images which we have fancied to occur in the mind of the man deliberating whether he shall write a check do not take place, each of them, in the course of a series of actual movements that are visible externally. But nevertheless, — and this is a crucial assumption for our whole hypothesis, — *there probably are, going on in his muscles, slight actual contractions.* So when we mentally run over a series of nonsense syllables that we have learned by heart, it must be supposed that slight actual movements of the articulatory muscles do occur. Introspection furnishes some evidence of the fact. Try, for instance, the following test: pronounce aloud or in a whisper the letter 'b' successively twenty-five times, and as you pronounce it try, absolutely simultaneously, to think of each of the other letters of the alphabet. You will find that, whether you think of them in auditory or visual terms, whether you mentally hear them or mentally see them, you have to slip them in between your pronunciations of 'b': the sequence of events in your consciousness has to be 'b a,' 'b c,' 'b d,' and so on. Or try James's old experiment of holding the mouth open and thinking of the word 'bubble.' In this case, to my introspection, the auditory image is impossible, but I can form pretty well a visual image of the word. In general, visual images of words are not so closely dependent on articulatory movements, whether strong or weak, as auditory images are, for all visual images are related also to other movements, as for example movements of the eyes.

Slight but actual movements occur when we are thinking. These movements it is difficult to christen by a suitable name, but for convenience of reference, we shall call them 'tentative movements.' A later chapter will be devoted to their consideration.

A train of associated ideas, each one suggesting the next by a process which travels directly from one sensory centre to another, rests according to this hypothesis on a train of movements each of which, by the kinæsthetic excitations its performance produces, sets the next one off, while delays in the process bring about, in sensory centres that have formerly discharged into the motor centres now partially excited, the processes on which the images are based. The case is fundamentally the same whether the movement system consists of movements that are being fully performed, though hesitatingly, or of tentative movements; whether the series of syllables is recited or only thought of.

Two points in favor of some such hypothesis may be noted. The older view demanded that there should exist nervous pathways directly connecting one sensory centre with another. Now, in those lower regions of the nervous system of vertebrates which have been the subject of exact physiological investigation and experiment, there is no evidence that sensory centres ever have pathways of direct connection with one another. 'Association pathways' connect an afferent or sensory pathway with an efferent or motor pathway. Several sensory pathways converge on a single motor pathway, their 'final common path,' or upon 'internuncial pathways' leading to a final common path, but nowhere does any path directly bridge across from one afferent path to another. Yet apparently such connections would be as useful in the lower regions of the nervous system as they are supposed to be in the upper, cortical regions. Simplicity would argue for the supposition that all parts of the nervous system are built on the same general plan, and that this plan involves the association of movements, but not the direct association of sensory processes.

A second argument for the kind of hypothesis we are trying to form is this: The older view supposed not only that direct pathways connected one sensory centre with another, but that when the two sensory centres were simultaneously excited, the resistances along the connecting pathway were lowered, so that at a later occasion, when a nervous process occurred in one of the centres, it travelled across to the other centre and 'centrally excited' it. Thus was explained the fact of experience that in order for one thing to recall another to our minds, by central excitation, we must have encountered the two things together. In order that the sight of a word printed in a foreign language shall recall its correct pronunciation, we must have heard the word pronounced on some former occasion while we were looking at it. But the older view neglected the fact that merely experiencing two stimuli together will not suffice to form a central excitation tendency. Stimuli may easily act simultaneously, each on its own sensory pathway, and the resistances between these pathways not be lowered at all. For example, one needs merely to suppose that when looking at the foreign word for the first time and hearing it pronounced, one hears it only inattentively. If the attention is not directed towards the sound, if both the look of the word and the sound of it are not attentively experienced, the look will not later recall the sound, nor *vice versa*. Not the simultaneous experiencing of two objects, but simultaneous attention to them, forms a tendency to recall.

It is clear on our theory why the formation of an 'association' demands attention. All association is association between movements. Now, when the association between movements is in process of establishment, the performance of the movements is necessarily subject to many inhibitions and delays, but of course it must be an actual performance. We must suppose then that the actual performance of movements — that is, something more than the mere innervation of the muscles — is what is involved in attention; the excitation being weakened and slowed by inhibitions, but nevertheless resulting in actual though slight movements. We have seen that there are two types of association between movements. The first type is characterized by the dropping out of movements, so that a stimulus takes on a new motor response and loses its old one. The second type preserves all the movements, and links them so that the performance of one furnishes the stimulus for the performance of another. Clearly, it is this second type of association that is the basis of trains of ideas, each one distinguished from the rest, for only where different motor responses are initiated are the sensory processes leading to them accompanied by distinguishable sensations.

One of many other points in favor of a motor theory of attention and the image is that it explains readily what we may call the transitory character of both. "The object of attention constantly fluctuates." We cannot hold an unchanging thing in the focus of attention: it seems to change of its own accord. Some years ago in the Vassar laboratory (124) an attempt was made to investigate experimentally a phenomenon that nearly every one has noticed: the fact that if you look steadily for some time at a printed or written word it takes on a strange and unfamiliar appearance. As our observers gazed steadily at a single printed word for three minutes, they noted that the word was constantly changing; constantly suggesting new pronunciations, new syllable divisions, and so on. 'Acre' would become 'ac-er,' 'a-cree,' and so on. This shifting of the object of attention has been referred to the fact that primitively a stimulus must be a change in the environment of an organism, and that an unchanging object cannot be a stimulus. But in fluctuations of attention it is not really the stimulus, not the external object, that changes. What changes is our reaction to it, and the reason for this constant change of response to a stimulus in attention is that the essence of attention is movement, and that the great majority of motor processes are of the phasic rather than the static or attitude type.

On our general theory, then, consciousness will depend on a certain ratio between excitation and inhibition of the motor response to a stimulus; while recall through association will depend on the motor response's being sufficiently innervated to be actually performed, though only in the weakened form of a tentative movement. We may tabulate the different ratios of inhibition and innervation of response which according to this theory correspond to different degrees of consciousness.

I. Motor response very slightly excited, not enough to produce consciousness. The effects of this excitation appear, however, in the phenomenon of 'readiness,' which will be discussed later. (See page 82.)

II. Motor response *more strongly* initiated, but *no actual performance of a movement, either tentative or full.* This is accompanied by *consciousness* of the stimulus, but *no associative activity* can take place, because associative activity requires the actual performance of a motor response, to produce the kinæsthetic excitations necessary to set other motor pathways into action.

III. Motor response *still more strongly initiated. Tentative movements occur slowly and with delays. Consciousness and associative activity both present:* this is attention.

IV. Motor response *still more strongly initiated. Tentative movements occur smoothly and without delay. Associative activity* occurs, with *comparatively little conscious accompaniment:* these are the conditions which we may think of as underlying *very rapid thinking,* which is nearly unconscious.

V. Motor response *fully initiated and entirely unopposed.* Performance of *full motor response without delay and without consciousness:* the situation in *secondarily automatic or habitual actions.*

Thus, by supposing five different ratios of excitation to inhibition, we can make a bridge between the apparently contradictory but equally true statements that unconsciousness accompanies total inhibition of movement and that it accompanies perfect freedom of movement.

Can we form any notion of what physiological process underlies the difference which we consciously experience between a peripherally excited sensation and an image? We have assumed that the degree of consciousness, what Münsterberg would call the vividness, of both is due to the same underlying cause, the relation between the excitation and the inhibition of the motor pathways with which their sensory pathways are connected. Now, just what makes the difference between the color red as I see it before me and the color red as I remember or imagine it? Certainly it is not a difference in consciousness degree. The degree of consciousness depends on attention: but I may be wholly inattentive to the colors I am actually looking at, and fully absorbed in the color imagery that my imagination conjures up. If you ask me afterward what I thought of a certain red cushion, I may have no recollection that any such object was near me, although I spent some minutes apparently looking intently at it.

All authorities are agreed that centrally excited sensations are much less steady and enduring than peripherally excited sensations. I cannot hold in consciousness the image of red nearly so long as I can be conscious of the red that I actually see. On our theory, this short duration of the image is due to the fact that the stimulus which initiates the motor response on which consciousness of the image depends is produced by another movement; while the stimulus which initiates the motor response on which the peripherally excited sensation depends is an outside physical force. It is obvious that a stimulus supplied by a bodily movement must be of brief duration, unless indeed the movement is not a true movement, but a static motor process or attitude. Much discussion has centred about the problem as to whether a difference in *intensity* is characteristic of the difference between a sensation and an image. To immediate observation it seems clear that the color or tone or smell one imagines is never so intense as an actual sensation. Now, it is not so easy as one might suppose to decide exactly what is meant by intensity.

Schaub's (122) observers, in an introspective study of the intensity of images, made the following reports: the images "lack volume, that is, concomitant muscular and organic sensations"; "with the sensations there are kinæsthetic accompaniments which are not present in the image"; "images exactly like the sensations in intensity, but . . . they did not give the kinæsthetic shock that accompanied the stimuli." There seems introspective evidence that when an outside stimulus acts on the organism, it sets up, not only a definite motor response that belongs peculiarly to it, but also a more generalized and diffused motor response, an 'all over' disturbance. This general disturbance is felt in consciousness sometimes as fused with the sensation proper to the stimulus, if the kinæsthetic and organic sensory excitations which it sets up do not produce a special motor reaction of their own; sometimes it is attended to on its own account, and more or less analyzed into localized components. Whether analyzed or unanalyzed, the kinæsthetic excitations coming from this general motor disturbance are probably the basis of a characteristic difference between the sensation from an outside stimulus and the recalled image; of what Ziehen (161) has termed the "sensual vivacity" of a peripherally excited sensation, and Stout (134) calls the "aggressive character" of a sensation as compared with an image. It is true that Stout, although he admits that when an outside stimulus acts, "the whole organism receives a shock giving rise to a mass of organic and kinæsthetic sensations," expressly denies that these can be responsible for the aggressiveness of the sensation. But his objection does not seem well taken. He says: "It seems evident that they [the kinæsthetic and organic sensations] cannot give an aggressive character to the experience unless they possess this character themselves, and as a matter of fact they are highly intrusive and obtrusive. But if organic sensations can 'strike the mind' in this way, there is no reason why other sensations should not do so too. The ultimate appeal must be to introspection. This shows in the case of the steam whistle [the example Stout has been using] that the sound itself is aggressive in the same way as the organic sensations which accompany it." But this reasoning confuses an unanalyzed experience with an analyzed one. We may reply that the so-called 'aggressiveness' of a sensation is merely the name we give to the unanalyzed 'feel' of the general organic shock produced by the stimulus; when this 'feel' is analyzed and certain sensational components are attended to by themselves, they in turn may perfectly well be accompanied by a diffused motor response in addition to the special motor response involved in attending to them; if they are so accompanied they also are felt as 'aggressive.' The same answer may be made to Stout's further suggestion that, "The organic sensations follow the beginning of the sound after the lapse of about a second, but the sound itself is aggressive from the outset." It is the analyzed experience that is thus delayed; not the unanalyzed feeling of aggressiveness.

When an actual outside stimulus, then, is responsible for the production of a sensation, the sensation has a certain vivacity or aggressive character that I shall assume to be due to kinæsthetic and organic excitations resulting from a general motor discharge. This character is quite evidently stronger, and the general motor discharge is more marked, the greater the amount of the stimulus: there is no reason why it should not be identified with the character of intensity. Shall we, then, say that images have no intensity?

Such a general motor response may be produced, like any other movement, not merely by an outside stimulus, but also by the setting up of another movement: that is, it can enter into a movement system. Thus, I can imagine a very loud sound, and when I do so, I feel certain sensations of shrinking and shock which are evidently the result of movements produced because they are associated with the motor processes involved in the idea, 'very loud sound.' They are associatively produced, and not caused by the action of an outside stimulus on my ear. An image may be more or less intense (as distinguished from being more or less clear, having more or less consciousness degree) according to whether these sensations correspond to a more or less diffused shrinking and shock. In this sense images may possess intensity: I may have the image of a louder or a weaker sound. But introspection seems to testify that the general motor responses thus associatively produced are not identical with the general motor responses that the original outside stimulus produced. The general shock and strain felt when I imagine a very loud sound are like but not identical with those I feel when I actually hear the sound. The difference very probably consists in the fact that the associatively produced shock involves merely the kinæsthetic and organic sensations which were analyzed out of the original, and that what is missing is the unanalyzed and more diffuse components: it would naturally be the components which were attended to separately that could readily enter into a movement system and so be associatively produced. In any case, while the intensity of a mental image consists of the kinæsthetic-organic 'feel' of a general motor response, the 'feels' of which image intensities consist are not identical with those of which sensation intensities consist. Thus, it is possible for Ziehen to say of "sensual vivacity" as a feature of the peripherally excited sensation that it "does not belong at all to the idea, not even in a diminished intensity," and for Schaub's observer to state that the image was just like the idea in intensity, but did not give the same kinæsthetic shock.

Before we proceed to a fuller discussion, much needed, of the subject of tentative movements, it will be well at this point to consider a little further the state of affairs described under II, above: the case where the motor response is very slightly initiated, not enough to produce any actual muscular contraction, either tentative or full. This, it was said, produces consciousness of the stimulus, but under such circumstances the sensation resulting can suggest nothing associatively. Now, suppose that a number of stimuli are simultaneously acting on the organism, and that each of them is exciting its appropriate motor response to precisely this degree. The result for consciousness will be a fusion or blending of sensations which is recognizably a complex phenomenon, but is not analyzed. We may say that when the conscious state at a given moment is felt to be complex and not simple, even though the complexity is not analyzed into its component parts, the reason is that a number of different motor responses are very slightly initiated. As soon as one begins to analyze such an experience, one of course attends to its parts successively, and the motor excitation belonging to each part attended to passes from stage II to stage III; to the stage, that is, where it becomes an actual tentative movement. Thus, for example, we hear a musical chord. It makes upon us a complex impression, even before we analyze it into its constituent tones; this complexity is due to the fact that a number of different motor responses are very slightly excited. When one analyzes the chord, one gives attention to its tones successively, making tentatively the motor response belonging to each.

All unanalyzed complexity of experience depends on the simultaneous initiation of different motor responses, none of them carried to the point of actual performance, even as tentative movements. A fine example of the truth of this statement is furnished by the phenomena of single and double images in binocular vision. When you hold up one forefinger about a foot from the eyes, and look at it, the other forefinger, if held at either a greater or a less distance from you, will appear double. Now, according to our principle, a single object is one which initiates a single movement; an object can be perceived as two only if it initiates two movements. The law under which objects are seen singly by the two eyes is generally stated as follows: if the images of the objects fall on corresponding points of the two retinas, they will blend into one; otherwise they will produce double vision. Corresponding points are points that would coincide if one retina could be placed directly over the

other; thus, evidently the centres of the two retinas are corresponding points, and so are any two points that lie at equal
distances from and in the same direction from the centres of
the two retinas. Now, it is clear that when the images of an
object fall on corresponding points, they suggest absolutely
identical movements of the two eyes. The movement that
regularly tends to be initiated when an image falls on a point on
the retina is the movement which would be required to bring
the image from that point to the centre of the retina, since it is
when an object casts its image on the centre of the retina that
it is most clearly
seen. If, for ex-
ample, the images
fall on the corre-
sponding points a
and a', the move-
ments $a - f$ and

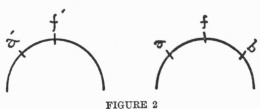

FIGURE 2

$a' - f'$ are initiated, movements precisely equal in extent and
direction: practically a single movement of the two eyes. But
if the images fall on points a and b', non-corresponding points,
then the movement $a - f$ will be initiated for one eye, and the
movement $b' - f$ for the other eye. These are movements in
opposite directions, unlike movements; hence, may we not say,
the object is seen as double?

Two further considerations may be noted. First, on our
theory of the nature of the associative process, evidently two
sensory centres or pathways must be connected with one and
the same motor pathway, to give rise to a centrally excited
sensation or image. For the centrally excited process is due to
the partial excitation of the motor pathway belonging to the
sensory centre which is centrally excited, through the action
upon it of another, a kinæsthetic, sensory pathway. In the
diagram, on page 30, we may assume that the sensory centre
S is kinæsthetic. The excitation of M, meeting a certain
amount of inhibition, sets up a process in S', which at some
former time has discharged into M; the accompaniment of this

process is a centrally excited sensation or image of the proper stimulus of S. At the same time, according to our theory, there should be peripherally excited consciousness corresponding to the kinæsthetic pathway's excitation. Thus, in every centrally excited or image process there would be two components, one kinæsthetic and one of the modality to which the image is referred; in every centrally excited visual sensation, for instance, there would be a kinæsthetic and a visual factor; in every centrally excited auditory sensation a kinæsthetic and an auditory factor. These factors need not, however, be for consciousness in any way distinct, since distinctness for consciousness involves the excitation of two different motor responses, and the kinæsthetic and non-kinæsthetic components of the process underlying the image need not give rise to different motor responses. The interesting point, however, is this. As the associative processes run more and more smoothly; as thinking becomes easier and easier along a familiar line, as the motor responses pass from stage III to stage IV, and the delay becomes less, it is easy to suppose that the non-kinæsthetic pathways become less and less involved, and that the conscious accompaniment of thinking becomes less and less composed of centrally excited visual, auditory, and other non-kinæsthetic processes, and more and more composed of peripherally excited kinæsthetic processes. Thus we may be able, in a later chapter, to understand the fact that thinking tends to become 'imageless' in proportion as it becomes more rapid.

Secondly, the most natural explanation, on a theory which bases the image on the movements made in connection with attention, for individual differences in type of imagery is that they depend on individual differences in the appeal of certain kinds of stimuli to attention. A person thinks in visual imagery habitually if he habitually attends to the look of things; he thinks in auditory imagery if he habitually attends to the way things sound; he is clearly aware of his own tentative movements if he is in the habit of attending to movements. What determines the habit of attending to visual stimuli more than to auditory stimuli may be either the nature of one's occupation, or the development of one's sensory apparatus. A person whose eyesight is not good would not be expected to have his attention readily attracted to the appearance of things, and would probably not belong to the 'visual type' as regards his imagery; if, however, with the aid of eye-glasses he were a great reader, his visual imagery for words would probably be far in advance of the rest of his mental pictures. A person with keen eyesight, whose profession did not involve the use of visual imagery, would probably have much less of it than, say, an architect or a painter. A person who has poor discrimination for musical tones and intervals, that is, whose auditory sensory apparatus is poorly developed, would have less auditory imagery for that reason, although he might increase his powers of imaging sounds if his profession demanded attention to sounds. 'Imagery types' and their variations and anomalies may, I think, be most readily explained as attention types, due to innate differences in sense discrimination and to habits formed by the nature of one's environment and work.

It is evident that this theory of the motor basis of consciousness, whether centrally or peripherally excited, requires, for a creature like man, with an immense variety of sensory discriminations, a great variety of movements. Every stimulus, in so far as it is discriminated from other stimuli, excites a motor response different from that which other stimuli excite. It is possible, indeed, that two stimuli may be consciously discriminated and still produce the same externally visible movement: a person may reach for two different kinds of food with equal vigor and enthusiasm and yet be perfectly aware of their difference. But the motor reactions in such a case are complex, and, while outwardly alike, the inner components may well be very different: the person, for instance, may be mentally naming the two kinds of food. If the whole motor response were the same for two kinds of stimuli, then our theory assumes that they would not be in any sense discriminated. To have a variety of sensations and images, then, demands a variety of

movements. Let us very briefly survey our motor stock in trade.

The muscles of the limbs acquire very few new movement systems in the course of a lifetime, and their movements have little variety. Those of the hands, however, are quite another matter. The most complicated and varied kinds of finger movement systems that we acquire are of two types. There is, first, the type where an object is held between the thumb and one or more other fingers, and moved in various directions. These are the movements which we use in forming written letters, holding a pen or pencil; in drawing, in using delicate tools. They form successive movement systems; in the case of writing or drawing, the movements leave behind them permanent visual stimuli, so that visual imagery tends to be lastingly associated with them. Secondly, there is the type of movement which consists in pressing down with the finger tips, using different fingers successively. In typewriting common words like 'and,' 'the,' and many others, firmly established successive movement systems are formed, and in learning a piece of music by heart the finger movements involved in various phrases become well organized into systems.

The muscles of the face have a certain number of innate movement systems. These were originally all phasic systems, it may be supposed, giving rise to changes of facial expression in connection with various stimuli of importance for welfare: Wundt has shown how, by the operation of the principle of analogy, movements originally connected with accepting and rejecting certain smells and tastes have become associated with other agreeable and disagreeable stimuli. It is noteworthy that facial expressions tend to become static rather than phasic. An expression originally appropriate to a temporary emotion becomes fixed and permanent. The reason for this is probably that the facial muscles are little needed and may remain at rest for long periods of time: a phasic system of arm movements, obviously, could not afford to become static, since the muscles would be called into activity in other combinations.

The eye muscles are an extremely interesting system from the point of view of the movement systems into which they enter. The fixation of the eye in any position may involve a simultaneous static movement system; that is, a true attitude, requiring the steady contraction of certain muscles. The unopposed contraction of the external rectus muscle, for instance, would move the eye away from the nose until the limit of the muscle's contraction was reached: if any point between the centre of the field of vision and the extreme side is fixated, the contraction of the external rectus is balanced by that of the internal rectus, and the contractions have to be maintained as long as fixation is maintained. Binocular fixation also means a static movement system, involving varying degrees of steady contraction on the part of the two internal recti, acting together and producing convergence of the eyes. The eye movements by which lines are explored are, as we have seen, while not successive movement systems themselves, the basis of the formation, between the other movements made in response to visual stimuli, of double successive systems with reversed order, the characteristic basis of spatial perceptions.

The articulatory muscles furnish us with the greatest variety of movement systems, a variety that is practically unlimited. We have only to consider that it includes at least all the words and phrases that can be uttered in any language spoken on the earth's surface, to realize its enormous range. There is nowhere else in the body a region capable of anything like such versatility: the movements of the fingers, complicated as their combinations may be, have not the same varied character to start with; their combinations must be formed out of a much smaller number of simple movements. In speech the single sounds are produced by means of simultaneous phasic systems. The sound of broad *a*, for example, results from the simultaneous vibration of the vocal cords and a certain position of the cheek muscles and the tongue. The guttural *g* is produced by a certain position of the glottis and a slight vibration of the vocal cords. A word involves a successive system made up of the

simultaneous phasic systems that constitute the letters; a phrase, a sentence, a stanza of poetry learned by heart, are still longer successive systems. The slight degree of physical effort which the use of speech muscles involves, and the fact that they are not often required for ministering to immediate practical needs, makes possible the repetition of a given movement system so often that it may be very quickly and firmly established. Another characteristic feature of articulatory movements is that they so commonly produce audible effects, which for a given movement are absolutely constant in character. Very commonly as a successive system is formed out of speech movements, the auditory pathways excited by the performance of the first movement join with the kinæsthetic pathways in exciting the second. This is surely the reason why kinæsthetic excitations from speech movements, if accompanied by consciousness at all, seem to involve some auditory imagery.

Of the greatest significance for the structure of our experience are undoubtedly the motor processes which go on in the internal organs. The general organic response to a stimulus furnishes masses of kinæsthetic excitation which we cannot analyze in many cases, but which are probably highly varied and capable of representing, in movement systems, the different individualities of many stimuli and combinations of stimuli. The possibility that the peculiar motor effect of a stimulus on the organism as a whole may be the basis of the recall of mental imagery has not escaped psychologists. Betz (11), in particular, says that one experience recalls another when they set up the same *Einstellung* or attitude, and this *Einstellung* seems to include the total motor effect of the experience, not only word movements, but "finer organic movements," and feelings. As an illustration of an *Einstellung* which in a given case accompanied the recognition of a face he mentions the tendency to laugh. Müller-Freienfels (92), also, makes the 'attitude' into which an object throws us, and which involves apparently as its most characteristic features organic processes, the essential thing for both perception and recall.

CHAPTER IV

TENTATIVE MOVEMENTS

THE point where the theory regarding the nervous basis of consciousness, attention, and the image which has just been outlined departs furthest from generally accepted psychological doctrine is in the supposition that when a stimulus is attended to, not only is there initiation of a motor response peculiar to that stimulus, but slight actual performance of the movement. Thus, to take a simple example, when one attends to the sound of a tone sung by another voice, our theory supposes that there is slight actual movement in the muscles required to sing the tone oneself. These slight actual movements give rise to kinæsthetic excitations, which when they affect consciousness are felt as kinæsthetic or movement sensations; thus, we can find some introspective verification of the existence of such movements when we listen to the tone; we can feel sensations in the vocal organs. But our theory would suppose that even when the kinæsthetic excitations do not affect consciousness and thus cannot be detected by introspection, they yet are present and perform an important function. I have chosen the term 'tentative movements,' for want of a better name, to indicate these slight actual movements, peculiar to a given stimulus, which accompany attention to that stimulus.

Let us see once more just why we have found it necessary to assume the existence of tentative movements. We get a peripherally excited sensation when a motor response belonging to the stimulus for the sensation is delayed. We get a centrally excited sensation when a motor pathway into which a certain sensory centre has formerly discharged is partially excited from some other source. Two sensations, whether peripherally or centrally excited, are consciously discriminated only when their motor responses are different. If their stimuli lead to the

same motor response, they are, for the time being at least, indistinguishably fused for consciousness. It follows, then, that the basis of a train of mental images or centrally excited processes must be the excitation of a train of motor responses: the sensory centres concerned with the images are not directly excited one by another, but are excited through the arousal of their motor responses one by another. And there is no way in which one motor response can directly excite another except through the kinæsthetic excitations it produces: that is, it must actually be performed; there must actually be some process in the muscles, to give rise to a sensory current that can excite the other motor pathway. This, at least, must be the case for all associations that are of recent formation. It may be that acquired movement systems become after a while so thoroughly organized that a direct connection is established between the motor centres concerned, so that the excitation of one immediately excites the others, without the intervention of any kinæsthetic processes; such is doubtless the case with innate movement systems. But trains of ideas occur on the basis of associations much less thoroughly practiced than they would have to be to arrive at this stage of organization. And these trains of ideas must, unless the whole motor theory is wrong, involve the kinæsthetic excitations resulting from actual movements.

It is only in certain cases, however, that we can get introspective evidence of the sensations from such movements. Sometimes, as we follow a train of thought or imagery, we can detect inner speech by slight movement sensations in the vocal organs, or slight sensations from eye movements, or slight shrinkings, strains, and relaxations in more widely distributed muscles. In other cases, one idea will give rise to another so quickly that no introspection can detect sensations from any motor process. Now, here is a curious point. When introspection has put on record such kinæsthetic accompaniments of thinking, it has commonly described the sensations as 'centrally excited,' as kinæsthetic images and not sensations from actually performed movements. All the introspective testimony to the presence of kinæsthetic factors is simply, it may be urged, testimony to the effect that we remember or imagine the movements concerned, not that we actually perform them. To prove that they are actually performed, we should have to argue that there is no such thing as a centrally excited movement sensation: that *all cases of so-called kinæsthetic imagery are really cases of peripherally excited movement sensation resulting from the actual slight performance of movements.*

It is universally admitted that kinæsthetic images have a marked tendency to result in actual movement, and thus to transform themselves into peripherally excited sensations. "Every representation of a movement," says James (57, Volume II, page 526), " awakens in some degree the actual movement which is its object"; a statement which we should modify by saying that the representation of the movement has no existence apart from the sensations resulting from the actual movement 'in some degree' aroused. "It is well known," says Beaunis (9, page 138), "that the idea of a movement suffices to produce the movement or make it tend to be produced."

Stricker has furnished psychology with a classic example of a person whose kinæsthetic processes are habitually clear in his consciousness; who is in the habit of attending to them and can readily detect them by introspection. He could easily note them, not only when he was thinking of objects as being moved, — when, for example, he lay on a couch and thought of a person walking, in which case "feelings in the muscles" were very clear to him, — but when he imaged any process of change. He says (136, page 18): "When I imagine that a yellow object becomes blue, I can imagine the yellow and blue side by side without thinking of a muscle. But when I think of the yellow as giving place to blue, I must have recourse to muscle feelings: the thing is done with the aid either of the eye muscles or the muscles of the back of the neck." Now, the possibility occurred to Stricker that these "muscle feelings" which were so noticeable a part of his experience in general were the results of actual muscular contraction, and that there is no such thing as a remembered or centrally excited kinæsthetic sensation. One might think, he says, that in the centre for muscle feelings there is no residue left behind which can make a memory possible: that when one associates a muscle feeling in memory it always has to be produced over again: precisely our position, that kinæsthetic processes are always peripherally and never centrally excited. And his objection to this conclusion does not touch our own theory. He urges that surely traces of past muscular feelings are left behind, for there is the fact of practice: there is the fact that when in humming an air he comes to a point where he can't remember it, he can often take his fiddle and play it (136, page 36). Evidently, we can reply to this, the fact of practice, that a movement is more readily performed each time it is repeated, has nothing to do with the power to call up a mental image of a movement without actually performing it. Indeed, the two processes of habit formation through practice and the recall of images vary inversely with each other in general: the more thoroughly a movement is practiced the less imagery of any sort accompanies it. We need not conclude, then, that because motor memory, in the sense of habit formation through lowered resistances at synapses, exists, therefore kinæsthetic image memory, which would require a fairly high degree of synaptic resistance, is necessarily possible.

In Ach's (2) experimental studies on the will, he develops a peculiar conception which he calls that of intentional movement sensations. They are one of the characteristic features, he thinks, of a voluntary act. They occur in the interval between the forming of a resolution and the execution of it, provided that there is such an interval of delay, occasioned either by opposition to the carrying out of the movement or by lack of practice in executing it. They determine the direction in which the movement is to be carried out: they can exist only weakly, as indications (*andeutungsweise*), without resolving themselves into actual movement, and the transition from them to actual movement is perfectly continuous. Hence, Ach says, they have often been wrongly called 'innervation sensations.' But they are not the peripherally excited results of actual movements, Ach thinks, for the following reasons. First, they occur before the actual movement. We might answer that the weak tentative movements which we are assuming may precede the actual movement, understanding by the latter term the full execution of the movement; and yet the tentative movements may be actual as well as the full movement. Secondly, Ach urges, they occur when no movement follows. This fact, we may reply, does not mean that they are not movements themselves. Finally, the most serious of Ach's arguments against the peripheral origin of his intentional movement sensations is that they were not abolished by suggested anæsthesia of the part to be moved. That is, a patient was hypnotized and given the suggestion that his hand and arm were insensitive: the suggestion was accepted, but intentional movement sensations were still observed. Even this argument is not conclusive, however, for it is hard to be sure that the suggestion abolishes all sensations from the part affected; suggestions are so difficult to make thoroughgoing. One recalls the case quoted by Sidis (128) where a patient was told under hypnosis to have no more slight headaches and proceeded to have a severe one.

In his *Experimental Psychology of the Thought Processes* (137), Titchener says that while he once wrote a paper in which he expressed his inability to discriminate between a kinæsthetic sensation and a kinæsthetic image, he has now found a criterion which distinguishes them. "Actual movement," he maintains, "always brings into play more muscles than are necessary, while ideal movement is confined to the precise group of muscles concerned. You will notice the difference at once — provided that you have kinæsthetic images — if you compare an actual nod of the head with the mental nod that signifies assent to an argument, or the actual frown and wrinkling of the forehead with the mental frown that signifies perplexity. The sensed nod and frown are coarse and rough in outline; the imaged nod and frown are cleanly and delicately traced. I do not say, of course," he continues, "that this is the sole difference between the two modes of experience. On the contrary, now that it has become clear, I seem to find that the kinæsthetic image and the kinæsthetic sensation differ in all essential respects precisely as visual image differs from visual sensation. But I think it is a dependable difference, and one that offers a good starting point for further analysis" (pages 20–21). We should say that this difference between the coarse, roughly outlined movement which brings into play more muscles than are necessary, and the clear-cut delicately traced movement that involves only a precise group of muscles, is the difference, not between centrally excited kinæsthetic sensation, remembered but not actually performed movement, and movement that actually occurs in the muscles, but between slight, tentative muscular movements, and large, visible, fully executed ones. And why, one must always ask the partisan of movement imagery, is it so hard even for Titchener to distinguish between the movement image and a slight actually performed movement? Perhaps, as he says, they differ just as a visual image differs from a visual sensation, but certainly he never felt moved to write a paper doubting the existence of a difference between visual image and visual sensation. My colleague Dr. Woods writes me with regard to her studies of the process of recognition (156): "My observers admitted an inability to distinguish imaged from real movements to such an extent that I abandoned the attempt to separate kinæsthetic image from actual movement, and used the term 'kinæsthesis' to cover both."

Since, then, it is so generally recognized that the border-line between image and sensation is obscured for kinæsthetic processes, is not the simplest explanation of this difficulty in discriminating between the mental image of a movement and weak sensations from actual muscular contraction, that the images really are sensations from slight actual muscular contractions?

If we grant that there often exists introspective testimony to the existence of tentative movements, what shall we say of the cases where introspection can find no trace of any kinæsthetic process, either sensation or image? Sometimes, as has been said, one idea suggests another when we can discover no muscular 'feeling' at all, either image or sensation. This is true of everybody at many moments of experience, and of some persons more constantly true than of others. Notice that Titchener says, "provided that you have kinæsthetic images"; and certainly some people are aware of little or no kinæsthetic 'imagery.' Stricker furnishes an instance of a person who had much awareness of kinæsthetic processes, and he went so far as to say (135) that his idea of a word was wholly an idea of the movements needed to pronounce the word: whereupon other psychologists promptly denied that their verbal ideas were kinæsthetic at all. There are evidently two problems for us here. First, can we believe that actual tentative movements occur of which even the most 'motor-minded' person is unconscious (ruling out, of course, movements of the internal organs which are never normally accompanied by consciousness)? Secondly, under what circumstances may we expect that tentative movements will be represented in consciousness by sensations?

There is a great mass of evidence to show that actual movements of slight extent take place in the voluntary muscles, without consciousness of them by the person who performs them. One needs only to refer to the literature of 'mind-reading' and to experimental comparative psychology. It is well known that many, and probably all, cases of so-called 'mind-reading' are 'muscle-reading'; that is, that the 'mind-reader' is able to distinguish by the senses of touch, sight, or hearing slight movements of which the subject whose mind is read is quite unconscious. A famous English mind-reader, Stuart Cumberland (26), said in a popular article written many years ago: "In my case 'thought-reading' is an exalted perception of touch. Given contact with an honest, thoughtful man, I can ascertain the locality he is thinking of, the object he has decided upon, the course he wishes to pursue, or the number he desires me to decipher, almost as confidently as though I had received verbal communication from him." That unconscious movements can reveal themselves to another person's sense of sight as well as to his sense of touch was well illustrated by the investigation which Pfungst made of Clever Hans, the trained horse of Berlin. In order to show that this animal's performances in the way of solving arithmetical problems and answering questions consisted really in the response to slight movements unconsciously made by his trainer, Pfungst (108) instituted a series of laboratory experiments with human beings, in which he found that he could discover what number they were thinking of, by beginning to tap with his hand and watching for a slight movement of the head that was unconsciously made when he reached the right number. When they thought of spatial directions such as up or down, right or left, or of 'yes' or 'no,' Pfungst could similarly determine what they were thinking by the head and eye movements they made. Certain thought-readers are known to have made use of auditory clues furnished by unconscious movements on the part of their subjects, and it is quite possible that the arithmetical performances of the Elberfeld horses, who are able to solve arithmetical problems even when they cannot see, are dependent on an acute sense of hearing. As a result of such experiences on the part of experimenters on animals, it is now a regular practice for the experimenter to be always out of sight and when possible out of hearing of the animal tested: no statements on the part of an investigator that he was sure he made no movements which could serve the animal as a clue are now accepted, for we know that he may have made such movements quite unconsciously.

Our second question was: Under what circumstances may we expect that tentative movements will be represented in consciousness by movement sensations? The answer to this question should explain why some persons are so constantly, and every one is occasionally, unaware of such movements when they nevertheless actually occur.

Let us suppose the case where a train of ideas passes through consciousness. On our theory, the nervous basis of this train is a successive movement system. The first reaction, made as a tentative movement, produces kinæsthetic excitations that excite the second motor centre: during any delay that occurs in the discharge of this centre, the sensory centre that belongs to it is centrally excited, and there occurs an image in consciousness. When the second centre discharges into tentative movements, the kinæsthetic excitations which these movements occasion excite the third motor centre: and the sensory centre belonging to this motor centre is centrally excited, giving rise to another image in consciousness. Each motor centre in the system is connected with two sensory centres: the kinæsthetic one which is excited by the performance of the preceding movement in the system, and its own proper sensory centre, visual, auditory, or of whatever nature. Now, the conscious image resulting from the excitation of a motor centre is thus a fusion of kinæsthetic elements with visual, auditory, or other sensational elements. In order that the kinæsthetic elements shall be distinguished in introspection, in order that the owner of the brain whose processes we are describing shall realize that any motor processes are going on, the kinæsthetic processes must be separately attended to: that is, they must have special reactive movements belonging to them. They must produce, not simply the next movement in the movement system, but a special motor response of their own: for example, the response of describing them in language, of saying that they are sensations in the larynx or in the eyes; of calling them sensations of strain or movement or relaxation.

Now, there are two cases where attention to movement sensations is necessary, and where, accordingly, the kinæsthetic excitations will be connected, not merely with the other motor centres in a movement system, but with responsive movements of their own. The first and least important is that where there is the special intention to introspect. The nature of a special intention or *"Aufgabe"* is considered elsewhere (see Chapter VIII). If our definite aim is to observe and discover the kinæsthetic factors that are present in, for example, a train of ideas, then, as we revive the experience for purposes of study, we are constantly interrupting the flow of events by saying to ourselves 'sensations in the larynx,' 'slight tendency to move the lips,' 'strain at the back of the neck,' and so on: that is, we make certain motor responses to the kinæsthetic excitations for their own sakes, instead of allowing them, as they ordinarily would, to excite the next movement in the series without themselves becoming apparent to consciousness. This situation is one peculiar to the psychologist, and is no part of the experience of the common man.

The second case where attention is given to kinæsthetic excitations for their own sake is the case where a full movement is to be made, and made with great care. In this case the movement first occurs as a tentative movement, and there is a slight delay before the tentative movement passes over into complete, externally observable movement. In this pause the kinæsthetic excitations coming from the tentative movement become clear in consciousness, are attended to, and thus when the full movement is made, and the same kinæsthetic excitations occur in greater intensity, the movement is identified as correct. (See the discussion of the feeling of incorrectness, page 202.) It is possible that this was the original function of tentative movements, to try a movement before fully executing it; and that out of this situation, where a movement is made experimentally before being made completely and thus endangering the welfare of the organism, has grown the function of tentative kinæsthetic excitations in producing ideas. If so, the later function has now largely overgrown the earlier one. And as Stricker has said, those individuals who can with especial ease attend to their own movement sensations are apt to be those who are much given to bodily exercises; who are, that is, much in the way of learning new and hazardous bodily movements which need to be performed with great care. It is necessary for such persons to be conscious of kinæsthetic excitations. But most of us, after childhood, perform few movements that are not thoroughly practiced; so we have lost the tendency to attend to movement sensations.

Upon the occurrence of tentative movements and their combination into simultaneous and successive movement systems will be based the whole theory, outlined in this work, of the nervous processes underlying the inner life of the mind. All thoughts and mental images, all the contents of consciousness, rest not simply on delayed full motor response, externally visible, but on delays in the systems of tentative movements. When these systems run smoothly, we have 'unconscious thought'; when delays occur, we have 'sensations' and 'images.' The precise nature of the physiological process which underlies a tentative movement, and the precise difference between this process and that underlying a full movement, it would be useless to conjecture. Is there simply a difference in the amount of the nervous energy sent along a given motor pathway to the muscles, a less amount producing the very slight contractions of tentative movements; or do full movements require the action of more neurones than tentative movements do? The latter alternative must be chosen if the 'all or none' principle, according to which a neurone acts either with full strength or not at all, holds for reflexes. (See for evidence against this supposition, Brown (16).)

The actual muscular contractions which we perform in the course of a day, then, are some of them full movements, visible externally, and some of them tentative movements. The latter are always going on; the former, save for the movements connected with organic processes, may be wholly interrupted by long periods of rest. Tentative movements are very economical of energy. They involve far less fatigue than full movements, and can be performed far more rapidly. They are also not likely to bring the organism into danger. A creature capable of tentative movements can remain in a safe place and escape observation, while if the movements were fully performed it would risk discovery.

The first requisite for the development of the nervous apparatus, whatever it may be, on which tentative movements are based, was evidently the ability to suppress or inhibit the full movements. A creature, to be capable of tentative movements, must be capable of resting apparently motionless under the influence of a stimulus which is nevertheless producing an invisible effect. Thus one of the great conditions of higher intellectual development, as Sherrington (126) and the writer (144) have both argued, is the development of sense organs that enable an animal to respond to an object not in actual contact with the body; distance receptors, to use Sherrington's term. The eye and the ear, for example, give warning of the approach of objects while they are still a great way off. Now, an object in contact with the body must be reacted to without delay: it must be seized or avoided, for it is capable of direct and instant benefit or injury. But to an object far off one may delay full motor response. And only when full motor response does not occur can tentative movements be performed.

Among the higher animals, whose distance receptors are well developed and which are capable of keen vision, hearing, and smell, tentative movements are still limited in their occurrence by the fact that most animals have a very limited repertory of movements. You cannot use muscles for tentative and for full movements at the same time. Most of the muscles of an animal are needed for purposes of locomotion: they have no such apparatus as our vocal organs, for example, capable of performing an almost infinite variety of movements without interfering at all with movement of the body as a whole or any other necessary movements. We can, and some of us do, accompany all our physical labors with talk. Moreover, eye movements are but little developed in the great majority of animals: where, as in the case of many vertebrates, there is no fovea or retinal region of clearest vision, there is no need for eye movements. We are so impressed with the skill and agility of movements of locomotion in the lower animals, whose motor performances in this line are so far beyond our own powers, that we overlook the comparative simplicity and lack of variety involved in their movement systems. But when we consider the number of articulate sounds in all human languages, taken together, we realize that they are based on a capacity for varied movement that all the movements of all the lower animals combined could not equal.

Finally, it would seem highly probable that the cortex is the organ for tentative movements, and that on the development of the cortex the development of tentative movements rests. The very interesting theory of Head (50) with regard to the functions of the cortex and the thalamus naturally occurs to one in this connection. He believes that consciousness, instead of being the accompaniment of only cortical processes in the brain, may also accompany processes in the optic thalamus. "There are two masses of gray matter, or sensory centres, in which afferent impulses end to evoke that psychical state called a sensation. One of these is situated in the optic thalamus, whilst the other consists of a considerable area of the cerebral cortex." When the thalamic centre acts independently of cortical control, the motor response is excessive and there is very poor discrimination; thus the resulting consciousness is of the emotional type. Attention and all the effects which depend upon it are due to cortical activity: "the cerebral cortex is the organ by which we are able to focus attention upon the changes evoked by sensory impulses." [1] These alleged differences be-

---

[1] Mr. S. Bent Russell (119), in a criticism of an article of mine (146), has suggested that kinæsthetic impulses from what he calls 'strain signals' may pass directly to cortical sensory neurones and give rise to centrally excited sensations of various modalities. His 'strain signals' seem nearly identical with what I have called 'tentative movements.' He says: "The theory of strain signals assumes that a motor discharge that is too faint to cause contraction is strong enough to excite certain sensory terminals in the muscles which have communication with cortical centres." His use of 'strain signals' differs, however, from my use of 'tentative movements' in that I make the kinæsthetic excitations act on motor centres to cause the association of movements: he makes them act on sensory centres to occasion images. That is, his theory is not based on the hypothesis that all association is association between movements.

tween thalamic and cortical consciousness are just what we should expect to occur if the motor responses from the thalamus had to be full responses, while only cortical motor responses could be tentative. And it is obvious that our theory regarding the function of tentative movements would explain also why in Head's words, "the sensory cortex is also the storehouse of past impressions."

CHAPTER V

THE SPONTANEOUS RECURRENCE OF MOVEMENTS: THE MEMORY AFTER-IMAGE AND PERSEVERATION

In what we have been saying about the possible nature of central excitation and the mental image, it is the revival of sensations some time after the action of the original, outside stimulus that has been considered. When, in attending to an object, we recall the circumstances under which we last encountered it, the assumption is that our previous experience with it may have been minutes, hours, days, or years ago. I can recall the front door of the house in which I lived ten years since, and which I have not seen since I moved away. Now, I can also, immediately after looking at the front door of my present abode, shut my eyes and recall its appearance. Is there any fundamental difference between a mental image recalled directly after the original stimulus has ceased acting, and a memory image recalled after a longer interval? Fechner (34) suggested, for the former kind of mental image, the term 'memory after-image.' When we glance at a picture and then turn away, for a few moments, unless our attention is distracted, it is as though the picture were still before us; or perhaps a clock has struck unheeded when we were absorbed in work, and presently our attention is drawn to its tones still echoing, not in the air, but in our consciousness.

In the case of a visual stimulus, we must evidently draw a careful distinction between the memory after-image and the sense organ after-image due to retinal processes continuing after the withdrawal of the stimulus. After looking at a bright object, such as an electric light or the sky out of a window, on closing the eyes we see for a while a bright image still lingering, and we are told that this image is due to a retinal process that goes on after the original stimulus has ceased to act. That this retinal after-image, as a phenomenon of consciousness, is dependent like all other conscious phenomena on the partial excitation of a motor response, is shown by the fact that we do not see it unless we are attending to it, watching for it; that is, unless the appropriate motor response is excited. Fechner mentions in that passage of his *Elemente der Psychophysik* where he uses the term 'memory after-image,' several points of difference between the visual memory after-image and the retinal after-image. Instead of considering these just as Fechner stated them, let us ask what differences would most naturally strike one in introspecting the two experiences.

First, it is of course only the positive retinal after-image with which the memory after-image could possibly be confused. A retinal after-image is sometimes positive, of the same brightness as the original, as when on glancing away from an electric bulb we see a bright image of the incandescent wire; and sometimes negative, or of the opposite brightness, as when we see black disks floating before our eyes when we have incautiously looked at the sun. Further, the after-image of a colored stimulus often appears in the color complementary to the original: if we look long at a red disk we shall see a green disk on looking away. The negative and complementarily colored retinal after-images could never be confused with the memory after-image, for the latter always resembles the original. This is one of the points of difference mentioned by Fechner.

Secondly, the positive retinal after-image produced by an object of ordinary brightness is very brief and often not noticeable at all. An object seen in the shadow, presenting no marked difference in brightness from its surroundings, will give no observable positive retinal after-image, but its memory after-image may be perfectly clear. If the front door of my house is in bright sunlight, as I close my eyes after glancing at it I may see a very brief positive retinal after-image; if it is shaded, I shall probably get no retinal after-image at all, but I can perfectly well hold in attention a very clear memory after-image of its appearance.

Thirdly, the memory after-image represents the original object in its proper spatial relations: solid objects are solid in the memory after-image, but the retinal after-image is always seen as flat. Fechner quotes from Purkinje's *Beiträge zum subjektiven Sehen* (page 166), a passage in which the latter contrasts what he calls the after-image and the dazzle-image (*Blendungsbild*). It is not quite clear just what Purkinje had in mind, but Fechner thinks the after-image is what he himself means by the memory after-image, and that the *Blendungsbild* is the retinal after-image. "The topic activity of the sense," says Purkinje, "the touch sense of the eye, places the after-image [memory after-image] outside the organ, as it appeared in actual vision; it can also represent images in three dimensions, and even with movement and twisting of the whole body, this image preserves its original position. The *Blendungsbild* represents surfaces only, is localized in the eye, and follows its movements." The last sentence gives a true mark of distinction between retinal after-image and memory after-image. While the localization of both kinds of images is a highly variable and complex phenomenon, it is clear that the retinal after-image is always seen as a flat, never as a solid object.

The most important point to be considered with regard to the memory after-image, when compared either with the sense organ after-image or with the revived image, is its relation to attention. Can a detail of the original object which serves as stimulus, unattended to in the original, appear in the image; or is the image the faithful reproduction only of what was attended to in the original? Much discussion has turned on this problem, and I think we shall see that sense organ after-image, memory after-image, and revived image form an ascending series with reference to their dependence upon attention for their details.

In the first place, a very little observation of the *retinal after-image* suffices to prove that in it details appear whether they were attended to in the stimulating object or not. Only the impression made on the sense organ, not in the least the impression made on attention, is the determining condition for the retinal after-image. We often note retinal after-images of objects which were quite unnoticed in our surroundings: with the eyes closed we see a green spot in the field of vision and trace it to a red object at which we have been looking with unobserving eyes, our attention occupied with something quite different. This, says Fechner, is a mark distinguishing the retinal after-image from the memory after-image: the former comes whether one has attended to the object or not, but the latter represents only what has been attended to. Whether this last statement is true or not, it seems highly probable from our ordinary experience that the *revived image*, on the other hand, that which recurs after an interval of time has elapsed since the original stimulation, contains only what was attended to in the original. We cannot recall a memory image several hours after an experience, and hope by examining it to note peculiarities which we overlooked when the experience was first received. Revived image and retinal after-image, then, represent opposite poles in this respect: the continued activity of the sense organ does not depend upon attention, but the activity of cortical centres will be revived only if that activity originally occurred under the conditions, whatever they may be, which underlie the psychic phenomena of attention.

Now, what is the case with regard to the *memory after-image?* There is some evidence that it resembles the revived image in so far that the elements in the original object to which most attention was given are the elements which most predominate in the image. Rousmanière (118), in her experiments on Certainty and Attention, exposed for two seconds various objects, such as black letters and numbers and colored geometrical figures, on a gray background. The observer was then asked to report what he had seen, stating the degree of certainty, on a scale of four degrees, with which he recalled each detail. The memory after-image must have been used in making this report. It was found that if the observers were instructed beforehand to attend to a particular feature of the figures shown, such as their color, the highest degree of certainty belonged to the reports with regard to that feature, indicating that they were most definitely represented in the memory after-image. On the other hand, every observer gave some judgments of the highest degree of certainty concerning details outside the field attended to; which may mean only that attention was involuntarily given to these details, and not that although unattended to in the original they were reproduced in the memory after-image.

In my own laboratory some unpublished and not very successful experiments were made to test the relation of attention to the visual memory after-image, in the following way.[1] We had made a number of cards, each card divided into nine compartments, and each compartment having drawn in it a nonsense figure of eight lines. The person experimented upon was asked to look steadily at the figure on the central compartment of the card for thirty seconds, but while she thus held her gaze fixed, she was to keep her attention fixed on some other figure, for instance, the one in the upper left-hand corner, which was of course indirectly and indistinctly seen, but which was to occupy the focus of attention for the thirty seconds. At the end of that time, the observer closed her eyes, and in pursuance of previously given instructions raised her right hand when she saw mentally the image of the figure she had looked at, and her left hand when the image of the figure she had attended to came into her mental vision. These instructions naturally suggested an alternation between the two images which very likely would not have occurred if no such directions had been given, but it seemed to us that if the figure which had been attended to, although it had been obscurely seen and the attention had been subject to the distraction of remembering not to look at it, appeared as a memory after-image for a longer time than did the figure merely looked at, we should have evidence that the predominant elements in the memory after-image are those which were attended to in the original impression. As a matter

[1] These experiments were performed by Miss Elvira Kush.

of fact, the results, obtained from more than twenty observers, showed that the figure attended to appeared alone in the memory after-image 1.3 times as long as the fixated figure appeared alone: some of the observers saw both together for a considerable part of the time during which the memory after-image was observed. It is obvious what the sources of error are here. The instructions to be followed during the period of observation were difficult, and the observer may have failed in two ways to carry them out. On the one hand, attention may have wandered to the fixated figure, and on the other, fixation may have momentarily shifted to the attended-to figure. The question arises whether attention or fixation can better be trusted to remain steady, and unless some answer to this question can be found the results of the experiment have little meaning.

Whether or not the predominant elements in the memory after-image are always those to which attention was directed in the original impression, there is good reason to believe that the memory after-image may, like the sense-organ after-image and unlike the revived image, contain elements that were unattended to in the original. The very curious experiments of Urbantschitsch (141) may be described in this connection. From his account of his method of experimenting it is hard to make out just how far he was observing the memory afterimage and how far the object of his study was a revived image, but on the whole, since the original object was frequently looked at, the process seems to have been essentially a memory afterimage, or at least to have involved in large measure the activity of cortical neurones which had been recently peripherally excited. His method was to ask an observer to look at a picture, word, or number for a time and then close the eyes. Sometimes, he says, the mental image came at once; sometimes only after repeatedly looking at the object. After spontaneous changes in the image had ceased and it had become stable, various external stimuli were applied to the observer: tuning-fork tones were conducted to his right or left ear, cold or warm applications were made to his face, the field of the closed eyes was illuminated by light flashed from a mirror, and so on. The curious effect of these outside excitants was to develop in the memory image details that had not been noticed in the original observation. But not only could such details be recovered by these, so to speak, artificial means: the unnoticed features would sometimes develop spontaneously in the memory image. Urbantschitsch's most striking results were obtained with pictures which were covered so that only vague spots of light, shade, and color showed through. In the memory image of such an object, the experimenter asserts, details of the picture quite unknown to the observer would develop, both spontaneously and when tones were used as stimuli.

The occurrence in the memory after-image of elements not attended to in the original is easily verified by introspection in the case of the auditory memory after-image. Ebert and Meumann (30) called attention to this fact; they point out that unlike the image recalled after an interval, the immediately recalled auditory image "reproduces all the concrete conditions of the impression: voice, accent, rhythm, tempo." They declare that in this respect it resembles the retinal after-image. The auditory memory after-image, as a matter of fact, is practically valuable just because it does regularly contain details that were unattended to in the original, or even, like the retinal after-image, calls our attention to the fact that the original stimulation has occurred. This is evident in the case where a remark made to us goes unheeded while the sound waves are actually operating on the auditory pathways, and only its cortical after-effect is responsible for its being finally noticed. The necessity, from a practical point of view, of some such arrangement is obvious. An object seen can often be looked at a second time; the characters not apparent at the first glance can be apprehended at the second. But a sound is usually fleeting; it is gone beyond recall in a few seconds, and what we did not apprehend while it lasted we must be able to catch in the memory after-image, or we shall lose it forever. A reason will presently be suggested for the superiority of the auditory memory after-image in reproducing unattended-to elements.

Upon the general tendency of any kind of a memory after-image to reproduce in some measure details that were not noticed in the original rests according to Ach (2) the function of this process for introspection. We can rely, Ach thinks, on having every experience, whatever its nature, left over, as it were, in consciousness for examination. The experience itself may occur untrammelled by the introspective attitude, and then, when it is over, it will spontaneously repeat itself, if attention is favorable, and may be introspectively studied. Ach's experimentation was done by the reaction method, that is, his observers were required to respond to the giving of a particular signal by making a particular movement. In each experiment he distinguishes a fore period, during which the person experimented on is waiting for the signal; a principal period, during which the reaction movement is made, and an after period. It is this last that is so valuable for introspection. The ideas which in the after period the observer has of his experience in the earlier periods are to be distinguished, Ach says, from associatively produced ideas (what we have called 'revived ideas' or 'memory images') both by their clearness and by the mode of their origin. It is as though the whole previous experience were present at once, and its details may be examined as if it were an external object; it may be analyzed without in any way interfering with it. Müller (88), on the other hand, who has given us an acute study of the sources of error involved in introspection and the best way to avoid them, objects to this basing of introspection exclusively on the memory after-image, for he thinks that, on the one hand, we may to some extent examine our experience as it passes, without waiting for an after period, and, on the other hand, that the memory after-image of an experience is not nearly so completely a reproduction of the original as Ach supposes, because, he says, it reproduces only what was attended to in the original.

We have seen that this last statement is certainly not true for the auditory memory after-image at least. Exner (33) is one of the psychologists who maintain the existence of an after-effect of conscious processes which is not dependent either on continued sense-organ excitation or on central excitation. He distinguished such an after-effect as a primary memory image. It returns, he said, immediately after the withdrawal of the stimulus; with unattended-to impressions, there is no secondary memory image. The latter occurs in the case of an object attended to for purposes of recall. That is, you have the best chance of observing a primary memory image, based purely on persistent excitation, in the case of impressions to which you did not attend: if you attended to them, you are more likely to have a memory image which is based on the associative connections set up during the process of attention. Daniels (27) in 1894 tried to base experimental observations of the primary memory image, or memory after-image, on a similar hypothesis. The person experimented on was required to read aloud, with entire attention, an interesting story. At a certain point in the reading, when his attention was fully occupied, the experimenter called out a number of three figures. The reader had been previously instructed not to stop at this point, but to continue reading aloud until the experimenter rapped on the table. The rap was given sometimes immediately after the figures had been pronounced, sometimes at five, ten, fifteen, or twenty seconds afterward. At the rap, the reader paused, and tried to recall the numbers that had been pronounced. If his attention had been wholly taken up with the reading, he had formed no associations which would help him to recall the numbers, and only their spontaneous lingering in consciousness would enable him to do so. When the interval between the giving of the numbers and the rap on the table was long, the numbers tended of their own accord to recur to the reader's mind. If they did not thus spontaneously recur, they could not be recalled when the rap came as long as fifteen seconds after they had been pronounced, indicating that the memory after-image under these circumstances did not last fifteen seconds.

Abramowski (1), in a research on the formation of the memory image, published in 1909, finds like Exner a twofold source for memory, but the primary memory image, or memory after-image, does not in his observations assume the character of an image at all. The image, containing distinguishable details, is in his opinion wholly a creation of the intellect, that is, of the associative processes. The directly persisting effect of the original impression is merely a vague feeling, not describable in language at all, but it is the basis of our recognition that we have experienced a thing before. Probably the reason why Abramowski came to this conclusion is that he overdid, in his experiments, the matter of distraction. He showed his observers very complicated 'nonsense' designs, with curves, dots, crosses, and much variety of color and shading. These were presented with different kinds of distractions, given sometimes together with the design itself and sometimes immediately afterward. It is not surprising that under conditions of such difficulty even the memory after-image, which, as not requiring the formation of any associations, should be reasonably independent of distraction, failed to appear in the form of an image. Although these distractions prevented the observer from reproducing the design he had seen, they did not interfere with his recognizing it when confronted with it a second time, from which the experimenter concluded that the primary memory process, while it could not appear in the form of an image, might be the basis of recognition. But of course there must be a limit to the power of a memory after-image to reproduce unattended-to details, if we grant that such a power exists. Undoubtedly Abramowski's method permitted the formation of the visual memory after-image only in so vague a state that its function was limited to bringing about recognition.

On the whole, the truth of the matter seems to be that the memory after-image, unlike the memory image produced by recall after an interval, may contain features that were not attended to in the original stimulus. It is very important to note, however, that the memory after-image will not appear at all unless attention is directed towards it beforehand. It does not force itself upon attention. Even in the case where we realize that some one has spoken to us, a few seconds after he has done so without attracting our attention, there is probably some other circumstance that has turned our attention in the direction of our companion: it may be doubted whether the lingering memory after-image of the sound of his voice ever could have 'attracted attention' by itself.

Our motor theory of consciousness, attention, and the image can be very simply applied to the explanation of the memory after-image and its characteristic difference from the revived memory image, with but one additional supposition, namely, that *a motor centre recently excited tends to renew its excitation spontaneously, provided only that incompatible excitations are not in progress.* Let us suppose that the original stimulus is complex, and that while certain parts are attended to, others remain unattended to: there is consciousness of them, but only vague, marginal consciousness. In terms of our theory, some of the motor excitations, receiving a moderate amount of inhibition, are giving rise to tentative movements, accompanied by kinæsthetic excitations; while others are getting an amount of inhibition that prevents tentative movements: the former excitations are the basis of attentive consciousness, the latter of inattentive consciousness. Now, the former excitations, through the kinæsthetic currents they set up, have the great advantage that they can not only begin to form movement systems among themselves, but can enter into movement systems already formed. Thus, when we look attentively at a design with intent to memorize it, we name the various parts in it, and the word associations thus called up will easily suggest previously formed associative systems of their own. Upon the basis of the formation of movement systems and the utilizing of old movement systems the recall of details after an interval is made possible: hence, only the attended-to parts of the impression can be recalled in the memory image. But all the motor excitations set up by the complex stimulus, whether they involved attention or mere inattentive consciousness, have, we may suppose, a tendency to recur after the stimulus is withdrawn, and in this recurrent excitation, the antagonistic processes that kept certain motor centres from discharge into actual tentative movements may have been removed. Thus, in the memory after-image details may be attended to that were unattended to in the original impression. To put the matter very briefly: those elements in the original stimulus which were not attended to cannot be recalled after an interval because, not producing the proper kinæsthetic excitations, they enter into no movement systems, new or old. They can, however, like all the other elements in the original, be revived in the memory after-image, because a motor centre that has just been active is likely to become spontaneously active again, provided that incompatible motor excitations are not in progress.

The fact that auditory memory after-images are less dependent on attention than visual ones; that is, that a visual memory after-image is less likely to contain details unattended to in the original than is an auditory memory after-image, I think may be explained by the fact that the proper reception of a visual stimulus rests so much more on attention than does the proper reception of an auditory stimulus. I mean by this that attention to a visual stimulus involves much more adaptation of the sense organ than attention to an auditory stimulus. An unattended-to portion of an object seen is often seen with the side of the retina and with a lens unaccommodated to its distance; thus an unattended-to visual object is often not properly seen at all. But the actual impression which an unattended-to auditory stimulus makes on the ear is not very different from that made by a sound to which attention is given.

The superiority of the auditory memory after-image to the visual is implied by many investigators. Calkins (19) found that the most recent of a series of auditory impressions which were to be immediately recalled had more advantage on account of its recency than the last of a series of visual impressions similarly recalled: the recent impression must derive its advantage in immediate recall from the memory after-image, so this result would indicate that the auditory memory after-images were clearer than the visual ones. Müller (88) says that short intervals between learning and testing verbal material lead to an auditory method of learning, because of the tendency to use the auditory memory after-image, which he thus implies is more striking than the visual memory after-image.

How long does the memory after-image last? There have been attempts to answer this question with regard to the auditory memory after-image by the following method. If a series of nonsense syllables or numbers is repeated to an observer at a rate too rapid to favor the formation of associations between them, and he is then asked to recite them 'from memory,' he can readily do so, in fact they almost recite themselves, provided the series is not too long. But there is a sharp and sudden limit to the number of syllables that can be thus correctly reproduced. This number has been called the auditory memory span of the individual. One of the earliest references to it was made by Jacobs (55) in 1887. He regards it as a measure of what he calls 'prehension,' and notes that in school children the length of the span increases with age and is fairly well correlated with school rank. Galton (41) appends the statement that it is extremely short in idiots. Bourdon (14) in 1894, using numbers, letters, and words, also found that the span increases with age, especially during the years from eight to fourteen, and that after fourteen no progress is made. On the whole, the length of the span appeared to be correlated with the teacher's estimate of the child's intelligence. The correlation with age in the normal child is so well established that tests of the auditory memory span have been incorporated into the Binet series of tests to determine whether a child is mentally as old as his physical age.

Now, theoretically one might suppose that when one comes to the limit of his memory span, he reaches the point of time at which the first impression of the series has just faded out of the memory after-image. Suppose that as many as eight nonsense syllables will faithfully repeat themselves in the observer's consciousness just after he has heard them pronounced. The first syllable, then, still exists as a memory after-image. When nine syllables are recited to the observer and he fails to reproduce them, we should naturally say that the interval of time since he heard the first syllable of the series is now so long that the memory after-image of the first syllable has disappeared. On this supposition it would be a simple matter to measure the duration of an auditory memory after-image. But unfortunately it is not the first syllable that regularly vanishes first from the memory after-image, leaving the rest intact. It may be any syllable, or group of syllables, or even the whole series that is gone in a flash as soon as the too-extended series has been presented.

The fact apparently is that some syllables have a longer memory after-image than others. In all probability this length is determined by the degree of attention given to a syllable in the original. The most 'striking' syllables persist longest in the memory after-image. As Poppelreuter (112), who makes the memory after-image or 'secondary process' the basis of all the higher mental processes, would say, the duration of the secondary process depends on the 'consciousness grade' it possesses. In terms of our theory, this would mean that the motor processes which have involved actual tentative movements preserve longer their tendency to spontaneous recurrence. To this advantage there is added the fact that such motor processes may have through their kinæsthetic excitations called old movement systems into activity. For instance, out of the series of numbers 8 2 7 1 4 5 3 the last four numbers may persist in the memory after-image because they are associated with the date of the fall of Constantinople: that is, an associatively revived memory image comes to the aid of the true memory after-image.

No satisfactory way of measuring the duration of a memory after-image has yet been devised. For, as we have seen, the memory span method fails because we cannot take for granted that the memory after-images of all the impressions in the series will be of equal duration, and it is useless to give an observer a single impression and ask him how long the memory after-image of that impression lingers in his consciousness. For he is certain under these circumstances to make more or less effort to recall it by means of associations; thus it will assume, as its duration lengthens, more and more the character of a revived memory image, its recall based on the connections between movements.

Alexander-Schaefer (4), by the way, showed that the memory after-image may be destroyed at its outset by a sudden distraction occurring immediately after the original impression, if that distraction be caused by a source as violent as a pistol-shot. He found that the effect of such a noise on the 'primary memory images' of colors on a rotating drum looked at through an opening in a screen was to make the observers 'forget' what the color was that they had just seen. A less extreme distraction, as the work of Daniels showed, does not have this effect, at least on the auditory memory after-image.

Few experiments on the changes undergone by the memory after-image during its course have attempted to distinguish between this type of image and the revived memory image, associatively produced. There are, on our theory, several causes which would especially tend to alter the character of the memory after-image. The first is the natural tendency of a motor excitation, spontaneously recurring after its original initiation, to weaken with time; this would produce a fading of the memory after-image. Lehmann (58), basing his conclusions on the mistaken assumption that one can recognize a standard stimulus and distinguish it from others only by comparing it with its own image, claimed to have demonstrated the fading of the visual memory after-image, or memory image. He showed his observers a standard gray disk, and then after an interval of five, fifteen, thirty, sixty, or a hundred and twenty seconds, he presented either the same disk, or a lighter one, or a darker one, the observers being required to recognize the original if it were given. The accuracy of recognition decreased as the interval increased, and this Lehmann thought was due to the gradual fading of the memory after-image of the standard. Later investigators, however, have shown that such comparisons can be carried out without the aid of any sort of image of the original standard.

Wolfe (155), acting on the same assumption of the necessity of images for recognition, reported the gradual fading of the auditory memory after-image, or memory image. He used tones as stimuli, sounding the standard tone, of either 496, 408, 320, 232, or 144 vibrations, for one second, and then giving a second tone, either four, eight, or twelve vibrations different from the standard, after an interval varying from one to thirty seconds. In a later series eleven different standards were used and the effect of longer intervals was investigated. The accuracy of recognition was greatest with an interval of two seconds, and from that on diminished as the interval increased. Lehmann noticed a peculiar refreshing of recognition and increase of accuracy at a point differing for different observers and lying between ten and twenty-five seconds. If this phenomenon really depended on a revival of the memory after-image, it might have been due to a later recurrence or 'perseveration' of the image, a phenomenon we shall discuss presently. Whipple (151) in his study of the auditory memory image gives data by which we can distinguish memory after-images from revived memory images in his results, though he uses the term 'memory image' for both. He used five standard tones, of 612, 724, 832, 928, and 984 vibrations, and after an interval of two, four, six, ten, fifteen, twenty, thirty, forty, or sixty seconds, a second tone was given, either the same as the first, or eight vibrations higher or lower. The presence of an auditory image was in many cases evident to introspection: it appeared spontaneously, without any associative supplementing. "Left to itself, it then decreases in intensity and clearness. To offset this, the observer has recourse to various memorial aids: he visualizes the instrument, contracts his throat, with incipient humming, . . . and exhibits all those muscular phenomena which characterize active attention." This is evidently the point at which the memory after-image is supplemented by the revived image. Despite this supplementing, it will hardly last more than a minute.

Secondly, the generalized motor responses on which the intensity of the original sensation was based may very naturally in their recurrence persist for a time which is less than the duration of the recurrent main motor response on which the image, itself, was based. This would make the image appear to decrease in intensity, as well as lose its clearness. Whipple, as we have just seen, speaks of a loss both in intensity and in clearness. Merkel (79) reports that the memory after-images of noises grow less intense.

Thirdly, changes in the quality of the memory after-image might be produced by the tendency of an unusual movement to be supplanted by a more practiced and hence an easier one. If two movements, that is, are both complex, and involve certain common components, and if one of these complex movements is of more frequent occurrence than the other, then the rarer movement, as it recurs, may easily slip into the commoner one, whose synaptic resistances are inherently low. Such a tendency on the part of the memory after-image to alter in the direction of a more frequent experience is indicated in the results of several experimenters: thus Shaw and Warren (143) found that when observers were asked to look at a square, and then go into another room, and pick out an equal square from among ten of different sizes, "for a smaller standard too large a square was chosen: for a larger standard too small a square." Thus, there was a tendency in the direction of a certain middle or average size. Leuba (69) found that brightnesses tended in a similar way to alter in the direction of a middle or average brightness, in experiments which seem to have involved both the memory after-image and the revived memory image. We shall later see that the true memory image has also this tendency to be changed into conformity with the most frequent and ordinary type of experience. Wolfe, in his experiments on tones, reports a tendency on the part of the memory after-image to grow lower in pitch, a fact which he explains as due to its weakening: "loud tones seem higher than they are, weak tones lower than they are." It may be that this was merely an illustration of the tendency of the more usual movement to supplant the less usual one. Since Wolfe's observers were all men, all of the tones he used were of a pitch above what they were accustomed to use in the speaking voice, and the tone reproductions might have lowered in pitch merely by the approximation of their underlying motor processes to habitual movements. Whipple's observers, however, were both men and women, musical and unmusical; their tendency to flat the image appears to have had no connection with either sex or musical practice.

Fourthly, the memory after-image may change its quality because the motor process on which it depends is altered by the action of other motor processes going on at the same time. Movements which are associated in systems with motor excitations occurring at a given time may tend to supplant the movements on which a memory after-image is based. Such a process of assimilation is common in the case of perception: it is the basis of the "proof-reader's illusion," whereby we fail to notice a misspelled word. In Bentley's (10) experiments on the comparison of shades of gray, it was found that when the field of vision was dark between the showing of the standard gray and the comparison gray, the mental image of the standard darkened during the interval; when the field of vision was light in the interval, the mental image of the standard grew lighter. As the research was not directed towards the investigation of the influence of the interval, however, the conditions were not such that assimilation of the image to the context can be said to have been demonstrated.

It is apparently a further peculiarity of the memory after-image that as its first appearance is spontaneous and independent of any effort to recall it by association, the mere fact that attention is not occupied with antagonistic material being enough to allow it to arise; so it tends more or less periodically to keep on recurring. Lehmann inferred that the auditory memory after-image thus recurred at intervals from the fact that the percentage of correct recognitions of the standard tone rose markedly when an interval of from ten to twenty-five seconds intervened between its first and second soundings: the accuracy of recognition was greater with this interval than for shorter intervals. A similar rise in the accuracy of recognition was found by Whipple, but as recognition does not necessarily imply the presence of an image, increase in its accuracy does not necessarily imply a renewed image. But the memory after-image of an auditory stimulus would naturally appear and disappear, for otherwise it would not faithfully represent the characteristics of the original, as it does ("it reproduces all the concrete conditions of the impression, voice, accent, rhythm, tempo"). The original impression is that of a sound having a definite beginning and end: the memory after-image then must have an end as well as a beginning, and must, to be like its original, recur rather than continue.

The visual memory after-image, reproducing an original that is not definitely limited in temporal course, might, one would suppose, fade away continuously, without any recurrences. Yet it too shows a periodicity. Meakin (76) in the Harvard laboratory exposed simultaneously two cards, each carrying a different design, between which the observer divided his attention impartially for five seconds. The observer then watched during the space of one minute the behavior of the memory after-images of these two designs. It was found that the two images alternated in consciousness. Murray (96) later simplified the conditions by presenting one design only, and the persons who took part in her experiments reported that the memory image of the design appeared "spontaneously at intervals which grew longer towards the close of the minute." This periodicity strongly suggests the relaxing and recovery of motor processes.

On the whole, the memory after-image seems to be an experience singularly ill adapted to be studied by introspection alone, and it is not surprising that Martin (75), whose studies of the memory image are based entirely on the introspective method, has no use for the term memory after-image. In one form of her 'projection method,' the observers looked at an object and then 'called up' a mental image of the same object alongside of the original. This image she thinks is composed of a fleeting positive retinal image and a lasting memory image; of a process intermediate between these two and based on the persistent or spontaneously recurrent activity of the cortical neurones, she finds no trace. Certainly her method would not favor the observation of the true memory after-image. She rejects the view of Ach that introspection is based on the memory after-image, for, she says, such images are too fleeting, and we have no evidence that anything like them occurs in other than visual experiences. This last is a surprising statement in view of the fact that hearing gives us most striking and practically valuable instances of the memory after-image, of which we make use many times a day.

The testimony of many psychologists in favor of the existence of the memory after-image is to be set over against Martin's rejection of it. In Lay's (65) study of mental imagery, published in 1898, 'memory images' are distinguished from 'mental images,' and are said to be nearer after-images in their character. Goldstein (43), investigating in 1906 the ability of normal and abnormal patients to recall a group of objects looked at for a brief time, emphasizes the part played by the 'pure impression,' aside from associative activity: the capacity for receiving a pure impression of the objects may stand in inverse ratio to the power of forming associations: the latter is valuable in delayed, the former in immediate recall. Radossawljewitsch (113) also stated that direct recall is a different function from delayed recall and may vary independently. In Moore's (87) study of the process of abstraction, where the observers were shown sets of figures, each set for a very brief interval, and required to recognize similar elements in the different sets, he says that the figures were held in mind in two ways, either by 'visualizing,' or by 'mental analysis': the former would involve chiefly the memory after-image, the latter the use of associations. Müller (88) says that the distinctness of the visual memory after-image is no guaranty of the permanence of visual ideas based on associations, thus evidently recognizing the distinction between the two.

On our theory, the memory after-image is based on the tendency of movements, whether full or tentative, to repeat themselves just after they have been performed. To this tendency there is due an effect of the greatest practical importance. Suppose that a series of movements has just been made, and that the members of the series are movements that could not possibly be performed simultaneously. For example, a series of words has just been repeated: of course, no two words could be pronounced at the same time. Now, all of these movements have a tendency to recur, for a short time at least: but evidently they cannot actually all recur at once. If one of them actually does recur, what shall we say of the state in which the motor centres of the others are? Their discharge even in tentative movements is being hindered by the performance of incompatible reactions, yet they are certainly in a different state from that of motor centres which have not recently been excited. We may describe this condition of theirs conveniently by saying that they have been '*set in readiness*' for further discharge. For example, suppose one is told that when a certain signal is given, one is to do either one of two things, the acts being incompatible with each other. Each of these alternatives is attended to in turn; that is, the movements involved are tentatively performed. If the wait for the signal is long, they may be thought of, that is, tentatively performed, again, but whether or not they are again thought of, if the wait is not *too* long, both will be in a state of readiness to be performed again, although no memory after-images are present to consciousness.

To the readiness involved in the memory after-image process

we must ascribe the fact that when two movements are linked in a successive system, besides the associative disposition whereby the first movement excites the second, there is apparently formed a reverse association, a weak disposition for the second to excite the first. Ebbinghaus (29) found indications of this fact, but it was not remarkable that he should do so, because in his rough method of experimenting more than one syllable was visible at a time. Müller and Schumann (91) gave the matter more careful investigation, and found that series of syllables in which the pairs which formed rhythmic 'feet' had the order of their syllables reversed, the pairs being selected from a number of different series previously learned, were learned in a much shorter time than series in which the syllables from the original series were presented in wholly random order. When, then, a system is formed consisting of the members $A - B$, the kinæsthetic excitation from A becoming the stimulus for B, there must be some way in which the excitation from B also gets a slight power to excite A. The only way in which it would appear possible to explain this is to suppose that the motor pathway for A, which has just been excited, is in a state of readiness to be excited again, and thus actually gets some of the kinæsthetic excitation produced by the movement B. As a matter of fact, the readinesses and the actually recurrent excitations on which the memory after-image is based must be held responsible for the fact that a successive movement system is not a series of events, each of which vanishes utterly from the scene as soon as the next one occurs, but a process whose parts overlap and hence have some of the characters of a simultaneous system. This, as we shall later see, is peculiarly true of successive systems that have meaning: the meaning is often itself a simultaneous system and helps to give unity to the successive system that expresses it. (See pages 141–142.)

The spontaneous tendency of motor processes to recur, in cases where they are not accompanied by imagery, but simply by peripherally excited kinæsthetic sensations, is very noticeable in many cases. The balancing movements made during a few days at sea persist, as every one knows, for a considerable time after the stimuli which occasioned them have been withdrawn. The persistence of organic attitudes is also a frequent experience. One finds one's self wondering what it was that a few minutes ago cheered or depressed one; the organic attitude is still there, although the cause of it has disappeared. Again, I have often had the experience of being reminded, on rising from a chair, to pick up some object that I had laid down by the side of it on seating myself, by the recurrence in the muscles of my arm of a slight tendency to reach down, the same movement that I made when I deposited the object.

Under certain circumstances, the normal tendency of a motor process to recur may become exaggerated, so that it continues through considerable intervals of time. The students of the diseased mind were the first to call this abnormal tendency by the name '*perseveration*,' since its striking manifestations are in the morbid recurrence of ideas and impulses in the insane mind. Later, psychologists observed it, less strongly marked, in normal subjects; for example, Ziehen (162) applied the term 'perseveration' to the disposition, which he observed in normal boys from eight to fourteen years of age, to use the same reaction word repeatedly in association experiments. It was Müller and Pilzecker (90) who in 1900 erected this tendency into a fundamental psychological law and connected it with the memory after-image. Every idea, they said, has a perseverative tendency; that is, it has a tendency, quickly diminishing with time, to return to consciousness of its own accord. As illustrations of this tendency they quote the running of tunes and phrases 'in the head,' the realization that one has misspoken one's self, the images that float before one's eyes in darkness of objects one has been gazing steadily at during the day, and the difficulty with which a person breaks off one task to take up another. The awareness that one has misspoken one's self is clearly a phenomenon of the memory after-image. The case of persistent retinal images is a peculiar one. The most striking phenomena of this description that I have ever experienced were images of microscopic animals that seemed to swim in the darkness before my eyes after many hours spent in watching paramecia; images of the weaving in and out of scratches on the ice after a day of skating, and images of the motion of surf, after long watching the waves break over the rocks. The last-named images were especially interesting because I got them in the field of the open eyes, intermingling with the images of objects actually seen. After spending some hours in looking at the endless variety of rock-distracted surf, I have found that on the walk home, the sandy surface of the road seemed to glide about before my eyes like the foam at which I had previously been gazing. These images all have much of the 'objectivity' and relative independence of attention that characterizes the retinal after-image, and seem to be a kind of cross between a retinal after-image and a perseverating memory image: I doubt whether anything corresponding to them occurs in other modalities. They remind us of the peculiar position which the retina as a sense organ occupies, in being an outgrowth of the brain itself. We may set them aside from the other phenomena of perseveration, to await explanation from the special student of vision.

The chief difference between the memory after-image and what is ordinarily known as perseveration is one of degree. Every process has a tendency to recur immediately after its first occurrence. Under some circumstances this tendency is exaggerated so that the process recurs again and again. Its first occurrence is probably never normally due to perseveration, but rather to the effect of an outside stimulus or to ordinary associative processes: that is, it is doubtful whether in a normal brain at least any process can spontaneously recur if a considerable interval has elapsed since its previous occurrence. When a tune runs in my head, as tunes invariably do, for like Professor Titchener (137, page 9) "I never sit down to read a book, or to write a paragraph, or to think out a problem, without a musical accompaniment," I can almost always trace the particular tune to some suggestion from within or without: the spontaneous feature of it is not its first occurrence to my mind, but the fact that after it has been suggested it keeps on uninterruptedly. That which distinguishes a perseverating process from any other process is apparently an abnormal duration of the tendency to recur. It may, indeed, be true that all the recurrences of a perseverating process are associatively suggested; for example, that not only the first recall of the tune is due to some suggestion, but each of the later recurrences of it as it runs in my head. For instance, it may be some rhythmic process like my breathing or heart-beat that keeps recalling the tune. As a matter of fact, at one time I made a record of my perseverating tunes and the conditions under which they appeared and disappeared, and found indications that a particular tune could be banished by the performance of some unrhythmic activity on my part, such as writing a letter. But in any case, even if each recurrence of a conscious process later than its first recurrence is due to an associative suggestion, there must be an unusual degree of readiness to be excited on the part of the perseverating process, or so very slight an associative current would not be sufficient to revive it.

The tendency to exaggerated recurrence or perseveration is greater in fatigue and in the case of abnormal minds. It is also found in association experiments where some emotionally disturbing suggestion has been made: the observer is apt to have recourse to some previously used reaction word or stimulus word when he is 'upset' a little by the new stimulus word. All these facts indicate that when there is interference with the free onward course of associative activity the tendency is for recently excited processes to recur. It is easier for some reason to repeat an old reaction than to perform a new one. When young children are made the subjects of association experiments, they show a tendency for the same reaction word to perseverate, because the smallness of their vocabularies makes it hard to recall new words. Rhythmic processes are especially likely to perseverate in states of fatigue, for rhythm, itself involving constant repetition of the same motor response, is especially a path of least resistance when fatigue has diminished the body's energies.

An individual who shows strong perseverative tendencies in association experiments is by no means necessarily a person who will show peculiar persistence in working out a problem. The perseveration of simple movement systems is no guarantee that very complex systems will have the same tendency. Lankes (67) has recently studied the correlation of perseverative tendencies shown in various laboratory experiments with estimates of the character of the observers for persistence in their work; the correlation, one might say, between perseveration and perseverance. It turned out to be slightly negative. He is inclined to explain this fact by supposing that perseveration is a native quality, while perseverance "is the result not of nature and the native system alone, but of that and the individual's own effort and will." In the chapter on the problem idea we shall try to get further light on this subject. Persistence in the performance of a task, we shall maintain, is due to persistence and perseveration of an activity attitude. The worst enemy of the activity attitude is fatigue, and since ordinary perseveration, involving the recurrence of small movement systems, is stronger in fatigue, the relatively more fatigable individuals who display it would be expected to show less persistence of the activity attitude and less perseverance in the solving of a complex task.

CHAPTER VI

THE CONNECTING LINKS IN MOVEMENT SYSTEMS: ASSOCIATIVE DISPOSITIONS

THE motor theory we have been working out assumes, on what seem good grounds, that when an 'association of ideas' is formed, — as, for instance, the association between the face of a person and his name, — the real connection in the brain is made between the sensory pathway excited by the performance of a movement in response to the first stimulus, the face, and the motor pathway which evokes a movement in connection with the second stimulus, the name. It is the movements that are made, fully or tentatively, in connection with the perception of the person's face, which by the kinæsthetic excitations they occasion get the power to produce the movements involved in the recall of his name. All association is the association of movements. It has been customary to speak of the process of learning, when it involves the recall of ideas, as resting on the formation of associative dispositions or tendencies. The non-motor theory of association supposes that when two sensory centres are simultaneously excited, resistances are lowered along a nervous pathway connecting them; thus, an associative disposition or tendency is formed between them, on the basis of which the later excitation of one is likely to spread to the other and produce recall of an image of the stimulus which formerly acted on the other. Our theory, on the other hand, makes the associative disposition consist of lowered resistances between the kinæsthetic pathway involved in the performance of one movement and the motor pathway involved in the performance of another.

We have now to consider some of the laws which govern the strength of associative dispositions, thus understood. This chapter will be divided into four sections: the first dealing with methods by which the strength of associative dispositions may be measured; the second, with the effect of repetition on associative dispositions; the third, with the effect of time upon them; and the fourth, with their effect on each other when called successively into play.

I. Measures of the Strength of Associative Dispositions

Evidently the first thing we need, in investigating the causes which strengthen and weaken associative dispositions, the connecting links between the members of movement systems, is some means of measuring the strength of these connections. The effects of their varying degrees of strength we constantly feel in ordinary life: there are facts that we have at our tongues' end, and can never forget, as I can never forget the list of counties in New York State, which I learned as a schoolgirl; and there are facts that seem to have vanished beyond hope of recall; as when, for example, we return to a place we have once visited, and, far from recollecting the circumstances of the former visit, we say that the place does not even look familiar. But the exact measurement of these degrees of strength can be carried out only in the laboratory, and under somewhat artificial conditions.

To begin with, we must note that an associative disposition may be too weak fully to excite the motor centre concerned, and yet be of influence in other ways. For example, I may have once formed associative dispositions between the words 'fall of Constantinople' and '1453.' At a later time, I may be asked when Constantinople fell, and the kinæsthetic excitations from the movements involved in pronouncing or attending to these words may be unable to set into activity the movements involved in pronouncing the date. I have 'forgotten' the date: the associative dispositions have weakened too far to produce recall. Yet if some one says, 'Was it in 1456?' I answer, 'No; that does not sound right'; and if the date 1453 is suggested, I know at once that it is correct. So the associative dispositions cannot have vanished altogether. Associative dispositions that are too weak to produce actual recall may be termed 'subliminal dispositions.' The name is not supremely well chosen, for it implies the sense of dispositions that function below the level of consciousness, and very strong associative dispositions may do this precisely because they are so strong. If a disposition is so strong or so unopposed that there is no delay in its functioning, it has no conscious accompaniment: the things we are fully accustomed to do we can do with attention elsewhere. However, for want of a better word we may use 'subliminal' for those dispositions which are too weak to produce recall, and term those which, because of their strength, function with little or no conscious accompaniment, 'automatic dispositions.'

If an associative disposition is *supraliminal*, that is, strong enough to produce actual recall, an obvious way to measure its strength would be to measure the *time it takes to effect the recall*. If we can give the date of an historical event instantly when we are asked for it, we feel that the associative disposition is stronger than is the case when we hesitate. It was Francis Galton (40), that man of suggestive ideas, to whom there first occurred, in 1879, the thought of measuring the time occupied by associative processes. He noted, with the aid of "a small chronograph," the time required for a word, which he looked at, to suggest "about a couple of ideas" to his mind, and found that with seventy-five stimulus words, "it took a total time of 660 seconds to form the 505 ideas" that occurred to him. He had no intention of measuring the comparative speed of different instances of association, however. Four years later, Trautscholdt (140) in Wundt's laboratory undertook to measure accurately the time required for one mental process to call up another by association. He used a Hipp chronoscope and finger keys, the experimenter pressing one as he called out a stimulus word, and the observer pressing another as soon as an associated word was suggested. With the simple conception which then prevailed of the processes involved in such reaction experiments, he thought that the actual time occupied by the functioning of the associative disposition in recall could be obtained by finding, in another series of experiments, the average time taken by the observer for the mere recognition of words pronounced to him, and subtracting this 'recognition time' from the total time occupied in the association reaction. We now realize that the processes which occur, when an experiment involving the measurement of the time of an association is performed, do not consist simply of the addition of an act of association to an act of recognition. If the observer has been instructed before the stimulus word is given that he must let it suggest an association to him and must press a key as soon as it has done so, his whole experience, from the receiving of the instructions on, will be quite different from what it would have been if he had been told at the outset that he was required merely to recognize the stimulus word. We must abandon, then, the hope of measuring the time taken by the associative process proper, the passage of the nervous current from one cortical region to another. Since, however, although the time required for other processes than association itself must always be included in the total time of an association reaction, these processes, if the conditions are properly arranged, may be considered as constant factors; since the time required to recognize the stimulus word and to make a reacting movement may be treated as constant if a sufficiently large number of experiments is made, we can regard marked differences in the total association reaction time as due to differences in the association process. Cordes (23) has raised the objection that all time measurements of this process are faulty, because it is impossible for the observer to make the reacting movement, whether it be the pronouncing of an associated word or the pressing of a key, at the exact instant when the mental process of association is complete. There is evidently truth in this statement, yet practice will enable an observer to fall into a regular habit with regard to the instant in the process at which he makes his reaction, so that the effect on his association time of various alterations in the conditions may be safely studied. For this and other reasons, however, it is not safe to draw conclusions regarding the peculiarities of the associative processes in different observers from differences in their average reaction times.

Later investigators have substituted various refinements in the way of lip keys and electrical devices for recording the time of stimulation, in place of Trautscholdt's finger keys, but as a matter of fact, the differences in association reaction time under different conditions are so marked that a simple stop-watch, in the hands of a practiced experimenter, will suffice for measurement purposes.

The evidence that the reaction time of an association is shorter, the stronger the associative disposition, is conclusive. In the first place, the reaction time required for a stimulus word to call up a given reaction word is shortened by new repetitions. This was found by Müller and Pilzecker (90). In the second place, since we know that associative tendencies may weaken and be almost entirely obliterated with time, the fact that the association reaction time is longer, the greater the age of the association, is a further indication that this time is a fair measure of association strength. Another piece of evidence is the following. Müller and Schumann (91) showed that when a series of nonsense syllables is learned, associations are formed not only between the first and second syllable of each pair, but also between the second syllable and the first; that is, in the backward direction. They proved this by demonstrating that fewer repetitions were needed to relearn a series in which the order of the syllables in the pairs was reversed than one in which the syllables were given an entirely new order. The results show, however, as we should expect, that the number required for the 'reversed' relearning was greater than that required for relearning the unaltered original series; that is, the backward associative tendencies are weaker than the forward ones. In harmony with this Müller and Pilzecker found that the association time when the first member of an associated pair calls up the second is shorter than when the second calls up the first. Finally, the fact that association time varies along with certain other measures of association strength, which we shall mention presently, deepens the conviction that the speed with which an associative disposition acts is a good measure of its strength. There are limitations, however, to its usefulness: evidently there will be a maximum speed beyond which it will be impossible to go, but beyond which association strength may still increase. Two recalls might both be made so rapidly that no chronoscope could record the time of the process, and yet their associative dispositions might not be equal in strength.

It is worth noting that the association time of a wrong association is on the average longer than that of a right association. A wrong association, that is, a case where the observer gives as the associate of a certain stimulus word or syllable one that was not associated with it in the original series, must, of course, rest on some other associative connection with the stimulus, or it may be a perseveration, based only to a very slight degree on associative connections. In any case, the tendency which gives rise to the wrong response is evidently the strongest tendency on the field at the time, and one would think that in series which have been very imperfectly learned, the wrong tendencies might be as strong as the right ones, so that the mistakes might be made with as much promptness in the wrong cases as the correct syllables in the right cases. But the tendency which leads to a mistaken association, though it may be the strongest one on the field, can never be very strong, otherwise the wrong syllable would be presented along with enough general associative energy to cause it to be immediately recognized as wrong.

The stronger an associative tendency, then, the more rapidly it works, up to a certain limit. Further, the stronger a tendency, *the longer it will last.* This is, of course, not a self-evident statement. But it is supported by several facts: on the one hand, it has been found that, the more repetitions given to material that is to be learned, the longer it will be remembered. Also, those associative tendencies whose reaction times are shortest are those which remain above the limen longest (Müller and Pilzecker, 90). The strength of a supraliminal associative tendency can then be measured by the length of time during which it remains supraliminal. Perseveration, or the apparently spontaneous tendency of certain ideas to recur to the mind, to 'run in the head,' would of course be a coöperating factor here. Pappenheim (103) gave his observers a hundred stimulus words, to which they were asked to respond by speaking the first word they thought of; at the close of the series he repeated it immediately, and counted the number of cases in which the same reaction was made to a given stimulus. These cases proved to have shorter reaction times than those where a different reaction was made, indicating that they were based on stronger associative tendencies. It has also been found to be true that if a given reaction word is used by a number of different observers in response to a particular stimulus word, — as, for example, 'mother' in response to 'father,' — the reaction times of these preferred associations are unusually short, indicating that the stronger an associative tendency, the more likelihood there is that it will be common to many minds (140). It would hardly be feasible, however, to measure the strength of an associative disposition by finding out how many people possess it.

Still another way in which the strength of a supraliminal disposition may be measured is by finding *how much resistance it offers to the formation and operation of a new disposition*. Suppose that a given word or syllable, A, has been associated with another one, B, and that one desires to measure the strength of the association at a given time. Let A now be presented a certain number of times with another word or syllable, C, and then let A be given as a stimulus word. How many repetitions of the experience A–C will be necessary before A will suggest C more readily than it suggests B? The number will evidently be greater, the stronger the disposition A–B. Experiments of this sort were tried by Müller and Pilzecker (90), who used the term 'effectual inhibition' to designate the tendency which the second disposition, A–C, would have to prevent the working of the earlier disposition, A–B, and the term 'generative inhibition' to designate the tendency which the previous existence of the disposition $A–B$ would have to prevent the formation of the disposition $A–C$ at all. They did not, however, attempt to measure the strength of $A–B$ by the number of repetitions required to make $A–C$ effective, but limited themselves to showing that an effectual inhibition did occur. Ach (3) used a similar method for solving a different problem: his observers were instructed to resist a tendency to give the reaction to which a certain stimulus word would naturally lead on the basis of certain previously formed associative dispositions, and to give a different reaction of a kind described in the instructions furnished at the outset. He then measured the strength of the effect of these instructions by the number of repetitions that had been used in the formation of the associative disposition that was successfully resisted. For example, in a given series a certain syllable occurs immediately before a certain other syllable: this series is repeated a given number of times. The observer is then presented with the first syllable as a stimulus, after having been instructed on no account to react by giving the second syllable, but instead to give a syllable that rhymes with the stimulus syllable. If he succeeds in doing this, the number of repetitions of the original series forms a measure of the effect of the instructions upon his mind.

Finally, an *a priori* estimate of the strength of a disposition may be roughly made by referring back to *the number of repetitions used to found it*. If equal times elapse between the founding of two associations and their functioning, then that one may be assumed to be the stronger in whose establishment more repetitions were used.

We may now turn from supraliminal dispositions to *subliminal* ones, and ask how it is possible to measure the strength of dispositions that are too weak to produce recall. The only satisfactory method of doing so is the so-called 'Saving Method,' where the effect of previous learning is measured by the saving of time in relearning. Let us suppose that in childhood a person learned a poem to recite at a school 'exhibition.' At the present time he can recall of that poem just nothing at all, not even the title. But suppose that he is set to learn it now, in company with a person of equal learning capacity to whom it is entirely new. If account is taken of the time the two individuals take to learn the poem, and the number of times each has to read it, the person who has learned it before will probably be found to have a distinct advantage. The old associative dispositions that are too weak to produce recall are yet existent, and it is easier for the new repetitions to strengthen them than for wholly new associative dispositions to be formed.

Ebbinghaus (29) used this method in his pioneer experiments on memory, in which he was his own observer and learned a remarkable number of nonsense syllables. The method in detail was as follows. Say that a series of twelve nonsense syllables is to be learned, and that after a certain number of repetitions eight of the syllables can be correctly given; say, the first five and the last three. The associative dispositions connecting the fifth with the sixth, the sixth with the seventh, the seventh with the eighth, and the eighth with the ninth are then too weak to function in actual recall. It does not follow that they are all of equal strength. Suppose that the entire series is read through again, and that the ninth syllable can now be given correctly. Since only one new experience was needed to bring it above the limen, it would appear to have been the strongest of the four subliminal tendencies. In like manner we can find the comparative strength of the other three by determining how many repetitions of the series are needed to produce recall of the correct syllables. Thus it can be determined what position in the series of syllables, the beginning, middle, or end, is most favorable to the quick forming of associative dispositions. Further, we may wish to measure, not the strength of dispositions that are subliminal because the learning process has not gone far enough, but that of dispositions which, originally strong enough to function in recall, have become subliminal with the lapse of time. Twenty-four hours after the first learning, some dispositions will have fallen below the limen of effectiveness for recall.

Their strength can be measured by finding the number of new repetitions needed to restore their power of recall. Thus we have a means of determining the speed with which associative tendencies fall off with time. If tests are being made of the effectiveness of different methods of memorizing, then we need a value which will represent the average strength or permanence of the associative tendencies in a given series of nonsense syllables. Such a value may be obtained, even for a series all of whose members are either still below the limen of reproduction or have dropped below it with time, by noting the number of repetitions necessary to bring the whole series above the limen; that is, to produce a perfect recitation of the series. If it is the representative association strength of the whole series after an interval that is wanted, evidently we ought to take into account the difficulty of originally learning the series. If it takes six repetitions to relearn one series of syllables, and only four repetitions to relearn another, it would not be fair to conclude that the associative tendencies of the first series have decayed more rapidly with time than those of the second, for the first series may be a harder series in itself. The ratio of the number of repetitions needed to relearn the series, to the number that were originally needed to learn it, is what we need to find; or the *percentage of repetitions that are saved in the relearning.* This latter value was the one used by Ebbinghaus and the method of finding it has been termed the 'Saving Method.'

A subliminal association, then, may have its strength measured by the number of repetitions needed to bring it above the limen. This measurement, of course, *assumes that the value of the repetitions is always the same in cases where the numbers are compared.* Evidently the conditions under which the repetitions occur must be carefully controlled, and in particular, the grouping or distribution of the repetitions must be taken into account.

While subliminal associative dispositions obviously cannot have measured the speed with which they function in recall, some interest does attach to the quickness with which one recognizes that an associative disposition is subliminal; the promptness, that is, with which a learner acknowledges failure in the effort to recall. In experiments, for instance, where non-sense syllables have been learned in pairs and the time is measured which is necessary for the first syllable of each pair to recall the second, the 'zero cases' have also had their times recorded. 'Zero cases' are cases where the observer ends by saying, 'I give it up,' or words to that effect. Can anything regarding the strength of subliminal dispositions be inferred from these zero times? If you decide promptly that you have forgotten the associated syllable, does this mean that the subliminal associative tendencies, which are undoubtedly there, and might be revealed by the 'Saving Method,' are weaker than in the cases where you spend a few seconds in a vain effort to recall? Müller and Pilzecker say that the association time for zero cases is longer, the better known the series; that is, it increases with the number of repetitions. This seems natural: in a better-known series the associations that are too weak to produce recall would be only a little below the threshold, and introspection often distinguishes faithfully between something that we can almost recall and something that is hopelessly gone. If the observer feels, with right, that the missing syllable is on the tip of his tongue, he is apt to take longer before deciding to give the matter up as hopeless. Ephrussi (32) also, who was comparing the effectiveness, for learning pairs of nonsense syllables, of repeating each pair a number of times in succession and of reading the whole series of pairs through an equal number of times, found that while the former method gave more right associates and shorter reaction times, the times of its zero cases were longer, another proof that a slow zero reaction means stronger subliminal tendencies.

Besides making relearning easier, subliminal associative dispositions may betray their influence in making it easier to *perceive* and to *recognize* objects. If the motor pathways for the tentative movements which are involved in attention to a given object are excited by kinæsthetic influences so weak that no actual movement, even tentative, results, they are nevertheless set in readiness, apparently, so that subsequent attention to and recognition of the object take place with more speed. Unfortunately, there has not yet been devised any satisfactory way of using this fact to measure the strength of subliminal dispositions.

The effect of such dispositions on perception was studied by Ohms (100). He employed series of pairs of German and Russian words. These were presented to the observer a certain number of times. The number of repetitions was chosen so that the majority of the associative tendencies should be below the limen after an interval of twenty-four hours: that is, the person experimented on, when shown a Russian word, could not recall the German word that had accompanied it. The subliminal associations which nevertheless existed were tested in the following way. Two six-pair series had been used on the preceding day. There were now shown eighteen Russian words in succession, the time of exposure for each being so short that the word could not, ordinarily, be correctly read. In the final form of the method, a German word was allowed to be read before each of the Russian words was shown. In six out of the eighteen cases, the German word preceding was the one which had in the preliminary experiments been associated with the Russian word shown. In six, the German word had had no previous association with the Russian word, but the latter had been used in the preliminary experiments. And in the other six, an entirely new Russian word was shown. Thus the effect of the associative dispositions connecting the German and Russian words shown in the preliminary experiments, which were not strong enough to enable the observer to recall the Russian word when its German companion was pronounced, was expected to show itself in producing readier and more accurate reading of those Russian words which were preceded, in the test, by their proper German associates. Evidently, there were two ways in which the subliminal tendencies might function: they might influence the *time* taken to read the Russian words, and they might influence the *correctness* with which the Russian words were read. The times required for reading were measured electrically, with a Hipp chronoscope and lip key. In a later series the person experimented on had to listen to the Russian words instead of looking at them, and the necessary indistinctness was admirably secured by the use of an old-fashioned telephone receiver. The results showed in both series that the Russian words were more correctly recognized when they were preceded by their originally associated German words; that is, when subliminal associations coöperated with the faint visual or auditory impression of the Russian word. On the other hand, the influence of these associative tendencies on the speed of recognition was less definite. There seemed, in fact, to be two types of observers: in one the recognition was quicker when the subliminal tendencies were working; in the other it was quicker when they were not. Ohms says that the former class of observers comprises those in whom the motor tendency — that is, the tendency to pronounce the words — was strongest. It is not clear just what this would have to do with the case. One would conjecture, rather, that the difference between the two types of observers may have depended on whether they did or did not make an effort to recall the Russian word in the interval before it was presented and after the German word had been given in the test series. Suppose that the German word given in the test, as a preliminary to a Russian word, was recognized to be one that occurred in the learning series. For some observers it might start, in the interval before the Russian word came, a tendency to wonder what the associated Russian word had been, and when the word was presented, a second or two of criticism might precede its being accepted. On the other hand, if the observer did not recognize the German word as having occurred in the preliminary series, he would simply make a stab at the Russian word without troubling to criticize his identification of it, and his reaction times would be shorter in those cases where the preceding word was unassociated. The second type of observer might make no effort, on having the German word presented, to recall its Russian companion, but might simply give, as soon as he saw or heard the Russian word, his best interpretation of it. In this case, where the working of the liminal associations is not interfered with by the effort to make them supraliminal, they might do good service in actually shortening the reaction time. In such a case only could the time required for a correct reading of the Russian word be regarded as a measure of the strength of the subliminal tendencies. As the results of Ohms stand, the only actual measure of this quantity which they furnish is the number of correctly read elements in the Russian words. Evidently one important source of error here would lie in the fact that the sounds or printed characters in one word might be intrinsically easier to recognize than those in another. In the part of the investigation where the words were spoken into the telephone, account was taken of this factor. Gutzmann had previously published a work showing experimentally which consonantal sounds are hardest to recognize, and care was used in forming the series to distribute these difficult consonants judiciously throughout. In the series with visual presentation no such precautions were taken. On the whole, the work gives rather evidence that subliminal tendencies do influence the perception of objects under these conditions, than a quantitative measure of the strength of such tendencies.

The effect of subliminal associative dispositions on *recognition* was demonstrated in the experiments of Reuther (115). Every one knows that long after an object has been forgotten, in the sense that one could not recall a memory image of it, it can still be recognized when it is actually presented. Evidently subliminal associative dispositions betray their existence in bringing about recognition of an object as having been met before. This effect was studied by Reuther, using a method which he called that of 'Identical Series.' Series of four-place numbers were presented to the observer a certain number of times. Then a series was presented, concerning which the observer was told that each of its members might be either identical with a member of the preceding series, or entirely new: the observer must decide which. As a matter of fact, these instructions were deceptive: the second series was exactly like the first, both as regards its members and their order. Reuther calculated the ratio of the number of members correctly recognized as old to the total number of members. This value evidently represented supraliminal as well as subliminal associative tendencies. Sometimes, when an observer correctly recognized a member of the series as old, he would be able, by virtue of supraliminal dispositions, to anticipate the next: sometimes he would simply be able, by virtue of subliminal dispositions, to recognize the next member when it came. The introspections of the observers could be appealed to in order to separate these two classes of cases; but the method furnishes no way of measuring the strength of the subliminal dispositions whose existence is thus indicated.

Another method of testing the effect of subliminal dispositions on recognition was that of Fischer (37). Here the observer read a series of nonsense syllables a given number of times. Five seconds after the last reading he tried to recite the series. If he gave a wrong syllable the experimenter corrected him. But if he was at a loss for a syllable, then the experimenter suggested one which might be either right or wrong; it remained for the observer to decide which. While subliminal dispositions must be influential in such a decision, there seems no way of measuring their strength. Nor does the 'Reconstruction Method,' as it is called by Gamble (42), serve this purpose any better. It was first used by Bigham (12) in 1894. It consists in presenting the material to be memorized in a definite order, and then, after a certain number of repetitions and a certain interval, presenting the members of the series simultaneously, with the order abolished, and requiring the observer to reconstruct the series by rearranging the members. Thus a series of nonsense syllables may be read to the observer, a certain number of times. Then, after an interval, he is given a pack of cards each bearing one of the syllables, and spreading out the pack before him he attempts to reconstruct the original order of the series. This method was used by Bigham for numbers, colors, and forms only; when words and syllables were the material, the observer was obliged to reproduce the whole series by writing it out, instead of being supplied with the members in altered order. Gamble used smells, nonsense syllables, and "Bradley colored papers" two inches square.

The process of reconstructing the order of a series when the members are supplied is in its psychic aspect rather complicated. In the first place, it probably involves association of a given member with its absolute position in the series. The observer, turning his attention to a particular syllable, would say to himself, "This was in the first half of the series," for instance. He would be practically certain to make such an association in connection with the first and last members of the series. We shall later consider just what is involved in the association of a member with its position as early or late in the series. Apparently it may occur without the operation of any supraliminal association of the member in question with other members of the series. One can be quite sure that a syllable belonged in the first part of the series without being able to reproduce a single other syllable. Besides associations with absolute position, supraliminal associations between members might also play a part in the rearranging. On looking at a certain syllable, one might recall the one that came next to it, and after picking the recalled syllable out of the pile, reconstruct the sequence. Finally, subliminal associations might help. That is, when one looked at a certain syllable, one might be quite unable to remember what came next. But glancing over the other members, one might recognize the syllable required, as soon as one's glance lighted on it, and this recognition would occur through the associative tendencies which had been too weak to bring about recall. But the Method of Reconstruction, like those just previously discussed, does not offer any way of distinguishing between the cases where the associations concerned were subliminal and those where they actually functioned in recall; hence, it cannot be used as a measure of the strength of subliminal associations. We may sum up the subject of such measurements by saying that the only satisfactory method is that which estimates the strength of a subliminal tendency by the number of repetitions necessary to bring it above the threshold; that is, the Saving Method. The functioning of such tendencies in recognition has never been satisfactorily measured. A further advantage of measurement by the new repetitions required is that it can be used for tendencies which are so weak that they could not produce any effect even on recognition. For the associative link between two experiences may have so far degenerated that it will not even make us recognize the second experience as familiar, and yet it may effect a saving in the number of repetitions needed to relearn the series.

II. The Effect of Repetition

An associative disposition is founded between two movements when the kinæsthetic excitation started by one movement coincides with the innervation of the other movement: the kinæsthetic stimulus energy then finds its way into the motor pathway belonging to the second movement, and the resistances along the path which leads from the kinæsthetic pathway of movement A to the motor pathway of movement B are lowered. Each time that movement A precedes or accompanies movement B, the resistances are lowered a little more, until movement A comes through its kinæsthetic excitations to furnish a sufficient stimulus to movement B. Thus, each repetition of the two movements in conjunction strengthens the movement system that is in process of formation.

Does each repetition do an equal amount towards lowering resistances and strengthening the movement system? The principal influence at work here is the amount of attention accompanying the repetition.

Just what on our theory is the difference between a repetition with attention and a repetition without attention? The essential feature of attention we have assumed to be the occurrence of tentative movements belonging especially to the stimulus attended to. Take the case of a series of nonsense syllables which is presented visually. Reading it to one's self without attention may mean neglecting to make even tentatively the movements involved in pronouncing it: in such a case the most important kinæsthetic currents needed to establish a movement system will be lacking. The same thing will be true if the syllables are read aloud to the observer: if he does not listen with attention, he will not be making the tentative movements that are necessary to the establishment of the associative dispositions. If, on the other hand, the observer has to read aloud the syllables himself, the kinæsthetic processes involved in pronouncing them will, of course, be present in full strength; yet apparently even here the absence of attention is a disadvantage. The reason for this would seem to be that when we attend to the impressions we are committing to memory, not only are new associative dispositions formed, but the various tentative movements which occur set old movement systems into activity and enter into auxiliary new ones. Thus *the greater the variety of tentative movements which a series of stimuli sets up, the better that series will be recalled*, because, on the one hand, a number of new systems will be formed, and, on the other hand, advantage will be taken of all possible old ones. A series of syllables inattentively read aloud will be connected solely by the associative dispositions set up between the movements involved in pronouncing them, while a series attentively read aloud will be connected by the movements involved in pronouncing them, the movements involved in listening to them, the movements involved in looking at them, the movements involved in noting their place in the series, and the movements involved in noting their associations with words, the words being already united in old movement systems.

That the first presentation of the objects between which an associative disposition is to be formed does far more than the rest in establishing the disposition is a fact ascertained by many experimenters. G. W. Smith (130), working at Harvard in 1896, experimented with ten-syllable series, read through a slit in a screen, and tested by attempts to reproduce the series after one, three, six, nine, and twelve repetitions. The results showed that the first repetition did more for the learning of the series than all the others put together. Ephrussi (32), in 1904, had his observers read nonsense syllables or words a certain number of times, and then tested the learning by the Method of Helps; that is, by counting the number of promptings the observer needed in reciting the series. The tests were made either at once, or after twenty-four hours; and the first presentation was shown to have more value than any of the others. Witasek (153) got the same result in comparing the value of reading and recitation. Pohlmann (111) reached a similar conclusion in 1906, counting the number of figures learned in three series, one presented once, the second twice, and the third three times. Knors (62) in 1910 used a similar method with syllables and words as well as figures, and confirmed the superiority of the first presentation; but he noted that it was not so marked when the testing was done by the Scoring Method; that is, by giving the odd-numbered syllables out of the series and requiring the observer to give all the even-numbered syllables that followed.

The first presentation has also more effect than any of the others in bringing about recognition. Reuther's Method of Identical Series, where the observer is tested by noting the number of elements in the series that he can recognize, confirms the superiority of the first impression, and Gamble, using smells as material and working with the Reconstruction Method, where the observer is given the members of the original series with their order destroyed and is required to rearrange them in the original order, tells us that in the first presentation the observer learned sixty per cent. of the series. Fischer (37) also noted the superior influence of the early repetitions in producing recognition.

The first repetition is evidently the one that is made with fullest attention, so that a part at least of its superiority may be due to this fact. If it should turn out to be true that a repetition reduces the resistance at synapses more, the greater that resistance is when the repetition occurs, this factor also would contribute to the effectiveness of the first repetition. We may next ask whether all the repetitions after the first have equal value, or whether there are any other preferred positions for a repetition besides the first position.

Hawkins (48), in 1897, testing the ability of sixth and seventh grade school children to recall groups of ten numbers immediately after hearing them, noted the curious fact that the recall was poorer after two repetitions than after one. This was evidently an experiment on the memory after-image rather than on associative dispositions; and it is conceivable that a second reading of the numbers might have been made with certain differences of tone and accent that would tend to blur the memory after-image. Reuther (115) also found the second repetition rather a disadvantage than otherwise: his work, it will be remembered, was on recognition. No one, so far as I know, has observed that the second repetition is a disadvantage where recall after an interval — that is, recall based on supraliminal associative dispositions — is concerned. But it does seem to be evident from the work of many experimenters that the repetitions which come immediately after the first one not only accomplish less than the first, but less than the repetitions which follow them.[1] Ebbinghaus (29) declared that the next few repetitions after the first caused little increase in the saving effected on relearning; and that afterwards increase in the number of repetitions caused increased saving, with certain fluctuations, until a limit was reached. The Saving Method, it will be remembered, measures the increase in both supraliminal and subliminal dispositions. Reuther, working on recognition rather

[1] Nagel (97) finds that the superiority of the first repetition is confined to its effect on the first and last syllables of the series, and that these owe their advantage to place associations, to the greater influence of immediate recall in the effect of the first repetition, and to their comparative immunity to the bad effects of perseveration. While he makes some valuable suggestions, his discussion on this point is far from clear to my mind.

than recall, — that is, on subliminal rather than supraliminal dispositions, — finds that the amount correctly recognized increases with the number of repetitions at first more slowly than later; the repetitions immediately following the first one are less effective than those that follow them. Fischer (37) got evidence that the earlier repetitions in a series had more effect on recognition — that is, on subliminal dispositions — than on recall, — that is, on supraliminal dispositions. In Fischer's method, the observer was allowed to recall the syllables of the series if he could: if he could not recall a particular syllable he was asked to decide whether one supplied by the experimenter was right or wrong. The errors in recognition decreased much more rapidly after the earlier repetitions than later; the errors in reproduction decreased steadily as the number of recognitions increased. There would seem to be a perfectly conceivable reason for the fact that the repetitions just after the first one contribute relatively little to the strengthening of the associative dispositions in the series as a whole. The syllables that are learned in the first repetition get for the next few repetitions more attention than the ones that have not been learned: the result is that these next few repetitions are more concerned with strengthening the dispositions of syllables already learned than in learning new ones. (A suggestion similar to this is made by Nagel (97).) The same thing may happen later on in the learning process, so that after a few repetitions have gone to the acquiring of new syllables, the next few may be devoted to the further establishment of those already learned. Thus, Ephrussi found that the rate at which the amount learned increases with the number of repetitions undergoes marked fluctuations.

Attention is the prime factor in still another aspect of the influence of repetition on the strength of associative dispositions; namely, the relation of the number of repetitions required to the amount that has to be learned. When a long successive movement system must be formed, as, for instance, when a long series of nonsense syllables is to be learned, of course a greater number of associative dispositions must be established than when the movement system is short. Now, if it takes, say, twelve repetitions to enable one to recite a series of ten syllables correctly after a given interval of time, it will need more than twelve repetitions to enable one to recite a series of sixteen syllables correctly after the same interval. This is a fact with which we have everyday acquaintance in our attempts to memorize, and it seems self-evident that more time and labor should be needed to establish fifteen associative dispositions than to establish nine. But is this, after all, self-evident? The case is not like that of a hungry family each of whose members gets less food the larger the family. The nine associative dispositions in the ten-syllable series each got twelve repetitions, and this was enough to bring them above the limen of recall: the fifteen associative dispositions in the sixteen-syllable series each got twelve repetitions, but for some reason they were not able to profit by their advantages as did the nine dispositions of the shorter series. Now, it will, of course, be true that only certain of the dispositions in the long series are left subliminal by the twelve repetitions. Others will be firmly established. The observer will be able to repeat a part of the sixteen-syllable series quite well, but not the whole. This fact, that the associative dispositions share unequally in the advantage of the repetitions they have received, points clearly to differences in attention. While, if the observer has to read the syllables aloud, the kinæsthetic excitations which form the main links of the movement system are all present, yet, if some of the syllables are read with less and some with greater attention, there will be differences in the tentative movements which may establish auxiliary associative dispositions and make use of dispositions established at some earlier time. For a fuller discussion of this subject the reader is referred to the treatment of "aids," in Chapter VII. Now, in a long series there is obviously more chance for variation in the degree of attention than in a short one; hence the number of repetitions which will suffice to make all the dispositions of a short series supraliminal, because they are uniformly attended to, will not suffice for a longer series because some of its dispositions must be established under unfavorable conditions of attention. Does the number of repetitions required increase proportionately to the length of the series? If you double the length of the series, must you double the number of repetitions in order to learn it? There is a curious contradiction in the results of different investigators here, but it is one that is not hard to explain. Ebbinghaus (29) declared that the number of repetitions increases much more rapidly than the length of the series. He found that while it took an average of thirty repetitions to recite a sixteen-syllable series correctly, it required fifty-five repetitions to recite a twenty-six syllable series correctly. But he was testing the learning by immediate recall of the series, which, of course, involves the memory after-image to a large degree, and this would naturally give a high advantage to the shorter series. Practically all later investigators, working with delayed recall, which involves only associative dispositions, find not only that the number of repetitions does not increase more rapidly than the series length, but that it increases less rapidly. Within limits, the more you have to learn, the more you can learn: if you are set to learn a series of twenty syllables, while you need more repetitions than are required to learn a ten-syllable series, you will not need twice as many. (Meumann (81), Weber (149), Radossawljewitsch (113), Knors (62).) This is especially true of practiced observers: they learn, as Meumann says, to adapt attention to the task. It holds also for the subliminal dispositions involved in recognition: Reuther found that the absolute quantity recognized by the Method of Identical Series increased with the series length, and Gamble reports that with the Reconstruction Method, practice actually tends to make the number of repetitions required for long and short series equal. This operation of "adapting attention" to the task is really an effect of what is called the 'problem idea.' The nature of the influence of problem ideas will be discussed in a later chapter. Probably the adaptation of attention involves the use of different methods and helps for long and short series, and this is why practiced observers, who are expert in the use of helps, show especial ability in adapting themselves to long series.

Another fact, connected with the influence of repetition on associative dispositions, which must be explained by referring to the effect of problem ideas, is the following. When successive movement systems are to be formed, as soon as a disposition becomes supraliminal, it gains more in strength from being used for recall than from merely being reinforced through a new presentation of the material to be learned. Every one must have experienced the good effect of an attempt to recite something that is partly learned. One may not get through without having to be prompted, but the associative dispositions that were strong enough to function seem even to introspection far more firmly established by having been depended on for recall. Witasek (153) in 1907 and Katzaroff (61) in the following year tested the beneficial effect of attempted recitations under laboratory conditions, and both found it to be far greater than that of a new reading of the material to be learned. Now, why should this be true? Suppose that a person is set to read through a series of words or syllables to be memorized. The sight of each syllable produces the movements of articulating it, and these movements produce kinæsthetic excitations. Gradually, the kinæsthetic excitations from one syllable make connections with the movements involved in pronouncing the next, so that the movement system is formed. Suppose that a sufficient number of readings has occurred so that weak but supraliminal associative dispositions have been founded; that is, the observer is able, with hesitation and uncertainty, to recite the series "without book." In the course of the recitation, the nervous process has to travel the paths of the associative dispositions that have been founded, and of course, as it travels them, it lowers their resistances. But why should it lower them more than they would be lowered by an additional reading? For in a fresh reading, too, the nervous process must travel along the paths where associative dispositions are being founded; otherwise a fresh reading would do nothing at all to strengthen the associative dispositions; whereas, of course, it does a great deal. The value of a recitation from memory as compared with that of a new reading seems to be a matter of the attitude of the learner; of the problem which he sets himself. As such, we shall discuss it in Chapter VIII.

The important question as to the most favorable interval between repetitions, since it involves the effect of time on associative dispositions, will be considered in the next section.

The effect of repetitions changes its character somewhat as all the dispositions of the movement system that is being established become supraliminal. In the earlier stages of learning attention is of the greatest value to a repetition; that is, each syllable, for instance, of a series to be learned must be attended to. In this process of attention a variety of tentative movements associated with the syllable are excited, and if any of these movements fit into old, already established movement systems, such systems act as aids to the establishment of the new one. When we begin to learn the names of the cranial nerves, attention to each name helps us to link their initials with the rhyme "On old Manasseh's peaked tops": the rhyme makes sense of a kind; that is, its words involve movement systems already formed. The first few times the list of nerves is recited from memory this auxiliary system comes much into play. But if the list is often repeated after it has reached the point of correct recitation, if it is 'overlearned,' then gradually the need for the auxiliary systems falls away. The new system becomes thoroughly established in its own right: the pronunciation of one name will be a sufficient stimulus to the pronunciation of the next. The process becomes 'automatic,' which expression means in this connection simply 'independent of aids from other movement systems.' At this stage it does not matter whether the repetitions are made with attention or not.

The effect of repetitions is different also when the movement system to be formed is very complex. Bryan and Harter (17) studied the effects of practice on learning to telegraph, and Book (13) made a similar study of the effect of practice or repetition on typewriting. Both these activities involve, first, the formation of a number of simple movement systems, and second, the formation of a number of complexer systems. In learning to typewrite, for instance, one begins by forming an associative disposition between a letter and a particular finger and arm movement, required to strike a particular key on the board. Writing a sentence means at this stage that each letter is attended to and sets off the proper movement. Later, words often recurring, like 'the,' 'that,' 'and,' have links set up between the various hand movements involved, so that the movements for each word become independent systems. The same process may later make independent systems out of the movements involved in writing familiar phrases. Now, at the point where the change, say, from the single letter or spelling-out type of association to the word-unit type occurs, an increase of attention and of effort is needed. It will not do to leave the repetitions to bring about improvement of their own accord. If left to themselves, they follow the older type, and the new systems will not be formed. The fact seems to be that repetition strengthens a single associative disposition first with the aid of older, already formed dispositions, aids, memory devices: this requires attention. Later it strengthens the disposition without such aids. The strengthening shows itself by increased speed in the functioning of the associative dispositions: thus, in a process like that of typewriting a sentence, the time required will diminish. After a certain number of repetitions the time will be reduced to a minimum: it will be impossible to perform the function any faster. Further repetitions beyond this point will doubtless have an effect on the permanence of the learning, but they cannot affect the speed of the performance. Now is the time for the formation of connections between the dispositions, for grouping them into systems of higher order, for typewriting, for instance, by words and phrases instead of letters. But the formation of these new systems requires attention, and so the process of having recourse to aids begins all over again; resulting often in a new access of speed as the new systems in turn become automatic.

The influence of fatigue is, of course, an important factor in the effect of repetitions. If the learning process is in a stage which requires attention, it is evident that the fatigue which attends it may be either fatigue connected with the attitude of activity involved in learning, or fatigue connected with the process itself that is being learned. Take for example the task of learning a series of nonsense syllables. To learn them quickly involves keeping steadily in action the problem idea of learning, the effort or will to learn. The fatigue connected with the maintenance of the attitude of activity which always functions whenever there is intellectual effort is discussed in the chapter on the problem idea. Its occurrence is probably responsible for those fatigue sensations which we call sensations of boredom or ennui: we are not really fatigued with repeating the syllables, but we are fatigued with attending to them: we should like to relax the activity attitude for a time. Later on in the learning process there may be set up actual fatigue of the processes of articulation involved in learning the syllables.

III. *The Effect of Time*

No feature of our experience is more familiar than the fact that *time* effaces the past from our minds; that the movement systems formed in the course of our experience gradually weaken in their connections; that associative dispositions sink by the mere lapse of time to that subliminal state where they can no longer function to bring about recall. As dispositions grow weaker they act more slowly: Müller and Pilzecker (90), in the research which introduced the Scoring Method to psychologists, found that the longer the interval which has elapsed since an associative disposition was founded, the more slowly it acts in recall. If nonsense syllables are learned in groups of two, and if later the first syllables of the various groups are given in altered order, the observer being asked to supply the correct second syllable in each case, it will take him longer to do so, when an interval of six minutes has elapsed since the learning than if the interval has been only one minute. And when the strength of dispositions is measured by the Saving Method — that is, by the amount of time and labor their existence saves in relearning — the decrease of their strength with the lapse of time is apparent.

But the falling off in association strength with time does not occur at a uniform rate. This fact is well known to all students of psychology. One of the first results of the modern experimental investigations of memory to find its way into the textbooks was Ebbinghaus's (29) alleged law with regard to the rate of forgetting, that the ratio of the amount retained to the amount forgotten varies inversely as the logarithm of the time that has elapsed since the learning. This means, of course, that one forgets very rapidly at first and much more slowly later. The truth of this latter statement has been confirmed by subsequent investigators using other methods, although the rate of decrease is probably not so fast as Ebbinghaus's law requires. Ebbinghaus's experiments consisted in learning eight thirteen-syllable series and relearning them after intervals of twenty minutes, one hour, nine hours, one day, two days, six days, and thirty-one days. The results were stated in terms of the ratio of the time saved in the relearning to the original learning time: thus it might take, say, twenty minutes to learn the series the first time, and sixteen minutes to relearn it after an interval of two days: then the strength of the associative dispositions after a lapse of two days would be represented by the fraction $\frac{4}{20}$. Radossawljewitsch (113) also used the Saving Method, with intervals of five, twenty, sixty, and four hundred and eighty minutes, and of one, two, six, fourteen, twenty-one, thirty, and one hundred and twenty days. But while Ebbinghaus, who was his own observer, counted a series learned, or relearned, if he could once recite it correctly, Radossawljewitsch counted it learned or relearned only if two correct recitations could be made. His results showed a much less rapid initial falling off with time than did those of Ebbinghaus. Finken-binder (36) employed a somewhat different method: the syllables were presented slowly, one every two seconds, and the learning or relearning was considered complete if the observer on seeing one syllable could just recall the next one. Practice and fatigue conditions were carefully controlled. The intervals used were half an hour, one, two, four, eight, twelve, sixteen, twenty-four, thirty-six, forty-eight, and seventy-two hours. The results lay between those of Ebbinghaus and Radossawl-jewitsch as regards the rate of forgetting. The comparatively slow rate at which the dispositions in the latter's experiments fell away with time thus seems to have been due to the fact that they were especially strong, since the test was two correct successive recitations.

In Müller and Pilzecker's (90) study with the Scoring Method it appeared that when the association times for syllables learned eleven minutes before were compared with those for series learned twenty-four hours before, the difference was slight. Apparently if an associative disposition maintains after the first ten minutes enough strength actually to reproduce the second term of the association, it will continue to perform its function with about the same readiness for at least twenty-four hours.

But before asserting on the basis of these experiments that weak associative dispositions fall off very rapidly just after they are established and more slowly later, while stronger ones fall off less rapidly at first ("When the over-learning has been carried to a very high pitch — to so high a pitch that a very large share of the associations involved have been reduced to a condition of automatic efficiency, then the onset of forgetting is extremely slow," say Ladd and Woodworth in their "Physiological Psychology," pages 576–77), we must consider the inferences to be drawn from experiments on another problem. This is the problem of the best distribution of repetitions. When Lottie Steffens (132) was engaged in finding whether the most economical method of learning is to read the material straight through from beginning to end a number of times (Whole Method) or to break it up into sections and learn each part separately (Part Method), it occurred to her that one among other reasons for the superiority she found in the Whole Method might be the fact that this way of learning made a longer time elapse between two repetitions of the same syllable. Is it perhaps true that if a given time be allowed for learning, the best results will be obtained when the repetitions of the material to be learned are most widely distributed through the interval? Ebbinghaus had found indications that such was the case. To test the supposition further, Steffens made her observers learn series of eight nonsense syllables according to three different plans, A, B, and C. By plan A, a series was read once: then there was a pause equal to the time of one rotation of the kymograph drum on which the syllables were being shown, then another reading, then another pause, and so on until there had been six readings and six pauses. Then the series was repeated without intermission until it could be recited without error. Plan B was to give three readings in immediate succession, then a pause equal to the time of three rotations, then three more readings, followed by a second pause equal in length to the first: there ensued as before repetitions in direct succession until the series was learned. In plan C, the series was given six readings in direct succession: then came a pause equal to six rotations of the kymograph, and then the learning proceeded as in the other cases. It was found that the number of repetitions needed at the end to produce perfect learning was least when plan A was used. Other experiments with longer pauses confirmed the superiority of distributed repetitions.

Jost (59) undertook to give the law of the superiority of distributed repetitions a more thorough investigation than it had had from either Ebbinghaus or Steffens. He compared the learning of twelve-syllable series by thirty repetitions on a single day with the learning of similar series by ten repetitions on each of three days, testing the learning each time by the number of repetitions required to relearn after twenty-four hours. The distributed series showed greater saving. The most obvious explanation for this result would be that thirty or more repetitions in immediate succession are so fatiguing that the last ones have little value. Jost in the following way excluded fatigue as an explanation. The thirty repetitions on a single day were divided into six groups of five repetitions each, and between each group and the next, ten repetitions were made of one of the series which were being learned at the rate of ten repetitions a day. Thus, the ten-a-day series should have been more fatiguing to learn than the thirty-a-day. But the former still gave a higher saving in the relearning.

Now, we have seen that the first repetition of a series has greater value than any of the repetitions which follow, because it gets most attention. If this is true not only of the very first repetition of all, when the series is first presented to the observer, but of the first repetition of any group of repetitions even when the series has been shown in earlier groups, then an explanation of the superiority of distributed repetitions would lie in the fact that they furnish a greater proportion of first repetitions. Jost rejects this explanation on grounds which do not seem satisfactory. He holds that the very first repetitions have not so much attention value as those coming a little later, because attention takes time to adapt itself. Hence he thinks if attention were the chief factor, a division into groups of four ought not to be so advantageous as a division into groups of, say, eight: but the results show that the smaller groups are most effective. There is however plenty of evidence that the very first repetition of all has superior attention value, and one cause of the advantage of distributed repetitions, it is natural to suppose, must lie in their greater proportion of first repetitions.

Jost himself finds the chief reason for the superiority of distributed repetitions in the influence of the age of associative dispositions on the rate at which they fall off with time. The relearning of the series learned by thirty repetitions in immediate succession was done twenty-four hours later. The relearning of the series learned by ten repetitions on each of three days was done on the fourth day: two-thirds of its previous repetitions had thus occurred at a longer interval before the relearning than was the case with the thirty-a-day series. "If two associations," says Jost, "are of equal strength but different age, a new repetition is more valuable for the older one." The truth of this statement he proved in the following way. The method of testing the strength of an associative disposition by relearning gives the material new repetitions: the method of testing by association time, the Scoring Method, does not. Now, suppose that two series of syllables be read n times, and tested after an interval t, one of them by the relearning or Saving Method, the other by the Scoring Method. Suppose, further, that two other series are read $n - x$ times, — that is, a smaller number than the first two series, — and are tested, one by the Saving, the other by the Scoring Method, after an interval $t - x$, less than the first interval. The associative dispositions of these last two ought to be of nearly equal strength with those of the first two, Jost argued, since, although they have had less time in which to decay, they were not so strong at the outset, having been formed with fewer repetitions. The two pairs of series therefore fulfil the condition of being equal in strength but unequal in age. If Jost's hypothesis is correct, the Saving Method of testing, which involves giving new repetitions, should give better results with the older series, while this result should not appear in the tests by the Scoring Method. Jost reports that the results of the experiment fall out in accordance with this expectation. And he explains his first hypothesis of the greater value of a new repetition for an older association, by a second one: "If two associations are of equal strength but different age, the older diminishes less with time." Lipmann (72), working by the Scoring Method, finds that if a young and an old series of associative dispositions give an equal number of right associates, the number of scores is increased by new repetitions more rapidly in the case of the latter; which confirms Jost's statement that a new repetition is more valuable for an older disposition.

The superiority of distributed repetitions has been found to exist in the case of movement systems which involve other muscles than those of articulation. In some instances, as in Book's (13) study of learning to typewrite, the factor of fatigue is obviously the dominant one, and the distribution of repetitions resolves itself into a matter of the distribution of periods of rest. In the Vassar laboratory, intervals of one minute were found to be more favorable than no intervals between repetitions in learning a series of hand and arm movements in shuffling cards (15).

Now it is evident that two distinct factors enter into all the manifestations of the 'strength' of an associative disposition. The functioning of such a disposition involves the excitation of a motor pathway by a nervous current which passes over certain synapses from a kinæsthetic sensory pathway. The degree of excitation thus produced will depend, first, on the lowered resistances at the synapses in question. This resistance is lowered each time the nervous current crosses the synapses: it is therefore a function of the number of repetitions of the series of movements. We may call this the frequency factor. But, secondly, the degree to which the motor pathway is excited will depend on its readiness to respond. We have seen that the memory after-image is caused, probably, by the fact that immediately after a motor pathway has discharged, it is in a state of readiness to discharge again on the slightest provocation. This readiness may indeed depend also on lowered synaptic resistances, but the synapses involved would seem to be not particularly those from the kinæsthetic pathway which has just discharged it, but any or all the synapses which lead into it. This factor of readiness to renew discharge, while it is strong enough to produce apparently spontaneous recall of imagery only for a short time after the original excitation, except in the cases of perseveration, probably continues with diminishing intensity for some time. It is clearly a function of the recency of the excitation of the motor pathway, and we may call it the recency factor.

When a series of movements has been repeated a number of times, the ease with which it can be immediately reproduced depends then on a combination of the frequency and recency factors. Now the recency factor falls off quite rapidly with time. We may suppose that the frequency factor falls off much less rapidly. Immediately after the learning, the rate of forgetting is rapid, because the recency factor is dropping out. The rate at which it will drop out depends on the various causes which strengthen the memory after-image; a set of conditions which has been quite inadequately investigated. If the number of repetitions has been just enough to produce one correct recitation, it is probable that the correctness of the recitation depends largely upon the memory after-image or recency factor, and we may expect a very rapid falling off with time. If two correct recitations are made the test of learning, the frequency factor will come more into play, and the falling off with time will be less steep. Where the number of repetitions is very great, much beyond that needed for even two correct recitations, the recency factor sinks to comparative insignificance, and the learning lasts indefinitely. In fact, the question may be raised as to whether time has any effect at all on the frequency factor, the lowered resistances at the synapses between the kinæsthetic pathway and the motor pathway: whether the process of forgetting is not wholly due to the decay of readiness on the part of a motor pathway to be excited. The fact is that we do not very often bring the frequency factor to a point where it overpowers the recency factor. Most of our learning is done more or less with a view to quick forgetting. We are satisfied if we can recall after a brief interval. It is mostly the movement systems connected with the larger bodily activities that get really enough practice to make frequency independent of recency. We never forget how to skate, how to swim, how to use the typewriter. Most of our verbal movement systems are formed with very few repetitions, indeed, compared with the amount of repetition given to such movement systems as these.

The rapid initial forgetting would then be due to the falling off in the recency factor, the perseverative tendency. This would be more marked, the less the frequency factor was involved; hence Radossawljewitsch, who required enough repetitions of his material to produce two perfect recitations, found a less rapid rate of forgetting at first than did either Ebbinghaus or Finkenbinder, who required only one perfect recitation.

Now what about the superiority of distributed repetitions? When a motor pathway has just been excited, it is in a state of readiness to discharge again. This must mean that all its synaptic resistances are low. The next repetition following immediately upon the first, and finding low resistances, obviously cannot lower them much more. Its effect on them, we may suppose, is therefore slight. Since the 'readiness,' the recency factor or perseverative tendency, diminishes with time, the learning that is done with no interval will naturally be short-lived in its effects: it will depend much on the recency factor and little on the frequency factor. The superiority of distributed repetitions may then be due, not only to the absence of fatigue and the large proportion of first repetitions with their high attention value, but to a law which seems inherently probable: namely, that a nervous process, in traversing a synapse, cannot produce any permanent effect on that synapse if little or no resistance is offered to it.

IV. The Interference of Associative Dispositions in Successive Systems

Associative dispositions which are called into action successively may interfere with each other, instead of readily forming themselves into a successive movement system. There is an especial difficulty of this sort about the case where the movement system to be formed involves the same movement repeated a number of times in different contexts. We all know that a passage of prose or verse is particularly hard to learn if the same phrase occurs in it repeatedly, set each time in different surroundings: in learning a part in a play one is especially likely to trip over speeches that begin with the same words but end differently, or that involve the same thought put in slightly different words. Bourdon (14) and Ranschburg (114), using numbers as the material to be learned in their experiments on memory, both found that numbers are more readily learned, the fewer like figures they contain. The effect of the repetition of like elements in different settings may be formulated by saying that immediately after the movement sequence A–B is presented, tending to establish the associative disposition A–B, another movement sequence A–C occurs, tending to establish the associative disposition A–C. Müller and Pilzecker (90) said that if A has just been associated with B, this fact exerts a *generative inhibition* on the formation of the association A–C. Physiologically, one may conceive that since the pathway for B is still in readiness, having been so recently excited, when A is given the second time its kinæsthetic energy is divided between the old path A–B and the new path A–C. When the time for recall comes, when we try to repeat from memory the material we have learned, then the two dispositions are simultaneously set into action by A. Now, it may happen that they lead to perfectly compatible movements, such, for instance, as those involved in seeing a word and hearing it pronounced: under such conditions we have the formation of a simultaneous movement system, a process which will be considered in the next chapter. But if they are not compatible movements, and cannot both be carried out at the same time, there occurs in recall the process of interference which Müller and Pilzecker called *effectual inhibition*. If A tends to set into activity the incompatible motor processes B and C, then there may be for a few seconds a deadlock, both responses being inhibited. This regularly shows itself, of course, in experiments where the time of recall is being measured, as a lengthening of the time. Hence many experimenters (for instance, Cattell (21), Münsterberg (93), Wells (150)) find that 'free' associations, where the observer is at liberty to think of any word he likes in connection with a given stimulus word, take longer than 'forced' associations, where the observer is directed beforehand to think of, say, a rhyming word or a word with opposite meaning to that of the stimulus word. Again, stimulus words that refer to recent experience are reacted to slowly because they set into action so many dispositions. Hirszowicz (51) reports that abstract words, also, which have fewer associative dispositions connected with them, are responded to more promptly in such association time experiments than concrete words.

A period of mutual inhibition of this kind may be terminated by the victory of the stronger associative disposition. Calkins (19) undertook in 1895 to study the relative strength, in such a contest, of dispositions which had the advantage of recency, those which had the advantage of frequency, and those which had the advantage of greater attention at the time of their formation. She presented to her observers colors followed or accompanied by numbers. One of the colors occurred several times in the series, once in an unimportant position, and once in some emphasized situation, either again with the same numeral, or at the beginning or end of the series (with another numeral), or with a numeral of unusual size or color. Other experiments were made where a given color appeared, in a long color-number series, three times followed by the same two-digit numeral and once followed by a three-digit numeral, which as the only one of its kind would naturally attract especial attention; or three times with the same numeral and once at the beginning of the series with a different number, which as the first number of the series would get more attention. Also there were short series where the color shown last had appeared once before with a three-digit number, or at the beginning with another number, or twice before with the same number, which was different from the one associated with it when it was shown last. After each series the colors were presented without their numbers, one at a time, in altered order, and the observer was asked what number the color recalled. Thus a color A had formed associative dispositions with two different numbers, B and $C;$ in some cases the disposition $A–B$ had the advantage of recency, when the color A and number B were the last ones shown; sometimes $A–B$ had the advantage of frequency, and sometimes B had been presented in such a way as to attract especial attention. Under these conditions, the results showed that frequency gave the greatest advantage; the degree of attention came next, and recency had third place only. It is not surprising that the recency factor was of comparatively little importance here, for all the numbers really had the advantage of recency. The series were not long enough to permit the recency or perseverative tendency to die out in any of the motor pathways involved.

Müller and Pilzecker called attention to the fact that when, after the associative disposition $A–B$ has been formed, A is presented with C, even such a presentation with a new associate may strengthen the old disposition $A–B$. For the instant after one reads the new syllable C, one may recall A's old associate B, and since it seems to be a law that the functioning of an associative disposition in actual recall does more to strengthen it than the renewed impression of its terms through the sense-organs, $A–B$ is more helped than it would be if B were actually presented. Closely connected with this fact, which Müller and Pilzecker called 'associative co-excitation,' is a curious result obtained by Müller and Schumann (91). Although, as we have seen, the disposition $A–C$ will not be so readily established if the disposition $A–B$ already exists, the establishment of the new disposition $A–C$ seems to do no harm to the one already on the scene. Müller and Schumann found that if the disposition $A–B$ has so far weakened with age as to have become subliminal; if, that is, A will no longer recall B, it can be reëstablished by even fewer repetitions, when A has in the meantime become associated with C, than when no new dispositions have been formed. For example, let us say that the syllable 'con' has been learned in connection with the syllable 'seb,' but that the learning occurred so long ago that 'con' now fails to recall 'seb.' In a new series, 'con' is learned in conjunction with the new syllable 'mup.' After this series has been learned, the old one, in which 'con' is followed by 'seb,' is relearned, and although in the first repetitions of this old series the new association 'con-mup' exerts some interference, the bringing of the old disposition 'con-seb' above the limen of recall takes place with fewer repetitions than if the new disposition 'con-mup' had not been established. It is hard to understand this except on the supposition that 'associative co-excitation' occurs below the limen of actual recall, so that the old dispositions are subliminally practiced while the new ones are being founded.

No such furthering effect occurs when, immediately after an associative disposition has been founded, other dispositions which do not involve either of the terms of the old one are established; if, that is, just after the disposition $A-B$ has been formed, the dispositions $C-D$ and $E-F$ are founded. If one fills the pause between learning a series and testing its learning, for example, with the learning of other series, or with any kind of intellectual work, the results of the test are unfavorably affected. This is of course one of the factors which make a long series of syllables harder to learn than a short series. It is termed by Müller and Pilzecker *retroactive inhibition*. It helps to explain also why the middle of a series should be the part hardest to learn. For the middle syllables of a series suffer interference from the memory after-images of their predecessors and retroactive inhibition from their successors. (Poppelreuter (112) uses the term 'anterograde detraction' to designate the interference exerted on associative dispositions by the memory after-image processes of preceding impressions, and 'retrograde detraction' to designate retroactive inhibition). The physiological cause of retroactive inhibition can hardly be conceived otherwise than as an interference with processes of recall that would, without the distraction, take place in the interval between learning and testing. It may be supposed that if one were not given the new material to learn just after the learning that is to be tested, one would occupy at least a part of the interval in recalling the old. So far as I know, no experiments have been made to disprove such a supposition. The only way in which such recall can be prevented is by giving the observer something to do in the interval, which would of course produce the effect of retroactive inhibition.

CHAPTER VII

SIMULTANEOUS MOVEMENT SYSTEMS

A SIMULTANEOUS movement system is one where the movements, instead of being dependent each on the one which preceded it in time, are mutually interdependent and occur together. The linking by associative dispositions takes place in both directions, or in all directions if the system is composed of more than two movements. Not only are the kinæsthetic excitations produced by the movement A the necessary stimulus to movement B, but the excitations resulting from B are the stimulus to movement A. It is evident that in such systems the component movements must be compatible. They must be of such a nature that they can be performed at the same time. Thus two articulatory movements could not enter into a simultaneous movement system: you cannot pronounce t and b at the same moment. But the movements involved in pronouncing a word ànd those involved in looking at the word printed, or calling up a mental image of its appearance, are compatible, and could enter into a simultaneous system. In our perceptions of objects, some of the movements are compatible and enter into simultaneous systems, while others do not.

An originally simultaneous system is formed by the actual occurrence of the movements together, and strengthened by each repetition of their synchronous occurrence. Meyer (83), in 1910, following a method suggested by Ach, tried to bring about the formation of simultaneous systems under experimental conditions. The observer was shown a series of cards, each card carrying two groups of simple figures, and each shown for the very short instant of 135 thousandths of a second: the interval between each card and the next was the same very brief time. In the test, the observer was shown one half of the card and required to draw from memory the figures that were on the missing half. The brief exposure was intended to keep the observer from attending successively to the two halves of the card, and force him to attend to them simultaneously. The short interval between exposures would, it was thought, in a similar way keep him from attending successively to the two parts of the memory after-image of the card. Learning and correct recall proved to be possible by this method. It is evident that only those parts of the card could really be simultaneously attended to which did not involve incompatible movements. It is also evident that most of the learning which we do in ordinary life is performed under conditions very different from these.

Where the movements which enter into the system are very simple, they may form themselves into simultaneous systems, probably, by actually occurring together. But in all the concrete examples one can think of where simultaneous systems are formed, one comes to do the two things together, or attend to them together, through a preliminary process of attending to them alternately. The leg and arm movements of a practiced swimmer form a simultaneous system, but in learning to swim they are performed alternately, and even after one really begins to swim one has difficulty in not attending to them alternately. The static movement system of holding the head perfectly still and the phasic system of the arm swing are formed into a simultaneous system when one learns to make a golf stroke, but their simultaneous performance is possible only by having attended to them alternately as a beginner. When one has perfectly learned a language, the sight of a word and its meaning are simultaneous; but in the beginning one attended alternately to the printed word and the idea of its meaning. When associative dispositions leading in both directions are formed between two movements, so that either one can excite the other successively, if they are compatible movements the tendency is apparently always for them to form simultaneous systems. The greatest aid to the formation of simultaneous systems is the association of each of the two movements with a common third. If C and B are compatible movements, and associative dispositions have been formed between A and C and between A and B, then when A occurs, there is a tendency for B and C to be simultaneously excited. Thus Müller and Pilzecker (90) found that if a syllable such as 'bez' were learned at one time in connection with the syllable 'gaf,' and at another time with the syllable 'jip,' when 'bez' was later given the observer might respond with a kind of hybrid like 'gap.' Both of the former associates of 'bez' were reproduced, but the incompatible movements were forced out and a compromise was reached in the combination of elements from both syllables. This method of forming simultaneous systems by linking each of several movements to a common motor response is of the utmost importance for our experience. It is precisely thus that those simultaneous movement systems are formed on which are based what we call perceptions of objects, as well as ideas of concrete objects and of abstractions.

The perception of an object consists of a number of sensations, some of which are peripherally excited, that is, caused by the activity of our sense organs at the moment, while others are centrally excited, that is, the revival of former sense experiences. A piece of ice looks smooth, white, hard, and cold: we realize that only the whiteness of it is the result of present sense stimulation, and that the hardness, smoothness, and coldness are the effects of former experiences with the senses of touch and temperature. Now the way in which we form such combinations of sensations into perceptions is evidently not so much by adding bit to bit to form a mosaic, as by digging one bit after another out of an original whole. In first making acquaintance with an object we respond to it as an undifferentiated whole: later we come to make specialized responses to various parts and aspects of it; but it is the fact that it can be still responded to as a whole that keeps these specialized movements together in a single system, and thus gives the object its unity. An orange, or a chair, or a tree, is a single object, and not a mere aggregate of qualities and parts, because it can be reacted to as a whole, and because every one of the movements involved in attending to its parts is associated with the movement of reacting to the whole object. Some of these movements which are associated with various parts or aspects of an object are compatible: the fact that they lead to the common outlet of a movement made to the whole object may thus transform them into simultaneous systems. Others are incompatible, and must be united in successive rather than simultaneous systems; thus, for instance, one cannot attend simultaneously to both ends of a pen, but the whole object is a unity because of the possibility of responding to the whole of it by a single movement or movement system. Of the motor responses thus linked together by their common outlet, the compatible ones become simultaneous systems, relating to those parts of the object that can be attended to together; while the incompatible ones become successive systems, either reversible or irreversible, relating to those parts of the object which must be attended to in succession.

On a non-motor theory of association, which would make the formation of an associative disposition result from a lowering of resistances at the synapses on a pathway directly connecting two sensory centres, and resulting from their simultaneous activity, it is commonly held that all associations are based on simultaneous rather than on successive experience. Thus Offner (98) says that when two successively occurring impressions are associated, it is because the second impression is simultaneous with the memory after-image or perseverative process of the first. Wohlgemuth (154) has recently maintained on the basis of experimental results that all association is between simultaneously occurring experiences. He required his observers to form an association between a color and a form (a) when the form was colored; (b) when a black shape was shown on a colored ground; (c) when a colored field was shown alongside of a black shape on a white ground; (d) when a colored field was shown followed by a black shape on a white ground, or *vice versa*. It was found that "the more the members of a group are apperceived as a whole, the stronger their association with each other," and from this it is concluded that "all associations are due to simultaneity." It is evident that the superiority of the associations in impressions that were apperceived as a whole, for instance, of the association between color and shape when the shape is itself colored, is due to the fact that besides the simultaneous responses made to the two factors of color and shape, there is a single response to the whole impression; thus the simultaneous impression has the great aid of a single unifying motor reaction.

Just as the unity of the perception of an object depends on the possibility of making a single movement or movement system in response to the object as a whole, so of course the possibility of reviving a memory image of an object as a whole depends on such a single response. Upon the strength of the simultaneous and successive systems thus linked together by their common outlet will depend the completeness and accuracy with which a memory image can be analyzed into details corresponding with the original. It is not necessary to emphasize the importance of a word or name as furnishing a convenient unifying response to the whole object. One cause of the low stage of intellectual development of animals is the very limited extent to which they can hold together the parts of their experience by making reactions to a whole group of such parts as a single group. Beasts that, like the monkey, the elephant, and the raccoon, have grasping organs with which to move things about have a great advantage so far as the formation of perceptions of objects is concerned. But the unrivalled instrument of unifying motor responses is of course language. By its help we can not only hold together into a system our responses to the various aspects of a single concrete object, but we can in a similar way form systems out of the aspects or features which a number of objects have in common. We can form those systems which are the bases of general ideas or concepts, such as the concept dog or animal. There is almost no limit to the complexity of the system combinations which can be formed through having a single motor outlet for an entire combination.

The process of learning practically always involves both simultaneous and successive movement systems. In trying to form a new successive system, such as a memorized series of nonsense syllables, one is of course really working not with single movements, but with systems of movements. Each syllable is not merely pronounced, which is a process involving comparatively simple simultaneous systems for each vowel and consonant, but there is very likely present a visual image of the syllable, betraying, if our theory is true, the presence of tentative eye movements; and there may be also other 'aids' to the learning process, each one involving its own movement systems.

When a number of stimuli, each calling for its own motor response, act together upon the organism, as of course they are constantly doing, one set of responses is prepotent, and other incompatible responses are completely inhibited. It goes without saying that the inhibited responses can form no associative connections. That which is wholly unattended to does not form associations. It is true that Scripture (123), working in the Leipzig laboratory more than twenty years ago, found that unattended-to parts of a picture, letters or small colored squares in the corner, for example, did when later shown alone recall the picture in a certain number of cases too large to be due to chance. But there is always a doubt as to whether, in these few cases, the elements which did the recalling were really unattended to, and Howe (53), repeating Scripture's experiments in the Cornell laboratory, failed to confirm his results. Ordahl (101) tested the question in 1911 by a better method: she had her observers learn the middle one of three ten-syllable series arranged in parallel vertical columns. After a short interval another set of three was presented whose middle series was one of the two side series in the preceding set. Would this middle series be better learned now because it was present, though unattended to, at the side of the series previously learned? The results showed that it was not any better learned; its presentation without attention had formed no associative dispositions.

A different problem, however, is furnished by the more ordinary cases of distraction. A thing to which we give no attention cannot be said to distract us at all: distraction occurs when our attention is forced to alternate between the movement system we are acquiring and another movement system quite unconnected with it. The effect of distraction seems to be greater, the more the two systems are, not merely disconnected with one another, but actually incompatible with one another. When they are really incompatible, if attention happens to be given to the distracting process the one to be learned is wholly shut out. Von Sybel (136a) says that distraction diminishes visual learning in favor of auditory-motor learning. Thus its effect in general seems to be that of simplifying the movement system that is formed. It prevents the stirring up of the more complex systems involved in visual imagery and in meaning connections. There are two ways in which one might conceivably explain this effect. One would be by supposing that only a limited amount of nervous energy is available in the cortex, and that if a part of it is occupied in the movements of the distracting system, there will not be enough left for other complex movement systems. The other explanation would rest on the possibility that the distracting system might contain movements incompatible with those of the system to be learned; and of course the more complex the system to be learned, the greater the likelihood that some of its parts would be incompatible with those of the distracting system. Both of these suppositions are very likely true.

The most concrete problems connected with the mutual relations of movement systems concern the way in which large systems are secure from distraction. The ability of any process that is going on in the mind to keep itself from being disturbed by distractions depends mainly on two factors. The first is the amount of effort or resolution that is put forth to 'keep one's mind on' the process to be attended to. This factor will be discussed in the chapter on "The Problem or Purpose." When the task is one of forming a new movement system, of learning, for instance, a series of nonsense syllables, nothing but effort will enable the material that is in process of being learned to hold attention against distraction. It will be suggested in the chapter just referred to that it is the naturally persistent character of the attitude of activity or effort which enables the task associated with it to be held to, despite distracting influences. But often, of course, it is the interest of the material that holds distraction aloof. Now, interest always means that some large, already formed movement system is back of the material attended to, and that its momentum, so to speak, is such that the associative dispositions not involved in it will be inhibited. The advantage is always with the older and complexer systems. Thus Toll (139) had his observers learn lists of words in which names of mammals alternated with names of American cities. The results showed that the tendency of one word was almost never to recall the word that followed it in the series, but rather to recall, if it were an animal name, the name of another animal; if it were a city name, the name of another city. The older and complexer systems had the right of way.

Levy-Suhl (70) used the ability of a well-established system of associative dispositions to resist distraction as a test of the normality of the mind. Insane and normal persons were allowed to start a train of ideas suggested by themselves, and when it was well under way, they were interrupted by pronouncing to them an irrelevant word. Only a hopelessly abnormal mind meekly accepted the distraction and followed the new line of thought without reference to the old. A curious instance of the effect of the problem or purpose involved in an experiment is shown by the fact that Baldwin (8), trying experiments by practically the same method, found that his observers, who were all normal, usually accepted the new train of thought almost at once. In his experiments the first train of thought, on which the interruption broke, was suggested by the experimenter instead of being self-suggested. The whole attitude of the observers was therefore that of attending to anything that might come from the experimenter, instead of really allowing an associative system to get possession.

An experiment of Poppelreuter's (112) well illustrates the independence of complex systems. He suggests that we take sentences from different stories and intermingle them, and that the result be read straight through from beginning to end. It is a fact that one will have at the end of the reading the two narratives side by side and each almost as clear as if it had been read without the other. Each system of movements has appropriated that which belonged to it, and each has in turn yielded place to the other. Thus we can carry on a conversation with a fair degree of intelligence while we read a story, and the story ideas do not mix with the conversation ideas except very occasionally.

Quite as important as the distracting effects of one movement system on another are the favorable effects of one system on another. One of the simplest ways in which we can make associative dispositions help each other is to attach some distinguishing mark to each member in a series of movements that are to be formed into a successive movement system. Thus each member of the series becomes a simultaneous system of some complexity, and the various members get more individuality. A few examples will make this clear. Gordon (44) found that nonsense syllables could be better learned if each syllable was printed on a ground of different color; Peterson (107) that figures were better learned if they differed both in form and in color. The introduction of these variations increases the complexity of the material to be learned, and thus increases its dissimilarity: now, the less alike two movement systems are, the less the danger that their associates will get confused. When the differentiating marks are themselves connected into a system, the advantage they furnish is very much increased. Very simple illustrations of this state of things are furnished by the effect of rhythm in learning and the effect of associating a syllable with its place in the series.

The influence of rhythm in learning has been many times noted in experimental studies and in everyday life: perhaps it was a little exaggerated in the days when schoolrooms full of children used to chant the multiplication table at the top of their voices, but it has its uses as a mnemonic factor. Ebert and Meumann (30) found that without rhythm, it took twenty-three repetitions to learn a ten-syllable series; with rhythm only fourteen were needed for a twelve-syllable series. Indeed, so strong is the innate tendency to make rhythmic all our motor processes whenever we possibly can, that material to be learned cannot be read over repeatedly without falling into rhythm. The attempt not to make it rhythmic operates as a strong distraction of attention: thus M. K. Smith (129) showed that when nonsense syllables are presented without rhythm, at irregular intervals of time, some sort of rhythm has to be read into them or they simply will not be learned. One reason, then, for the value of rhythm in the presentation of material to be learned is simply that we can't help making it rhythmic, and the attempt to do so distracts the attention. But another reason, and the one which concerns us at this point, lies in the fact that when material is presented rhythmically, the words or syllables are differentiated by being associated with differences of accent, just as in Gordon's experiment they were differentiated by having differently colored backgrounds. Thus Müller and Schumann (91) proved that it took more repetitions to relearn a series of syllables in which the accented syllables were those which had been unaccented in the original series, than to relearn the original series with its accents unaltered. The association of a particular syllable with a particular stress helped to individualize it. A third reason for the advantage of rhythm is that it forms especially strong associative dispositions between the members of a single rhythmic foot; thus dividing up the whole system to be formed into a series of smaller systems. That a particularly strong disposition connects the two syllables which belong to the same rhythmic foot was demonstrated by Müller and Schumann. After a series had been

learned in trochaic rhythm, new series were presented, in some
of which the 'feet' of the original were preserved although their
order was altered, while in others new 'feet' were made by
putting together a syllable that had ended one foot and the
syllable that began the next one. The learning of the first kind
was helped by the associations already formed between the
syllables belonging to a single foot; that of the second kind was
helped by the associations already formed between syllables
which were not parts of the same foot. The results showed that
series of the first kind were learned more quickly than those of
the second kind; therefore, presumably, the associative dispositions between syllables in the same foot are stronger than
those between neighboring syllables in different feet. The
exact reason for this is not so easy to make out.

The association of each member of a successive movement
system with its place in the series is an aid to the formation of
the system. What constitutes the association of a particular
part of the material to be learned with a particular place in
the series? How do we recognize that a certain syllable came
near the beginning of a series formerly learned, or near the middle, or near the end? The syllables at the beginning and end of
a series are apt to have distinguishing marks: thus, if the syllables were presented on a rotating cylinder, as is often the
case in experiments where syllables are to be learned, the first
and last syllables may be associated with the blank spaces at
the beginning and end of the series.

Vaschide (142), as long ago as 1896, made a special investigation of the process of associating an impression with its place
in a series. He used series of eight, ten, twelve, or twenty words,
sometimes visually and sometimes auditorily presented. A few
seconds afterwards, the observer having first tried to recall the
series, the words were given to him in altered order, and he had
to assign to each its original place in the series. The localizing
was done in various ways. Usually only the first and last words
could be immediately placed, no doubt by some association
with stimuli which occurred at the beginning or end of the

series, although Vaschide implies that the placing was done directly and not through the aid of consciously realized associations. Other words were localized in groups, or by association with a number, or by some associative scheme such as a story, or forming the initials into a word; in still other cases a 'sentiment' was the localizing mark, such as that of effort or difficulty connected with words in the middle, or of relief at nearing the end. Sometimes the marks which determined the place of a word were too indistinct to be analyzed; sometimes it was localized negatively, so to speak, as belonging, for instance, neither to the beginning nor the end and therefore necessarily to the middle. Thus in many ways an impression in a series can enter into simultaneous movement systems which stand for its place in that series. That these marks of absolute position form associative dispositions which aid learning a series of nonsense syllables was proved by Müller and Schumann. After having learned, on one day, four series of twelve syllables each, they learned next day a series in which the feet were those of two of the series previously learned, six feet being taken from each of the two, and each foot being in the position it had held in its original series. That is, the first foot was the first foot of Series I of the preceding day; the second foot was the second foot of Series II, the third foot the third foot of Series I, and so on. They also learned another series made up in like manner of feet from Series I and II of the day before, but with these feet not in the absolute position which they had occupied previously: thus, the first foot was the second of Series I, and so on. The learning of the series in which the feet preserved the same absolute position which they had had on being previously learned in a different series showed a saving of 15% of the repetitions necessary to learn the series with the absolute position changed. It was not the *order* of the feet that was maintained, since the new series had feet selected from two different old series, but their absolute position, as at the beginning, middle, or end. Each syllable must in the first learning have entered into certain simultaneous movement systems, perhaps with the varying degrees of effort, fatigue, and relief characteristic of different positions in the series; and these must have aided the relearning with absolute position preserved. Müller and Pilzecker (90) found them so influential that sometimes instead of the right syllable another would be substituted which had nothing in common with it except the fact that each was, say, the fifth syllable in its series. Such associations with absolute position are naturally, as Nagel (97) showed, more influential with nonsense material than with sense material, where the movement systems formed are so much more complex.

The association of a visual object with a definite position in space nearly everybody will attest from personal experience is a help to remembering it. One recalled a certain rule in one's Latin grammar by thinking of its position on the lower part of the left-hand page. Jacobs (56) conceived the idea of trying the effect of a purely mental localization of visual images on learning: he provided a series of circles in which the observer was to imagine placed the nonsense syllables that were read to him. Such a method involves too much distraction of attention, and it is not surprising that it offered no advantage over simply listening to the syllables. Gordon (44) actually presented the syllables in particularly striking spatial arrangements. They were shown either in a straight line with equal intervals, or in a straight line with unequal intervals, or around a circle with equal intervals, or around a circle with unequal intervals. The circle with equal intervals gave the best results: the spatial positions of the syllables were varied enough to distinguish them, and not so varied as to be confusing. There is a limit to the effectiveness of distinguishing marks added to the material to be learned. If the marks are too complicated, the formation of the movement systems which they involve may interfere with the formation of the new successive system which is the main object: too many sidewise dispositions may detract from the straight-ahead dispositions. This was clearly shown in Peterson's (107) experiments, where the observers remembered colors better if the colored objects had different forms, but were not helped when a size variation also was introduced.

The best way to make simultaneous systems aid in the formation of successive systems is of course to have the auxiliary simultaneous systems themselves linked into a succession by already formed associative dispositions. This constitutes the enormous superiority of material that makes sense, over nonsense material. 'Sense' always means already formed associative dispositions. No matter how new an idea may be to us, if it has any meaning at all it evidently appeals to something out of our past experience. There is an overwhelming tendency to bring old and already formed movement systems into activity whenever new ones are to be formed. If you open the pages of a dictionary at random, and select any two disconnected words between which to form a new associative disposition, you have only to attend to them for a few seconds and by some hook or crook, some byway of past experience, you will find that they are already connected. Even nonsense syllables, selected, because of their freedom from old associations, for use in experiments to discover the laws under which new systems are formed, constantly stir up old systems. Take the syllables 'bap' and 'dif'; almost immediately an old system springs into activity and one thinks, 'The Baptists differ from other sects.' It is with the greatest difficulty that students in a psychological laboratory can be induced to learn nonsense syllables without 'making sense' of them.

These already formed systems in some cases help the formation of a new system by breaking it up into units, each unit forming part of an old movement system. This process of using aids to the learning of nonsense material has recently been exhaustively studied by Müller (89). When the aids are simultaneous systems, "apprehended by a single act of attention," Müller calls them complexes; when they are successive systems he calls them associative groups. All kinds of links are used in the formation of these subsidiary groups. Several syllables may be held together in a group because the first and last ones rhyme, or because the first and last ones have tall consonants, or by means of any sort of meaning association. In recall, a whole group will present itself as a simultaneous unity, and can then be turned into a successive group by having its several members successively attended to. But aids too have their disadvantages: the old systems on which they rest may sometimes transform and falsify the material presented. Müller says they may cause certain elements to be neglected by attention; moreover having too many aids at one's disposal may occasion hesitation, and one may sometimes reject a right syllable because one does not remember using it as an aid and thinks one would have done so had it been there. All this simply means that if one sets old systems into activity, instead of depending on patient repetition to form the new one, the old systems may become so very active and so numerous that they interfere with one another and with the formation of the new system.

When material is learned with the help of any kind of aid, it belongs to two or more movement systems when the learning is complete: one, the new system which has been established, the others, the old systems which functioned in the learning. Its recall when the point of correct recitation has been reached is due to the combined effect of all the systems, the newly formed and the older ones. When a number of associative dispositions thus combine to produce the same result, we may use the term 'constellation,' by Ziehen's (161) suggestion, to designate the process. Many times, when a disposition would be too weak to bring about recall unaided, it may be made the dominant one by the coöperation of others: the word 'plant' might call up an image of something with stem and leaves, and set going other vegetable reminiscences if it did not occur in the phrase 'manufacturing plant,' in which case we may get instead an image of machinery and smokestacks. Constellation is really the most important influence in determining recall. Even the action of a subliminal disposition may so aid another disposition as to secure its victory in a contest. This was shown by some curious experiments of Müller and Schumann's. Those patient learners committed to memory four twelve-syllable series in trochaic rhythm. Later, enough later for these series to have been partly forgotten, other series were learned which consisted of the accented syllables of the former series. Immediately afterwards, a third set of series composed of the unaccented syllables of the first set was learned, and the number of repetitions required to learn this third series indicated that it was actually helped by the previous learning of the accented syllables; apparently the unaccented ones had been 'set in readiness' by the presentation of their accented companions.

When the material to be learned has meaning, as in the case of a series of words, the tendency to link the words with a connected and ready-made system through their meanings is irresistible unless a great effort is made to counteract it. The words, however randomly chosen, are made into a story. And when the material has connected meaning, forms a coherent narrative or exposition, the influence of these previously formed simultaneous and successive systems is so great that a single reading is often enough to establish the new system. The experimental evidence that meaningful material is learned more readily than meaningless material is plentiful. Ogden (99) found sense material learned about ten times as fast as nonsense material, and Balaban (7) got a corresponding result; the latter and Radossawljewitsch (113) report that it is forgotten much less rapidly. The speed with which different individuals learn sense material is more uniform than the speed with which they learn nonsense material: Michotte (84) says that while four observers had very different capacities for the mechanical learning of pairs of words, they all four accomplished about the same amount of learning in a given time when they were instructed to think of relations between the meanings of the words; that is, to make use of old associative dispositions.

An important effect of meaning associations is that they

unify successive movement systems. We noted in the chapter on The Memory After-Image that weak backward associative dispositions are formed, through the influence of the tendency of a movement just performed to be re-excited, between the second member of a successive movement system and the first. Now a much wider opportunity for the functioning of associative dispositions in such an apparently reversed direction is given when the successive movement system is associated as a whole with a simultaneous system as its meaning. Thus the latter part of a familiar quotation can easily suggest its beginning; the words 'falling fast' may instantly call up the whole line, 'The shades of night were falling fast.' When a successive movement system, each of whose members normally could produce only the next following one in the series, aside from a much weaker tendency to produce the preceding one through the memory after-image process, is associated as a whole with a meaning, that is, a simultaneous system, the latter part of the successive system may suggest the meaning and the meaning may serve to revive the whole successive system beginning with its first members. This 'initial tendency in recall,' as Arnold (6) has called it, is due not to any reversal of the action of associative dispositions, but to the fact that the latter part of the successive series calls up the first part through the mediation of a simultaneous system with which the successive system as a whole is associated.

The influence of meanings, that is, of old and ready formed movement systems, on recall will account for a difference which McDougall (73) regards as fundamental between two kinds of memory, and which he takes as a convincing proof that a motor theory of association is impossible, and hence that psycho-physical parallelism in general must be abandoned. Parallelism, he says, will be discredited "if it can be shown that habit and memory do not obey the same laws." As an argument in support of the belief that they obey different laws, McDougall supposes himself to be set the task of learning a series of twelve nonsense syllables in a certain number of repetitions. After the learning is complete, he says, "I can throw my mind back and remember any one of the twelve readings more or less clearly as a unique event in my past history. I can remember perhaps that during the fifth reading I began to despair of ever learning the series, that I made a new effort, that someone spoke in the adjoining room and disturbed me disagreeably; I may perhaps remember what he said." "If the repetition by heart of the nonsense syllables and the remembering of any one of the readings of the series are both to be called evidences of memory, it must be admitted that two very different functions, two very different modes of retention, are denoted by the same word."

The chief differences between them he states to be the following: —

(1) The syllable learning involves the formation of a habit to which each repetition contributes a little; the recall of the events which characterized a single repetition "depends wholly on a single act of apprehension." The reason for this, we should say, is simply that the syllable learning involved the formation of a wholly new movement system, while the events of a single repetition are already related to many old movement systems; in other words, they have meaning. We have often before felt weary and discouraged when half way through a task; we have been interrupted and have felt annoyed on many previous occasions. These happenings are so readily recalled because they are *relevant*, and to be relevant means to be already imbedded in the same movement systems.

(2) Reproducing the syllables involves a forward-looking attitude; recalling a particular repetition involves a backward-looking attitude. To this we should agree; it is immediately related to the next point of difference.

(3) Recalling the syllables is not helped by any effort to cast back thought to the moment of apprehension; recalling a particular repetition is aided by "voluntary rummaging in the past." Naturally, we should answer, since the syllables form a wholly new movement system, and the memory of a partic-

ular repetition is as we have seen largely interwoven with older systems.

(4) The syllable learning involves the connecting of eight simple impressions only, yet it requires twelve or more repetitions: the remembrance of a particular event involves a very complex set of impressions, yet it depends only on a single act of apprehension. Naturally, because it is aided by the old movement systems of meanings.

(5) The series is quickly forgotten; the particular event may be recalled for a long time. Naturally, for the same reason that meaningful material may be longer retained.

Another instance of the effect of auxiliary movement systems is furnished by the location that is assigned to visual imagery. There seem to be two sources from which the systems are derived on which such localization is based. One is the actual surroundings of the individual at the moment; the other is what he recalls of the actual location of the real object that is being imaged. Milhaud (85) reports that some observers localize the mental image of an object with reference to their own position at the time, while others feel themselves transported to the real position of the object represented: the difference, he suggests, is due to the fact that observers of the former type are more interested in their own kinæsthetic sensations and cannot lose the sense of their actual position. Martin (75) enumerates no fewer than twelve different ways in which a mental image may be located, and a great variety of conditions which determine the localization, all of which, however, seem to fall into two general classes, namely, those due to actually present objects and the position of the observer's body, and those connected with the memory image itself, such as the recollection of having last seen the original object in a particular situation.

The distinction drawn by Perky (106) between a memory image and an image of imagination is based on a difference in the complexity of the movement systems involved. Perky caused the persons she experimented on, sitting in a dark room with one eye closed, to call up what she called a memory image and an imaginary image of the same object. By a memory image she meant the image, say, of a particular horse recently seen; by an imaginary image she meant the image of a horse not connected with any particular occasion of past experience. This use of the terms memory and imagination may have historical justification, but it is surely not the ordinary one. Imagination forms new combinations out of past experiences: one may imagine a centaur, but one has to remember a horse, and one remembers, not imagines, it, whether it is thought of as with or without a context. Baldwin and Stout, in the former's "Dictionary of Philosophy and Psychology," say of the term 'imagination': "It seems better to adopt the current usage of popular language, and to restrict the term to that forming of new combinations which is made possible by the absence of objective limitations confining the flow of ideas." Perky found that the 'memory images' of her observers required more eye-movement and more kinæsthesis generally, than their 'imagination images'; also that "in imagination consciousness is narrowed and there is inhibition of irrelevant associations, while in memory attention wanders and the image is unstable." This is what we should expect: if an observer is required to call up, besides what we should call the memory image of an object, memory images of its surroundings and attendant circumstances on a particular occasion, the motor systems will naturally be more complicated than when the object is recalled alone.

Finally, a profound influence is exerted by old movement systems upon new ones in the processes which underlie the alteration of memory images with time. It may be laid down as a law that whenever in a movement system it is possible for an old associative disposition, based on much repetition, to take the place of a new one whose strength lies rather in recency than in repetition, the substitution occurs. This is of course precisely the fundamental law of perception. If the third and fourth fingers are crossed, and a pencil is laid between them, the patient's eyes being closed, he will have excited the tentative movements that belong to two pencils rather than those belonging to one, even though he knows there is only one pencil: the associative dispositions recently set up by the sight of the single pencil are not able to withstand the old dispositions connected for life with the stimulation of two points on the skin that are not normally reached by a single object at the same time. On this tendency of old dispositions to supplant new ones is based the tendency of memory images to alter in the direction of the ordinary and normal experience; to lose their peculiar and unusual features. Thus Warren and Shaw (143) found indications that the memory image of a large square tends to grow smaller and that of a small square to grow larger, both being as it were attracted towards a mean. Leuba (69) and Lewis (71), working by entirely different methods, noted a tendency in the memory image of a bright light to grow dimmer and that of a dim light to grow brighter, or rather to be judged as the image of a brighter light than that which had actually produced it. Phillippe (109), who had his observers look at a collection of five small objects and then draw them from memory after various intervals of time, reports that the images "seem to tend towards a type pre-existing in the mind" which exerts an attraction: thus the features on a Japanese mask tended in the memory image to resemble the European type. Kuhlmann (64) says that the memory images of the picture of an object tend towards representing the object itself, which of course involves older movement systems than those of the picture. Some time ago I saw at an exhibition of the National Academy of Design Waugh's painting called "The Knight of the Holy Grail." I remember that the parts of the picture which impressed me most were the sky, with a single faint star and the line of mountains underneath, the red glow of the Grail, and the very faint halo around the Grail. A stanza from Tennyson's poem was inscribed on the frame, and the last line, "And starlike mingled with the stars," ran in my mind, 'perseverated,' for several days after, which probably accounts for the persistence of the memory image of the sky and the Grail. For this is the part of the picture which is now clear in my memory; next come the figures of the angels, while the figure of Galahad I can scarcely get at all. When I attend to the angel figures, I see them grouped around the Grail in a way that I know must be incorrect, because it is inconsistent with my image of the Grail seen against the sky. I think this wrong grouping of the angels has been borrowed from another picture in which the angels are carrying a little child: I have a vague tendency to complete the angel group in this way. As I let my attention dwell on the angels, suddenly the image of a mast at the bow of the boat appears, at first with an air of authority about it; but presently I reject it. I do not believe it was in the picture: some other boat picture has 'contaminated,' as the philologists say, the Galahad one. I now fix my attention on the figure of Galahad. I see him in profile, kneeling, with hands pressed together in the conventional attitude of prayer. His face is like that of the Galahad in the Abbey pictures. Now, in order to test the accuracy of the memory image which I have thus called up and developed, I can fortunately appeal to an illustrated catalogue of the exhibition. I find that the mountains are much higher and wilder in the real picture than they were in my memory image; that instead of there being a group of two or three angels at the same level, there are two pairs, one above the other, an angel of the upper pair holding the Grail against the sky; that the figure of Galahad is not kneeling but sitting, though with the hands folded in prayer as I had remembered them; that my memory image had placed him near the centre of the picture instead of at the extreme left where he really is, and finally that the lower pair of angels carry in their hands tall wax candles in still taller candlesticks. It occurs to me that these candlesticks are responsible for my picture of the mast at the bow of the boat. There is no mast. My rejection of the mast image when it presented itself was accompanied by the incipient, undeveloped thought that a mast in that position would spoil the picture. Was it perhaps not the long, straight, nearly vertical lines of the candlesticks in the bow that suggested a mast? Now, almost all the errors in my memory image are in the direction of making it more commonplace, more generic. The rugged wildness of the mountains was softened; the unusual distribution of the angel figures became the more familiar image of two or three figures at the same level, and tended to blend with other pictures of the same general kind, as is shown by the intrusion of the child's figure. The figure of Galahad was shifted towards the centre to make the composition more commonplacely symmetrical; the correct image of the hands pressed together suggested the ordinary accompaniment of a kneeling rather than a sitting figure. Finally, the candlesticks were so unusual a feature of the bow of a boat that they transformed themselves into a mast.

CHAPTER VIII

In the preceding chapter we have considered some of the ways in which movement systems may interact with each other, and associative dispositions, the tendencies of one movement to excite another, may influence one another when they are simultaneously set into action. Upon such mutual influences the wandering of our thoughts at random, the play of fancy, depends. But much of our thinking is not random; it is, rather, directed toward a definite end. Is it possible to explain directed, controlled, purposeful thought, without introducing any new principles and laws beyond those which govern the mutual relations of associative dispositions?

Psychologists in the last few years have been much occupied with this subject of the exact nature of the problem or purpose, as directing the course of mental phenomena. It was Watt (148) who in 1905 first used in the sense which has recently become technical the German word '*Aufgabe*,' to indicate the idea of a problem to be solved, as affecting the associative dispositions that follow upon its acceptance. The term was used in the same year by Ach (2) to designate certain features of the reaction experiment. For instance, it has long been customary to distinguish in such experiments between the sensorial reaction and the muscular reaction: in the former the reagent's attention is beforehand directed towards the stimulus, which he is instructed to expect and to discriminate accurately when it occurs; in the latter his attention is directed beforehand wholly towards the movement that he is to make when the stimulus occurs. Ach pointed out that this is a difference in the problem, the *Aufgabe*, which in the sensorial reaction is, "React when the stimulus is fully apprehended," and in the muscular reaction is, "React as quickly as possible." The influence of the problem, once attended to, upon subsequent associative dispositions and movements Ach explained by saying that to associative dispositions and perseverative dispositions we must add a third kind of disposition in the nervous system, namely, determining dispositions or tendencies. A determining tendency proceeds from the idea of an end, and is responsible for the fact that the same stimulus may suggest different ideas under the influence of different problems. The strength of determining tendencies differs with individuals; it is modified by opposing associative and perseverative tendencies. An ingenious method of measuring the strength of certain determining tendencies was devised by Ach and has already been mentioned.[1] Associative dispositions between certain syllables were formed by a number of repetitions of the syllables. The observer was then given certain syllables of the series as stimuli, having been previously instructed that instead of responding by the *next* syllable of the series he was to give a new syllable that *rhymed* with the stimulus syllable. That is, he was to overcome an associative disposition by means of a determining tendency proceeding from his instructions. If he failed to carry out the instruction, and simply gave the syllable associated with the stimulus in the series learned, then the determining tendency was too weak to overcome the associative disposition. The strength of the associative disposition was measured by the number of repetitions used to form it, and the strength of a determining tendency could be measured by the number of repetitions needed to found an associative disposition that just overcame the determining tendency.

The question for us is evidently, 'What is the physiological basis of determining tendencies?' If associative tendencies or dispositions are based on lowered synaptic resistances between the kinæsthetic centres excited by the performance, either tentative or full, of one movement and the motor centre belonging to another movement, upon what are determining

[1] See page 95.

tendencies based? And a necessary step towards the solution of this question is as evidently a consideration of what constitutes a problem idea.

It would seem that the distinguishing characteristic of a problem idea, which differentiates it from other kinds of ideas, is the *persistence of its influence*. In disordered revery, we fly from one thought to another: each thought is responsible for the occurrence of the next, but beyond the next its influence hardly reaches, except occasionally. Thus we find at the end of our train of fancy that we have reached a conclusion we never anticipated: we started with the thought of the European war and we have arrived at a mental picture of a barn where we hunted for eggs in our childhood. A problem idea, on the other hand, exerts its influence often for a very long time: the problems connected with writing a book pursue us for months and years.

The degree of persistence required of a problem idea's influence of course varies within wide limits. The shortest duration of such influence is demanded when the problem is simply that of attending to a particular aspect of a stimulus about to be given. If an observer is told to notice especially the color of a design that is to be placed before him, the influence of this problem or task need persist only a few seconds. If all problems could be solved so quickly, we might need nothing but the *memory after-image* to explain their influence. As a matter of fact, Groos (45) in 1902 suggested that what he called the 'after-function' or 'secondary function' of nervous elements accounts for the difference between ordered thought and revery, and prevents us from being always the sport of wandering ideas. His pupil Schæfer (121) undertook to measure the strength of a person's secondary functions as a general individual characteristic, by calling out a stimulus word and requiring the observer to write all the words he thought of during one minute. The number of times the observer broke away from the influence of the starting word was taken as a measure of the strength of that word's after-effect. But the secondary function, or the memory after-image, is something that belongs to ideas whether they are problem ideas or not: for instance, Schaefer finds that ideas with emotional suggestion have much stronger secondary functions than ideas without it. If it is said that problem ideas have stronger secondary functions than ideas that are not problems, the question remains as to the reason for this difference; and besides, the conception of the secondary function or memory after-image process as the source of a problem idea's persistent influence would hold only for very short-lived problems. One could not explain the hold of a complicated mathematical difficulty on the mind, whereby it works itself out through months of labor, by anything so fleeting as the secondary function of the original putting of the question.

Müller (89) and Offner (98) both think that the persistent influence of the problem idea is to be explained by *perseveration*. It has a spontaneous tendency to recur to the mind, through considerable intervals of time, and not merely immediately after it has first been attended to. But obviously the point to be explained is why problem ideas as such have this perseverative tendency. It is not as uncertain an affair as the perseverative tendency of a tune which 'happens' to run in one's head: the human mind would be a very inefficient instrument if its plans and purposes had as fitful a tendency to recur and persist in their influence as the perseverative tendency of a tune. What is it that gives the problem idea such an especially good chance of recurring and persisting? Watt (148) said that the problem idea was simply a greater and stronger 'reproduction motive' than other ideas, and that he did not know its physiological basis. Müller appears to think that its relatively permanent influence is due to a combination of associative tendencies; to 'constellation.' That is, the problem idea is one which starts into action a movement system so complicated that it naturally takes some time to work itself out. The activity of such a system has a strong tendency to recur. This conception seems to apply well enough to certain kinds of problems, but not so well to others. It describes the case of a problem which like a complicated mathematical theorem has to be developed step by step, but not the case of the addition of a long column of figures: here the associative system is not complicated at all. The same simple kind of association has to be made to each of the figures in the column and the one before: the constellation involves only three factors, the two numbers and the problem of their sum. If we say that the performance of such a task as this is due simply to the persistent after-effect of the preceding step in the addition, to the fact that, as it were, we get in the habit of adding, that adding runs in our head, we evidently do injustice to the steady purpose that is in our mind. We do not add because we have got into the habit of adding, simply, but because we formed the 'resolution' at the outset to add. In this 'resolution' something more than ordinary associative processes, whether simple or complicated, and something more than the perseveration of associative processes, seems to be at work. Thus we find several authorities implying that there is an *affective or emotional aspect* to the problem idea. Claparède (22) declares that logical thought is distinguished by the presence of a "sentiment of the end." Meumann (81, 82) says that the capacity of fixing attention on the idea of the end is connected with affective life, and has developed this conception most ably in his "Intelligenz und Wille."

We shall take it for granted that the most essential thing about a problem idea, as distinguished from other ideas, is the persistence of its influence, and that to explain this persistence we need to invoke something over and above ordinary associative dispositions: in other words, that an associative tendency becomes a determining tendency through the operation of some factor that is not itself an ordinary associative tendency.

Let us take a very simple case of the operation of a problem idea, that where a person is instructed to direct his attention towards a particular aspect, say, the color, of an impression that is to be given him, and to note whether the impression contains a particular color, red. Now, according to our general theory, the words of the instruction set up the tentative movements belonging to the color red. These tentative movements, however, are not set up merely for an instant, but persist until the impression to be judged is actually given; or if they lapse momentarily, when there is a long wait between the giving of the instructions and the presentation of the impression, they renew themselves spontaneously. We may call tentative movements which thus endure and recur, *persistent tentative movements*. I think we shall find that they are characteristic of all cases where a problem idea is operative; of all cases, that is, where mental processes are directed and not random.

If we pass from this very simple problem to the consideration of complexer problems, we shall find it convenient to divide them into two classes. In one class of problems, we have to do with what we have called 'sets of movements'; in the other class with what we have called 'systems of movements.' In a set of movements, it will be remembered, a number of different movements are associated, each in the same way, with one and the same movement. For instance, all the names of colors are associated with the same word, namely, 'color.' The word 'color' will call up any or all of the particular color names, such as 'red,' 'green,' 'blue.' These names have no connection with each other except through the common name color or through other common features: there is no necessity that when one thinks of red one should also think of blue or of green unless the movements belonging to color in general are exerting an influence. In a set of movements, the movement associated with all the members of the set is like the string tied around a bundle of straws: without the string, there is no unity. Now in a movement system, on the other hand, the movements are linked among themselves, either in simultaneous or in successive systems. For instance, many persons know the names of the colors in their spectral order: violet, indigo, blue, green, yellow, orange, red. Such a series of words is a movement system: the performance of one movement leads directly to the performance of another, and so on.

A simple illustration of a problem that involves sets of movements rather than systems of movements would be the case where a person is instructed to observe the color of a picture to be shown him. He is not told to look out for a particular color, but just to note what color or colors may be present. The persistent tentative movements belonging to 'color' tend to excite all the motor centres connected with particular colors: many of these movements are incompatible, of course, so they cannot be actually executed at the same time, even as tentative movements, but they may be excited in rapid succession and thus all be in a state to recur readily when the colors of the impression to be judged actually appear.

Again, suppose a person is put to adding a column of figures. The word 'add' similarly places in readiness a set of tentative movements, those connected with the adding process: for instance the words 'two and three are five,' 'three and seven are ten.' Or suppose that the task is one that is familiar in the psychological laboratory: suppose a series of words is given to an observer with the instruction that he is to react to each word by giving the word expressing the opposite idea. To 'high' he is to respond 'low,' to 'short,' 'long,' and so on. Here, too, evidently, the persistent movements connected with the word 'opposite' put in readiness the motor responses connected with a whole set of opposite words.

On the other hand, perhaps the simplest illustration of a problem idea which involves a system of movements rather than a set of movements is the effort to recall a forgotten name. Here one usually tries to reinstate entire situations in which the name was formerly experienced; that is, one tries to recall a whole context, and the parts of the context are linked with each other in the interdependent fashion of movement systems. Of course, one may try to get the name by reconstructing several situations in which the only common element was the name in question: in such a case the systems themselves form a set of movements; but each situation is itself of the nature of a movement system. The persistent tentative movements are those of the system, and 'constellation,' or the operation of simultaneous systems, is the best means of effecting recollection. The process is the same, only more complicated, in the highest operations of creative thought. When the inventor solves his problem, he does so through the persistent influence of certain tentative movements that set in activity whole systems of movements: each step of his reasoning is dependent, not only on the step immediately before it, but upon the whole series that has preceded. Upon the power of forming such very complicated movement systems creative power rests in part; but also on the power of sticking to one's problem until one has got it solved. This latter capacity relates, evidently, to the same character of persistence in the influences set at work by the problem idea.

Persistent tentative movements, then, are characteristic of the problem idea. Whence do they get their persistence? Partly from perseveration and the memory after-image, but largely from another source.

In the chapter on types of association between movements, we distinguished movement systems as phasic and static. The former are simply complex movements, requiring the coöperation of a number of innervations. The latter are not movements but attitudes, that is, what is required in them is the steady maintenance of innervation. Holding up the head is a static movement system: it requires not only the simultaneous but the continued innervation of a whole set of muscles. In such cases, as Sherrington has pointed out (126, pages 338–39), the stimuli to the continued innervation of the muscles are the kinæsthetic excitations resulting from the innervation of the other muscles in the system, and these kinæsthetic or 'proprioceptive' excitations, instead of ceasing to be effective as stimuli according to the law of sensory adaptation by which the effectiveness of a long-continued stimulus is reduced, seem to be able to preserve their influence unimpaired for long periods of time. Two causes, in fact, limit the duration of a static movement system. The first is fatigue. The second is the occurrence of a stimulus which demands of the organism a motor response prepotent, that is, having by inherited arrangement the right of way, over the motor innervations involved in the static system. In the case of those typical static movement systems, the external bodily postures, such as standing or sitting erect, a stimulus leading to actual movement always tends to be prepotent over the static system stimuli. An internal static movement system, not involving the muscles of locomotion, would be less liable to interruption from prepotent stimuli. If an internal static movement system, relatively permanent by virtue of its essential character, can be associated with any other motor excitation, it would have the effect of making the latter persistent, and constantly tending to renew it. In other words, *if the motor excitation on which an idea is based can be associated with an internal static movement system, it will acquire the persistence needed to transform the idea into a problem idea.*

Now, what happens at the critical moment when an idea is adopted as a problem idea? What, in other words, is the nature of a *resolve*? What is the difference between merely having the idea of an act occur to one, and deciding that the act shall be carried out?

According to Ach (3) the adoption of a purpose, — that is, the making of a resolve, — which constitutes the difference between the directing or problem idea and an ordinary idea, is characterized by four factors, which he terms the image moment, the objective moment, the actual moment, and the *zuständliche* moment, a term that is difficult to translate, but may perhaps be appropriately rendered as 'affective moment.' The image moment consists of strain sensations. The objective moment, which may also, rather confusingly, consist of an image, is the idea of the end, and of the means, oftenest verbal, sometimes merely an awareness.[1] The actual moment involves an activity of the self. The I-side of the psychic process be-

[1] See page 191.

comes prominent in quite a different way than is the case in other experiences, and in the moment where the will-act is present in its energetic form, a uniquely determined change in the state of the I is experienced. Moreover, this consciousness of the activity of the self involves not merely an 'I will,' but an 'I really will,' which excludes every other possibility. Finally, the affective moment consists of a conscious attitude of effort. What relation this bears to the strain sensations which formed the image moment is not stated, but we may suppose that the difference is simply that the conscious attitude of effort is unanalyzable, and not to be located as strain sensations are.

It will be seen that the actual moment introduces a factor which cannot be reduced to sensation, image, or affection. The discovery of this factor rests simply upon Ach's interpretation of the introspections of his observers. No suggestion as to the possible psychophysical basis of this activity of the self is offered.

Meumann's (82) analysis of the resolve also introduces, or discovers, a unique factor. For Ach's actual moment, he substitutes a process of *inner assent* to the end of the action. Besides the idea of the end and of the means of reaching it, we judge this end and give our assent to it. Moreover, and this is an addition to Ach's actual moment, we must be conscious that this inner assent is the real cause of the voluntary act; that without the assent the act would not be performed. The inner assent is the symptomatic manifestation of "an elementary active reaction of the Ego." Again we are left wholly without any clue as to the physiological process involved.

The fact is that in order for an idea to be accepted as a problem idea, and in consequence to obtain relatively lasting influence upon associative processes, it has in ordinary language to appeal to a need, a desire. All desires are ultimately connected with the great motor outlets of instincts. If we examine introspectively what happens when an idea 'arouses a desire' that cannot immediately be gratified, we find, I think, that motor effects of either or both of two different kinds are produced. The one effect (not necessarily first in time) is that we 'feel restless,' 'uneasy.' The restlessness seems to be produced by diffused and shifting motor innervations, which apparently have no useful connection with each other, and seem rather to be the effects of a common cause than to form a true movement system. The other effect that may be connected with the arousal of desire I shall call the *activity attitude*. In its intenser degrees it is revealed to introspection as the 'feeling of effort,' which is recognized as the accompaniment of active attention. Introspection further indicates that it is not due to shifting innervations, but rather to a steady and persistent set of innervations. It appears from introspection, also, to be in its intenser forms a bodily attitude, involving a kind of tense quietness, a quietness due not to relaxation but to a system of static innervations. We should then class it under the head of 'static movement systems.'

The writer would like to suggest that a problem idea becomes the starting-point of effective and directed thought towards its solution only when the incipient motor innervation which the problem involves connects itself, not simply with general restlessness and uneasiness, but with the steady innervations of the activity attitude. Through their inherent and characteristic persistence, as members of a static movement system, the problem innervation is kept from lapsing and may continue to exert an influence upon associated motor innervations and to arouse imagery which bears on its solution.

We must, indeed, if such a view be accepted, go a step beyond introspection. The 'feeling of effort,' the form in which the activity attitude reveals itself most clearly to introspection, is connected not with smooth and easy thinking but with interruptions and obstacles to the course of thought. If such obstacles are insurmountable, the activity attitude either resolves itself into the shifting movements of restless desire, or drops into an attitude of relaxation. But if the obstacle is successfully surmounted, the activity attitude, we must suppose, does not cease because it is less evident to introspection, but is most effective in securing the persistent influence of the *Aufgabe* when the kinæsthetic sensations to which the activity attitude itself gives rise are not themselves the objects of attention. In fact, just in proportion as it is evident to introspection, that is, attended to for its own sake, it is less effective in securing the persistence of the problem system. Is this only another way of saying that thinking implies active attention and that active attention is characterized by the presence of the consciousness of effort, or the feeling of activity? Yes; but it is saying more: namely, that the motor innervations underlying the 'consciousness of effort' are not mere accompaniments of directed thought, but an essential part of the cause of directed thought. It is the static, mutually reinforcing innervations of an organized movement system which, associating themselves with the incipient innervation set up in connection with the problem idea, keep that excitation effective and prevent it from lapsing. What is required to transform an idea into a problem idea or *Aufgabe* is the association of the incipient motor excitation which it involves with some excitation relatively static and enduring in its nature. And *a determining tendency is an associative disposition one of whose exciting influences is the activity attitude.*

All students of the learning process report the great influence of *effort*, the 'determination to improve.' Thus Bryan and Harter (17) say, "It is intense effort that educates"; Johnson (58) ascribes plateaus or periods of no improvement in the learning to pauses in the effort, and Book (13) says that "less effort was actually put into the work at all those stages of practice where little or no improvement was made." Now the actual causative influence of effort on learning has usually been regarded as due to a more or less mysterious will process, of which the bodily attitude characteristic of activity or effort was merely the accompaniment. The theory here suggested is the first, so far as I know, to explain how a bodily attitude like that of effort can actually be the cause of improved mental work, by prolonging, through its own persistent nature, the influence of the problem on associative processes.

In the section on "The Effect of Repetition on the Strength of Associative Dispositions," we left unexplained the fact that in learning a series of words or nonsense syllables, a recitation from memory does much more to strengthen the associative dispositions which it brings into play than a new presentation or reading of the series. The reason for this difference would be found, we said, in the different attitudes involved in reciting from memory and merely reading. Following a suggestion from Katzaroff, we find that it is in fact the activity attitude that is, in large measure at least, responsible for the great value of recitations in memorizing. "In the readings," Katzaroff says (61, page 257), "the subject is passive, calm, indifferent; in the recitations he is active, he has to seek, he rejoices when he has found and gets irritated at the syllables which evade his call. Hence a crowd of sentiments of affection for certain syllables, of antipathy for others, which contribute to enrich the associative nexus and favor conservation and reproduction. . . . When a pupil has read a fable many times without ever reciting it, he is thrown off the track when he has to say it by heart before the teacher: the active attitude in which he finds himself at the moment of the recitation, being different from the passive attitude in which he found himself at the time of the reading, is an obstacle to the revival of his memories." There can be no doubt that while one may not be wholly passive during the reading of a series to be memorized, one has much less of the activity attitude than during the effort to recite. Thus an attempted recitation forms an association between the series as a whole and the attitude of activity, which is of the utmost value when the final recitation is made that is the test of the learning: while a mere reading forms such an association either not at all or in a much less degree.

On this theory it is possible to explain, or at least to find a plausible description of, certain individual variations in the effectiveness of directed thought. The activity attitude, we may suppose, will not ordinarily be set up in connection with an idea that does not, directly or indirectly, appeal to some instinct. An idea that does so appeal may stir up merely a state of unrest, involving diffuse and shifting innervations. In certain individuals, this is the common result. Owing to causes lying in his physiological constitution and not accessible to his consciousness, ideas in such a person habitually set up unrest rather than activity attitudes: they come

> " Close enough to stir his brain
> And to vex his heart in vain."

In other natures, unrest quickly yields place to the fruitful and useful attitude of activity; while still others are so phlegmatic that even those ideas whose connection with instinctive outlets is fairly close will not so much as stimulate to unrest.

In the same individual, readiness to assume unrest attitudes and the activity attitude varies from day to day. Our physiological condition determines the intensity of instinctive appeals: where these are weak, both unrest and activity attitudes will fail to be aroused. A constant crux of discussion has been the lack of correlation between unrest and the activity attitude. In debates on the determination of the will, the 'strength of motives' has commonly referred to the intensity of the unrest set up by certain ideas. And it has often been pointed out that we sometimes act on a motive weaker than that which at another time fails to move us to action. Hence the illusion that we act without a cause; that will is not determined by the strongest motive. The facts, in my opinion, are as follows. Our physiological condition at certain times is unfavorable to the production of the activity attitude. The instincts may be alive: the motor pathways connected with them may be ready for use. The unrest aroused by an idea indirectly connected with an instinctive outlet may be intense. But the activity attitude is not assumed; and if the idea's connection with the instinctive outlet be so indirect that 'thinking' is necessary to willing, then the 'will' is lacking despite the strength of motive. Since no introspection can certainly determine whether the organism is or is not in the proper physiological state for the assumption of the activity attitude, the relation of motive and will is uncertain, contingent. At another time an idea that stirs up a far weaker unrest attitude may give rise to the attitude of activity and so dominate associative processes to a successful working out of its problem.

The question naturally occurs as to how on this theory the influence of a particular problem idea is terminated. Obviously we stop mental work on a problem under two conditions: when the problem is solved and when it is not. If a problem reaches its solution, the persistent tentative motor processes find their fulfillment. The result is of course that if the problem idea is later suggested, there will be no suspension of the motor processes, but the passage to the solution will be immediate: only if the solution has been forgotten, through the effect of time in heightening resistances at synapses, will the motor innervation remain obstructed, and if conditions are favorable, the activity attitude will come into function and the problem be worked through again.

But a problem is often dropped without having reached a solution. And the dropping may be temporary or final. A problem that requires a long train of thought for its solving is usually dropped and resumed several times before it is finally worked out, if it ever is. On our theory, the interruption of mental work on a problem before the solution is reached must be due to relaxation of the activity attitude. The usual causes bringing about such a relaxation are (1) the occurrence of a prepotent stimulus demanding an entire shift of attitude (the dinner-bell calling the thinker to food), or (2) fatigue. Really the second is but a special case of the first, since the stimuli produced by fatigue are prepotent when they reach a certain degree of intensity.

The relaxing of the activity attitude, and consequent interruption of directed thought on a given problem, may be followed after an interval by the resumption of active work on the task. Judging from introspection, such a resumption may be started either by the associative suggestion of the problem to our minds once more, or by the 'spontaneous' or perseverative recurrence of the activity attitude itself, which recalls the problem. We resume our task either because some other idea or something in our surroundings recalls the task to our minds and the task sets up the activity attitude; or because we 'feel like work,' and casting about for something to work at, we find that the activity attitude, thus recurring 'spontaneously,' suggests either the task most recently associated with it, or the task which the context and surroundings combine to suggest. If the activity attitude recurs when I enter my study, the unfinished task it suggests is that which belongs to those surroundings; if it recurs in the laboratory, it sets in excitation the centres connected with my unfinished laboratory tasks. This spontaneous recurrence or perseveration is familiar in the case of organic movements such as desires or regrets: it often happens that we have in consciousness first the 'awareness' of wanting something, or that something pleasant or unpleasant has happened, and these recurring motor states call up the idea of their own cause. We remember in a few moments what it was that we wanted, or that pleased or displeased us.

The experience of extreme unpleasantness in connection with any problem seems to break the connection between the incipient motor innervations connected with that problem and the activity attitude. A special and practically very important case of this occurs when work on the problem has been pushed to the point of great fatigue. The fatigue of mental work is rather generally acknowledged to be essentially the same as that resulting from physical work. We may assume that it is fatigue induced by too long continuance of the activity attitude. The worker has dropped his uncompleted task because the fatigue poisons, acting as prepotent stimuli, compel an interruption of the activity attitude. If the fatigue is moderate in amount, an attitude of relaxation supplants the attitude of activity. But if the fatigue is great, the stimuli which it produces give rise not merely to an attitude of relaxation but to the general negative response accompanying marked unpleasantness. The negative response, as many phenomena connected with the learning process in man and the lower animals inform us, has the ability to substitute itself for responses that produce it. So a task, dropped in the midst of the unpleasantness of great fatigue, will later call up not the activity attitude that would ensure its continuance, but a reaction of aversion: we 'want never to think of it again.'

The efficiency of a mental worker is thus directly connected with his sensitiveness to fatigue stimuli. Not merely is the too fatigable individual, whose activity attitudes relax before the problem has governed associative processes long enough to progress towards solution, a failure; but the worker who is insensitive to fatigue until its products have accumulated so that the reaction when it does occur is violently unpleasant, is in danger of still greater disaster from the point of view of efficiency. For the problem that is dropped under the influence of a slight degree of fatigue may be resumed, but the problem dropped under the influence of profound fatigue is likely to be abandoned permanently.

When fatigue puts an end to the activity attitude too soon for the highest degree of efficiency in work, it may be because the fatigue processes are really intense, owing to some temporary or permanent physiological weakness on the worker's part, or it may be because he has the bad habit of paying too much attention to fatigue sensations. As it is disastrous for efficiency when a worker disregards fatigue influences until they have become very intense, so it is in a less degree unfortunate if his limen for a special reaction to fatigue sensations is too low. There are some persons, and the present writer is one of them, who can never work without giving a disproportionate amount of attention to the fact that they are working. Hence, indeed, they avoid nervous breakdowns and do not tend to abandon unfinished tasks finally and forever, as do some of their too enthusiastic friends after uninterrupted long periods of work; but they waste a good deal of time by dropping their tasks after very short periods of work because their attention is directed to slight sensations of fatigue. I do not know whether any reader can verify this experience from his own introspection, but I have repeatedly noted that on a morning when I am generally fatigued after loss of sleep, I produce an unexpectedly large amount of work; and I am inclined to lay this to the fact that, starting out tired, I take my fatigue sensations for granted, as it were, and pay less attention to them than usual. Thus I am enabled to avoid the many needless breaks in my work ordinarily caused by the fact that I am distracted by the sensations caused by the activity attitude.

It would seem highly probable that to differences in innate and acquired or habitual permanence of the activity attitude and the proper amount of fatigability and attention to fatigue sensations are due differences in 'general ability.' There is more and more accumulated evidence in favor of the supposition called by Spearman (47) the theory of two factors; namely, that individual excellences in various kinds of mental work are due partly to special ability and partly to general ability. There can surely be no single condition so important for all kinds of work where mental ability is involved as the proper degree of persistence of the activity attitude.

Our theory is, then, that the persistence of the motor innervations connected with a problem idea is connected with the persistence of the activity attitude, a static movement system which associates itself, under favoring physiological conditions, with the attitude of unrest stirred up by the partial inhibition of a motor innervation connected with an instinct. It is a well known fact that a problem idea's influence will continue to be exerted after the idea itself has dropped out of consciousness. When the task is, for instance, the adding of a column of figures, the worker does not have constantly to remind himself to add. Several careful studies have been made of the stages in the disappearance of the directing idea from consciousness, under various conditions. A comparative examination of the results of these studies indicates that such stages are of three different types. There is, first, the case where the problem idea is fully conscious at the time when it exerts its effect: the observer says to himself, 'I must add,' or, 'I must think of an opposite,' whatever the case may be. In the second type of effectiveness of the problem idea, it appears somehow fused with the stimulus that is to be responded to, and the stimulus is apprehended in a particular way, or has certain features added to it, as the result of the problem idea's operation. Thus in Ach's (2) experiments where the task consisted of simple arithmetical operations, the numbers were visualized with a plus sign between them, or one over the other to facilitate the operation of subtraction. The third type of case differs from the second rather in degree than in principle: it occurs when, with more complicated problems, a certain means of solving them, a certain method which aids in the fulfilling of the task, is adopted: this method may be in consciousness while the problem idea itself is not. Thus in Grünbaum's (46) experiments, where very complicated sets of figures were shown for a very brief interval and the observers had to detect similar figures in the groups, they devised various schemes to help themselves. The second and third types are only cases where some other innervation has substituted itself for the innervation which the problem idea originally involved, and this substitute motor process persists in the place of the original one. Thus instead of saying each time, 'I must add,' the verbal formula, '—— and —— are ——,' remains in readiness, or the plus sign persists, or the more elaborate scheme which aids in solving a more complicated problem remains in a state of persistent readiness to be excited. Of course the processes underlying the memory after-image and perseveration, the readiness of movements to be repeated, are strong factors aiding in the solution of problems, but the peculiar feature that distinguishes either the original problem idea, or the surrogate that later comes to replace it, is association with the activity attitude.

There are cases where apparently the whole physiological process underlying directed thought ceases to have a conscious accompaniment and yet proceeds effectively, as later conscious processes show. In many such cases the activity attitude persists: there are times when I am puzzling over a difficulty, and remain for an appreciable interval conscious of the activity attitude, of strained attention, but of little else in the way of imagery, verbal or otherwise; yet at the close of the interval I find my associative dispositions have combined in a new pattern. Sometimes the activity attitude itself is absent: a new idea, the solution of a problem, flashes on one in the midst of idle revery on other subjects. Here it is evident, since there is no persistent attitude to help the persistence of the problem's influence, that it must be due entirely to perseveration.

Clearly the more practised a set of movements is, the more it will tend spontaneously to repeat itself, or to perseverate. Thus it is along lines in connection with which we have done much thinking that unconscious 'thinking' goes on: we do not have sudden inspirations on subjects about which we have done little conscious meditation. So the simpler tasks, such as adding or rhyming or thinking of opposites, very quickly come to depend entirely on perseveration, because they are tasks already so familiar and so well practised. So, too, when a task is set that can be solved in a number of different ways, not only does delay occur because a variety of movements is set in readiness, but such a task has to depend longer on the activity attitude than does a task that can be solved by only one set of movements, for in the latter case the single set of movements through being repeated and practised gets much help from perseveration. The fact that a fully determined problem is performed with greater ease and speed than a vaguely determined one is called by Ach (2) the 'Law of Special Determination,' and he derived it from experiments by the following methods. His observers were required to make one set of reactions with predetermination. These were as follows: simple reactions to white cards as stimuli; reactions where sometimes other stimuli were given to which no reaction was to be made; discrimination reactions, where two kinds of stimuli were intermingled and the observer was to react as soon as he recognized what a particular stimulus was; reactions where one kind of stimulus was to be responded to by a movement of the right hand and the other by a movement of the left hand; reactions where there were four different kinds of stimuli to be responded to by four different movements. Another set of reactions was made without determination. These included two classes, those where the stimulus was indeterminate and those where the response was indeterminate. In the first case, two stimuli were shown together, and the observer's instructions were to choose which one he would respond to, but always to make the same movement in response to the same kind of stimulus. Thus if a red card and a blue card were shown together, he might respond to either one, but if he chose to respond to the red card he must do so by a movement of his right hand. In the second case, cards with numbers were shown to the observer, who might perform any of several different arithmetical operations he chose with the numbers presented. The more complete and particular the instructions, the less liberty of choice left to the observer, the shorter was the reaction time.

Just the same law is shown in experiments on so-called 'forced associations.' When a word is given to an observer and he is told to answer with the first word that occurs to him, it regularly takes him a little longer to do so than if he is instructed beforehand that he must respond with a particular kind of word, for instance a rhyme, or a word denoting the class to which the object named by the stimulus word belongs. This at least is the testimony most generally given by those who have compared 'free association times' with 'forced association times': thus Wells (150) says that controlled associations, if simple, are always shorter than free ones. Wreschner (159), on the other hand, says that a given type of association occurs more rapidly when it is free than when it is prescribed: that is, for example, an observer would respond to the word 'dog' with the word 'animal' more quickly if he just 'happened' to do so than if he had been previously instructed to think of a superior concept to dog. "Every *Aufgabe*," says Wreschner, "exerts a certain inhibiting influence, in consequence of which the idea corresponding to it comes to consciousness a little late." Wreschner does not limit this statement to the complexer tasks, but it would certainly appear that he should do so. If a problem is simple, it certainly ought to be performed more quickly when the movements which it involves are set in readiness beforehand. If it is complex, one can see why the more complicated set of movements should involve delay as compared with a free reaction. The Law of Special Determination holds without exception: if a forced association means that only a few movements have been set in readiness, and a free reaction means that a great many movements have been set in readiness, then the free association will take longer than the forced one. But as a matter of fact the reactions given under the instructions to say the first word that comes into one's head are often not free at all in the sense that many possibilities are previously excited: for in the first place, when the stimulus word is not known, the expectation is wholly vague, and in the second place the reaction word that is given is often based on an associative disposition of such strength through much repetition that no other possibility can claim the field. The person who is given the stimulus word 'black' is likely to respond 'white' with no interference of other associative dispositions, because no other disposition is of anything like equal strength. The Law of Special Determination is clearly illustrated in the fact that it regularly takes longer to pass from a more general idea to a less general one, as from 'animal' to 'dog,' than from a less general to a more general idea. 'Animal' may suggest many subordinate classes besides 'dog,' but 'animal' is by far the most obvious superior concept to 'dog.'

The advantage of definite preparation and of the perseverative tendency that is involved in having a special and fully determined problem at the outset is further shown by the fact that when a person is given vague and indefinite instructions he very soon helps himself out by adopting a stereotyped method and sticking to it; that is, he adds self-imposed tasks to the one he has been set. In the very interesting experiments of Koffka (63), where the instructions were quite general, such as, "React, by making a signal, when the stimulus word has suggested an idea to you"; or, "React when it has suggested an idea and this idea has suggested another"; the observers imposed on themselves more special tasks, such as those of reacting as quickly as possible, or of reacting only with words, or of reacting always with synonyms, or of thinking of individual examples. Koffka therefore adds to Ach's conception of 'determining tendencies,' or the influences which proceed from problem ideas, that of 'latent attitudes' which have the effect of determining tendencies but do not proceed from problem ideas. It seems to me that these self-imposed problems can be explained simply in the following way. A very general problem sets in readiness a number of methods for its solution. One of these methods happens to be the first one adopted, and simply perseverates: since the influence of perseveration involves so much less fatigue than the influence of the activity attitude, it is not interfered with and becomes increasingly strong.

CHAPTER IX

THE FORMATION OF NEW MOVEMENT SYSTEMS UNDER THE INFLUENCE OF PROBLEMS

In this chapter we shall attempt very briefly to sketch an account of the way in which movement systems become broken up and new ones constituted out of old ones under the influence of purposes. That is, we shall consider the processes of thinking. And it is not primarily with the conscious accompaniments of such breaking up of old systems and formation of new ones that we shall be concerned. These conscious accompaniments will be discussed in the chapter that follows. It is rather with the mechanism of thinking than with the way it feels to think, that we have just now to deal.

The logician says that an act of reasoning is a complex act of judgment, consisting in fact of three judgments, which he calls respectively the minor premise, the major premise, and the conclusion. Thus if I reason that the weather must be cold this morning because I see steam rising from the nostrils of horses, my process of thought may be resolved into the minor premise that steam is rising from the horses' nostrils, the major premise that whenever steam thus rises the weather is cold, and the conclusion that the weather is cold to-day. It would certainly appear that the process of judgment, by which we make the assertion that a thing *is* something else, that *A is B*, must be fundamental to processes of reasoning which can thus be reduced to series of judgments.

What, then, is the essential nature of a process of judgment? We are, as has just been said, not concerned just now with the question as to the nature of the conscious processes that accompany judgment. Marbe [1] wrote a monograph whose conclusion is that there are no conscious processes which

[1] *Experimentell-psychologische Untersuchungen über das Urteil.* Leipzig, 1901.

especially characterize judgment. Our present point of attack is this: how are movement systems related and constituted when, instead of applying the verbal formula '*A* suggests *B*,' we use the formula, '*A* is *B*'?

When *A* suggests *B*, either the two movement systems, *A* and *B*, form part of one and the same system, so that there exist associative dispositions between them as wholes, or some movement or smaller movement system contained in *A* is identical with a movement or smaller movement system contained in *B*. In the language of the older psychology, either *A* and *B* are linked by contiguity, as having been once experienced together, or they are linked by similarity, as having a part in common. The sight of one person may suggest another with whom he is frequently met, or it may suggest some one whom he has never seen but who has a likeness to him. We get the typical cases of '*A* suggests *B*' in unguided revery, and it may be noted that when *A* has suggested *B* its influence generally stops. Gazing at a chandelier in a hotel lobby, I find myself thinking of Galileo; the chandelier has ceased to concern me and my attention has flown to ideas connected with the beginnings of modern science.

Now, one difference between '*A* suggests *B*' and '*A* is *B*' is that in the latter case *A* does not drop out of the account. It really was the slow swinging of the chandelier to and fro that suggested Galileo watching the cathedral lamp. The movement systems succeeded each other in approximately the following order: (1) systems concerned with the chandelier as a whole; (2) systems concerned with its slow movement to and fro; (3) systems concerned with Galileo and linked, as the chandelier was, with the 'slow swinging' systems. Now, did I, in the process of making this connection, say to myself, 'That chandelier is swinging'? Or did I pass at once on to Galileo without pausing to notice the connecting link? If I said, 'The chandelier is swinging,' I made a judgment: if not, the case was one of mere 'association of ideas.' The peculiar feature of making the judgment about the chandelier would be that *the movement systems concerned with the chandelier as a whole would recur for an instant.* The sequence of movement systems would in this case be: (1) systems concerned with the chandelier as a whole; (2) systems concerned with its slow movement to and fro; (3) a recurrence of the systems concerned with the chandelier as a whole ('the *chandelier* is swinging,' not merely 'swinging' as a phenomenon ready to detach itself from this particular context). In a judgment, a part of the movement system concerned with the subject lasts over after the rest has ceased to act (the swinging of the chandelier is attended to after the rest of it has dropped from attention). This smaller system, a component part of the subject system, is the predicate system. Its emergence and persistence is followed by a recurrence of the subject system as a whole. Thus, the sequence is 'A—B—B-as-a-part-of-A.' And the subsequent associative dispositions will be determined not only by the predicate B, but by the predicate in connection with the subject A. If in the train of revery in which I passed from the chandelier to Galileo, I had really stopped to make the judgment 'The chandelier is swinging,' my thoughts for the next instant or so would have dwelt with the phenomenon of the swinging chandelier, and not merely with swinging objects in general. I might, for instance, have wondered if it were securely hung.

Note that I spoke just now of 'stopping' to make a judgment. It always involves delay to make a judgment, because it always involves going back on one's tracks, as it were, to revive the movement systems connected with the subject of the judgment after one has passed on to the predicate systems. For this reason, judgments are most commonly made under the influence of a problem which secures the persistent influence of the subject system. Thus for example if I were a builder or an electrician, with a permanent problem of investigating chandeliers and such objects, I should be much more likely, after noting the swinging, to recur to the chandelier instead of going on to Galileo. The judgments we make in the course of a day are usually determined by our problems: if one is a painter, on going into a room one makes judgments about the pictures on the walls; if one is an electrician, one makes judgments about its lighting arrangements. Thus Watt (148) could say that determination by an *Aufgabe*, a problem idea, is the characteristic feature of a judgment.

Now, a process of reasoning or inference is a judgment made indirectly. When for any reason I cannot put my head outside the window and feel for myself that the weather is cold, I have to arrive at the conclusion by inferring it from some such fact as that the horses are steaming. It is self-evident that if a simple judgment means delay, a process of reasoning means a longer delay; and it would be almost impossible for so long a delay to occur without the influence of a problem idea, and, in more complicated processes of reasoning, the activity attitude.

In reasoning, as in judgment, we start of course with the subject we are reasoning about. And always in reasoning, as often in judgment, we start also with the thing we want to prove about our subject; the predicate of our conclusion. I have an interest in knowing whether the weather is cold before I begin to reason about it: if "cold" had not entered my mind there would be no reasoning about it. Professor James, calling the predicate of the conclusion P, says, "Psychologically, as a rule, P overshadows the process from the start. We are *seeking* P, or something like P " (57, Volume II, page 338). This means, of course, that P, the predicate of the conclusion — coldness, in the example we have been using — acts together with the subject as a problem idea. We have, then, in operation two systems of tentative movements, those connected with the subject (the weather to-day), and those connected with the predicate (cold). The outcome of reasoning is the setting into action of movement systems that are connected with both of these systems; any other movement systems will be inhibited by the persistent recurrence of these two as the problem idea. We want to continue our thinking and planning on the basis of the ascertained fact that it is or is not a cold day.

Now, surely, it may be supposed, if we have both the subject and predicate systems excited, if we are attending to the weather and the possibility of its being cold, these two systems must have old associative connections so that the processes of association can go on without any reasoning being necessary. We have experienced cold days before, and we know what can and what cannot be done on them. This is what is called proceeding on an hypothesis. But the difficulty is that these old associative dispositions do not really connect 'to-day's weather' with the predicate 'cold'; they only connect 'weather' with 'cold': If the movement systems connected with our true subject, 'to-day's weather,' remain active as a part of the problem, the mere hypothesis that it is cold will be soon inhibited by a return to the full problem. Not until some member of the full movement system which constitutes 'to-day's weather,' a very complicated system involving much more than 'weather' in general, proves to have associative dispositions in common with 'cold,' will the delay and constant reference back to the problem cease. Until that time, while we may be saying to ourselves, "If it is cold, I'd better take a closed cab, and have more coal put on the furnace before I go," these meditations will constantly be interrupted by the recurring question, "But is it really cold?"

But what about fallacies, mistakes in reasoning? We cannot fully describe the process of correct reasoning without examining the ways in which it may go wrong. Reasoning or inference proceeds by the discovery of what the logicians call the middle term (the steaming breath of the horses, in our example), which has associative dispositions linking it with both the movement systems of the problem, the subject system and the predicate system. Now, does the correctness of the reasoning depend on the *strength* of these associative dispositions? Does it, in our example, for instance, depend on the number of cold days on which we have seen the horses' breath rising like steam in the air?

Not so much on the strength of these dispositions, it may

be said in answer, as on the absence of any dispositions connecting the terms of the inference with incompatible movements. It does not so much matter how often we have noticed steaming horses on cold days, provided that we have never seen this condensation of breath vapor on a warm day. If we have, it cannot be used as a trustworthy middle term. For the movement system corresponding to the subject about which we are reasoning and that corresponding to the predicate, in order to combine to determine future systems, have to form themselves into a simultaneous system. And a simultaneous system cannot contain incompatible movements. They may perfectly well enter into successive systems, but not into simultaneous ones. Therefore the existence in any effective strength of a single associative disposition representing a 'negative instance' will injure the functioning of the whole system.

Yet people do ignore negative instances, and do guide their conduct by highly fallacious reasoning? Yes; by a loss of the original and true problem idea. They forget that their reasoning is about this particular case, and not about some other case which more or less resembles it. The subject or the predicate of their reasoning, by the many ways in which older dispositions and systems can modify and corrupt newer ones, gets altered; as my memory image of the painting adapted itself to older associative dispositions. Old prejudices and even mere verbal associations exert their contaminating effect. This is especially apt to be the case if the first attempt at reasoning out the situation fails: the activity attitude is fatigued, and the easier path is taken of reasoning about something more or less like the true subject of the problem, or accepting a somewhat different predicate which is less incompatible with the subject.

That fallacies do arise by such modifications and contaminations of the subject and predicate movement systems which should act jointly as the directing or problem idea, or more accurately, as its motor basis, may be illustrated by taking examples of the typical and classical fallacies which the logicians term respectively the fallacy of the undistributed middle term, of illicit process of the minor term, and of illicit process of the major term. Suppose a naturalist should argue that a new specimen brought in for him to examine was a bird because it had wings. His argument would be formulated by the logician as follows: "Birds have wings; this creature has wings, therefore this creature is a bird"; and the logicians would say that the naturalist had committed a fallacy known as that of 'undistributed middle term,' in that only part of the middle term, 'creature having wings,' is referred to in each premise. Now the psychological process underlying this fallacy is something like the following. The naturalist starts with attention to the specimen before him and to the idea of several different classifications for it, 'bird' among the rest. Attention to these objects involves the activity of certain movement systems; and the system corresponding to 'bird' combines with the system corresponding to 'this specimen,' to strengthen the movements corresponding to 'wings,' which form a part of the total system for 'this specimen.' But the movements corresponding to 'wings' belong also in other systems which contain elements incompatible with the 'bird' system; insects have wings. The fallacy is committed because the 'wing' system is not allowed to develop far enough to excite these incompatible movements. In other words, the middle term is not really 'wings,' but 'bird wings'; since the reasoner started with birds in his mind, it is easier and involves less delay to think of bird wings than to think of wings in general, which would recall to him the other winged creatures that are not birds, and prevent him from committing the fallacy. Here it is the strong influence of the predicate, birds, the haste, as it were, to reach a conclusion as soon as possible, that contaminates and limits the middle term system.

As an example of illicit process of the minor term, take the case of a person who argues from one specimen of a class that all members of the class are like it. A person meets an ill-informed college student, and proceeds to write a letter to the newspaper about the failure of college education. His reasoning formulates itself thus: This person is ill-informed; he is a college student, therefore all college students are ill-informed. Here the trouble evidently is that the middle term, 'this person,' has contaminated and practically substituted itself for the minor term, 'college students,' the true subject of the reasoning. The reasoner has not allowed the system corresponding to 'college students' really to develop itself; if it had, surely negative instances would have been suggested. But a little more time and patience would have been needed for the full development of the 'college student' system, and the system 'this person as a college student' is already on the field; so it is allowed to assume the functions of a minor term when its true function is that of a middle term.

Illicit process of the major term is committed when the predicate of the conclusion is contaminated and altered. Suppose that one is occupied with the question as to whether a particular piece of property is or is not exempt from taxation. The idea of its being exempt suggests the idea of church property, which is exempt; but this property is not church property. It is therefore rashly and fallaciously considered to be not exempt. The trouble here is that the system underlying 'exempt from taxation' is not allowed to develop fully; instead of becoming the 'exempt from taxation' system, it is really the system corresponding to 'church property exempt from taxation.' If it developed as it should, there would be suggested other kinds of property, such as public school property, that are exempt and that contain no features at all incompatible with the property about which one is reasoning.

In all three of these fallacies which the logicians call formal fallacies, one of the terms contaminates and alters another, which is not allowed to develop fully. In the 'undistributed middle' example, the major term contaminates and limits the middle term; in the 'illicit minor' case the middle term limits the minor term, and in the case of 'illicit major' the middle term limits the major term. In the so-called 'material fallacies,' as contrasted with these 'formal fallacies,' the contamination of the systems underlying the terms has its source in the influence of systems *outside* the argument; in the thinker's general habits and prejudices. Take as a single illustration an example given by Creighton of the so-called fallacy of ambiguous middle term: "Partisans are not to be trusted; Democrats are partisans; therefore Democrats are not to be trusted." "The middle term, 'partisan,'" says Creighton, "is evidently used in two senses in this argument. In the first premise it signifies persons who are deeply or personally interested in some measure; and in the latter it simply denotes the members of a political party" (25, page 160). This transformation of a term into a different term does not show the influence of any of the other terms in the argument: the influences which bring it about may be almost infinitely varied, and may include, as was said above, the thinker's habits of mind and also the influence of the situation as a whole, or of some suggestion from his antagonist in argument. As Creighton points out, the fallacy would not be very likely to occur in so simple an example as the one just given, but might easily be produced in the course of a long train of reasoning.

Fallacies, whatever their immediate cause, always have as one of their causes laziness. Correct reasoning, involving the full development of movement systems, requires more delay than incorrect reasoning, which involves a restricted and imperfect development: delay means that the activity attitude must be longer continued, and the activity attitude is fatiguing. When it relaxes, associative dispositions take the easiest way.

The whole process of creative thinking may be conceived in some such fashion as the following. The thinker has first in mind the idea of his problem or purpose. This usually involves at least two great movement systems, which are as yet disconnected. Tarde[1] says that invention always results from the interaction of two needs: two beliefs, two desires, or a belief and a desire. The essential necessity for the creative thinker is that

[1] *La logique sociale.* Paris. 1898.

he shall hold in activity both these systems in their full complexity, never allowing either one to become contaminated by the other or by his mental habits and prejudices. In each of the systems every component part must be allowed in its turn to become predominant: that is, both parts of the problem must be fully analyzed. The failures in creative thinking, whether it be the formation of a scientific hypothesis, the construction of a machine, or the production of a work of art, always come from suffering a part of the problem to be neglected or falsified: some essential condition is overlooked. As the various component parts of the two problem systems come into especial activity, they find various common motor outlets, the tentative hypotheses or suggestions towards the solution of the problem. But each of these must be inhibited while the other parts of the problem systems are allowed to come into activity, until a direction of motor discharge is found which is common to them all, and a solution is reached which leaves no part of the problem out of account. Constant reference back to the problem ideas in their uncontaminated purity; the acceptance of no partial solution, no working out of a problem which is a little changed from the original one; this is demanded of successful creative thinking, and it is possible only through the persistent dominance of the problem ideas, with the aid of a persistent and recurrent activity attitude.

The difference between creative imagination and creative thought is described by Meumann (82, page 14) as consisting in the fact that for imagination, imagery is an end in itself, while for thought imagery is only a means to an end. This statement should be modified, I think; the only form of imagination where the image can be called even relatively an end in itself is æsthetic imagination, and even here it is not really the creation of the imagery that is the end. Can an image ever be an end in itself; can anything, in an organism formed for the purpose of reacting adequately upon its environment, be an end except a movement? The scientific theorist's aim is to construct a system of tentative movements that will lead to a series of successful full movements in response to the world outside: the inventor's aim is to construct in thought a machine that will work upon the outer world. The creator in the field of æsthetics is indeed contented that his work shall have no effect in the larger movements which influence the external world: he is satisfied that his product shall continue to influence only the realm of imagery and the tentative movements upon which imagery is based. But we must remember that the æsthetic creator seeks to produce not only imagery but the affective reaction to imagery: not merely tentative movements, but the full motor response of those pathways which lead to the movements involved in emotion. The true statement, then, of the distinction which separates, not imagination from thought, but æsthetic imagination and thought from other forms of imagination and thought, is that the problem of the creative thinker in other than æsthetic fields involves the production of movements which affect the external world; the problem of the æsthetic creator involves the production of movements which remain as it were concealed within the other human organisms who contemplate his work: the tentative movements on which their mental imagery rests, and the full but self-limited movements which constitute their emotional responses.

CHAPTER X

"IF," said the philosopher Hume, "you cannot point out *any such impression*, you may be certain you are mistaken, when you imagine you have *any such idea*" (54, page 65). For a long time this principle virtually ruled psychology, and an idea that was vague and obscure, and could not trace its origin directly to sensations, was dismissed as no proper object of scientific study. It was James who, in a chapter familiar to every student of psychology, declared his wish for a "reinstatement of the vague to its proper place in our mental life" (57, Volume I, page 254). For it is evident to any one who carefully observes his own conscious experience that much of our thinking and feeling cannot be adequately described as made up of the colors and brightnesses which the eye supplies, the many tones and noises that the ear gives, the four taste qualities, the possibly nine smell qualities, the four qualities from the skin. The inner life of the mind, all that varied and eventful complex of processes which may occur when, lying in a silent and darkened room, we review the experiences of a day and decide on a course of action for the morrow, is not recognizably describable as a kaleidoscopic pattern of colors, tones, smells, tastes, and skin sensations, centrally excited. James has enumerated for us some of the parts of our conscious experience which especially, he thinks, refuse to be identified with sensations from the old five senses. He divides them into 'transitive states,' or relational feelings, and 'feelings of tendency.' In discussing 'transitive states' he says: "There is not a conjunction or a preposition, and hardly an adverbial phrase, syntactic form, or inflection of voice, in human speech, that does not express some shading or other of relation which we at some moment actually feel to exist between the larger objects of our thought." "We ought to say a feeling of *and*, a feeling of *if*, a feeling of *but*, and a feeling of *by*, quite as readily as we say a feeling of blue or a feeling of cold." Under the head of 'feelings of tendency,' he enumerates such experiences as the feelings occasioned by the words 'wait,' 'hark,' 'look'; the vague consciousness that represents a forgotten name, a consciousness sufficiently positive to reject a wrong substitute; the experience of recognizing a thing as familiar without being able to 'place' it; the feelings corresponding to 'naught but,' 'either one or the other,' 'although it is, nevertheless,' 'it is an excluded middle, there is no *tertium quid*,' 'who?' 'when?' 'where?' 'no,' 'never,' 'not yet'; "that first instantaneous glimpse of another person's meaning which we have when in vulgar phrase we say we 'twig' it"; "one's intention of saying a thing before he has said it"; "that shadowy scheme of the 'form' of an opera, play, or book, which remains in our mind and on which we pass judgment when the actual thing is done"; "the awareness that our definite thought has come to a stop" and the 'entirely different' "awareness that our thought is definitively completed"; finally, the awareness "that we are using such a word as man in a general and not an individual sense." This list was no doubt intended by James to be merely illustrative and not exhaustive. Every one will recognize these experiences as being highly important, and as not obviously, at least, analyzable into colors, sounds, tastes, smells, and skin sensations.

Many psychologists, some following James's lead, others independently, have contended for the existence of non-sensational or imageless conscious processes.

Stout (133), for example, says: "Professor James dwells only on the part played by psychic fringes in higher cognitive states. He fails to bring out its importance for sense perception also. But a little consideration shows that complex sensible objects do not appear to the percipient in all their sensible detail. When I look at a house, what is actually seen together with what is mentally pictured constitutes only a small part of the object as it is perceived. . . . An imageless representation of the whole is conjoined with the sensible appearance. . . . At the most, only the last two or three notes of a melody are perceived at its close, and yet the musically gifted are aware of it as a whole. . . . All perception of a series of changes as forming a whole involves imageless apprehension." The imageless processes in which Stout is most interested are the feelings of tendency in thinking, involving "not only consciousness of whither our thought is going, but backward reference to what it has already achieved."

Spencer (131) divided conscious processes into two classes, which he called 'feelings' and 'relations between feelings.' By feelings he meant sensations, peripherally or centrally excited. James's feelings of 'if' and 'but' would evidently be classed by Spencer as relations between feelings. The differences between feelings and relations between feelings, according to Spencer, are, first, that the latter have no duration, "occupy no appreciable part of consciousness"; they are "momentary feelings accompanying the transition from one conspicuous feeling to another"; and secondly, that as a result of their fleeting character they are unanalyzable: "whereas a relational feeling is a portion of consciousness inseparable into parts, a feeling ordinarily so-called is a portion of consciousness that admits imaginary division into like parts which are related to one another in sequence or co-existence."

In 1901 Calkins (20), accepting the doctrine of James and adopting the term 'relational element' from Spencer's 'relational feeling,' gave as an enumeration, admittedly incomplete, of such non-sensational components in our experience, the following list: feelings of one and many, of 'and' and 'but' (connection and opposition), of like and different, of more and less, of generality, or that which, added to a percept or image, makes it a general notion; of clearness (which feeling constitutes the process of attention: an attended-to percept is the percept *plus* the feeling of clearness); a feeling of the combination of elements in a percept; the feeling of familiarity (which is really a fusion of two relational elements, namely, the feelings of sameness and pastness); and the feeling of wholeness (which is a distinguishing feature of the process of judgment). Most of these feelings are not further described, and Calkins, like James, emphasizes the great difficulty of observing them introspectively: the feeling of pastness, however, is depicted as "the consciousness of an irrevocable fact, linked in two directions with other facts."

Woodworth (157) in 1906, as a result of experiments where the observers were asked to go through certain simple thought processes, reached this conclusion: "In addition to sensorial elements, thought contains elements which are wholly irreducible to sensory terms. Each such element is *sui generis*, being nothing else than the particular feeling of the thought in question. . . . There is a specific and unanalyzable conscious *quale* for every individual and general notion, for every judgment and supposition. An image may call up a meaning, and a meaning may equally well call up an image. The two classes of mental contents differ in quality as red differs from cold, or anger from middle C." Non-sensational processes were discovered in another direction by Mach (74) in 1886, when he posited, coordinate with colors, tones, and the other ordinary sense qualities, space and time sensations. A visual object like a house, he maintained, gives us, besides color sensations, space sensations of a certain size and form. The perception of a melody involves, over and above the tone sensations, a sensation of its temporal form. This general position was later greatly developed by Ehrenfels (31), Meinong (78), Cornelius (24), and Witasek (152): the opinion which they all have in common is that when sensations occur in a group, a new conscious element is produced which represents the togetherness of the elements, the form and character of their combination. Thus, a melody played in different keys has all its tonal elements quite different, but the form quality is identical and is recognized as such.

Still another development of the notion of conscious processes which are not reducible to sensations as elements was suggested by Mayer and Orth (76) in 1901. They made an introspective study of the processes that intervene between the giving of a stimulus word to an observer and the pronouncing by the latter of some word suggested to him by the stimulus word. These processes they classified as ideas (made up of centrally excited sensations), will processes, and what they termed, at the suggestion of Professor Marbe, '*Bewusstseins-lagen*,' 'consciousness attitudes,' or, more briefly translated, 'conscious attitudes.' They defined these merely negatively, as being neither ideas nor volitional processes. In his later work, "Gefühl und Bewusstseinslage," Orth (102) says of the conscious attitudes that they are unanalyzable. They fall, he holds, into two groups: first, those of which introspection can only declare the existence without characterizing them further, and second, those whose significance for the psychic process can in some degree be determined. As an example of the first, the indescribable class, he cites the following introspection. The observer (no less skilled an introspector than Professor Külpe) was given the task of subtracting 217 from 1000. He reported: "Distinct visual images of 1000 and 217, the latter written under the former. They elicited the spoken word 'seven hundred,' and after a little pause the words 'eighty-three.' The pause was filled with a peculiar conscious attitude, not further to be described." To the second class belong such states as doubt, certainty, uncertainty, contrast, agreement. Conscious attitudes are "something quite peculiar, which I find in my consciousness, without being able to call them feeling, sensation, or idea, because they are entirely unlike these psychic processes." They are obscure, ungraspable. They have more to do with knowledge than with feeling. To the suggestion that they are only ideas in an obscure state, Orth replies that even so, since they are unique for introspection and since an idea as such cannot be obscure, they have a right to a special name. He would include under conscious attitudes the feeling of familiarity or knownness; he describes doubt as a conscious attitude accompanied by organic and kinæsthetic sensations, and mentions also conscious attitudes of remembering, knowing, effort, belief, uncertainty. Some of these remind us strikingly of those "ideas of reflection" which Locke posited, in addition to sensations, as fundamental materials of our experience: "by reflection," he said, he meant, "that notice which the mind takes of its own operations." [1]

Messer (80) in 1906 gives a very long list of conscious attitudes. He suggests that they are of two kinds. The first kind includes those which are connected with words and represent the meaning of the words. He gives as illustrations the attitudes of understanding, ambiguity, and synonymity: one would say that these represent rather the relation of a word to its meaning than the meaning itself. Messer's second class comprises the attitudes which occur when words are lacking, but one knows what one is going to say: here one may go to logic for the kinds of attitude concerned. Some examples are attitudes of reality, spatial properties, temporal properties, causal connection, relations such as identity, difference, similarity, 'belonging together,' 'lacking connection,' coördination, subordination, supraordination, 'more general,' 'more concrete,' whole and part. These all represent relations between the objects of thought. There are also attitudes which represent the relations between the object of thought and the subject, that is, the thinker: such are the attitudes of knownness, strangeness, and positive or negative value. Again, there are attitudes which represent the relation of one's ideas to the problem one is thinking on; such as the attitudes of 'suitable' or 'not-suitable,' 'meaningful' or 'meaningless,' 'correct,' 'wrong,' 'inadequate.' Finally, there are attitudes representing states connected with the process of problem solution itself: seeking, questioning, deliberation, doubt, certainty, uncertainty, difficulty, ease, compulsion, 'ought' and 'ought not,' readiness, possibility and impossibility, success and failure, fullness and emptiness of ideas, puzzle and confusion. As a cross-principle

[1] *Essay on the Human Understanding* (1689). Frazer's edition, Volume I p. 124.

running through all the classes of conscious attitudes, Messer suggests that they may be divided into the more intellectual and the more emotional or affective.

Another type of imageless or non-sensational process was postulated by Ach (2) as a result of experiments on reaction time. The observers were shown white or colored cards, and received varying instructions: they were to press an electric key sometimes as soon as they had apprehended the character of the stimulus, sometimes as soon as they were aware of any stimulus at all: sometimes they were shown cards with two letters on them and told to choose either one as their stimulus, reacting to one with one finger and to the other, if they chose it, with the thumb. The observers reported the occurrence, in the interval between the instructions and the stimulus, of certain imageless processes to which Ach gave the name 'awarenesses.' They were, he says, complex experiences, in which no 'anschaulich' elements, such as visual, auditory, or kinæsthetic sensations, or memory images of such sensations, could be demonstrated as determining the quality of the experience (2, page 210).

Awarenesses, Ach maintains, are a "function of the excitation of reproductive tendencies." He groups them into four classes: awarenesses of meaning, that is, the awareness of the meaning of a word without its being present in the form of images; awarenesses of relation, whether an idea is the right one, that is, is in harmony with what we meant to think; awarenesses of determination, the awareness that an act is in harmony with what we meant to do; and awarenesses of tendency, the awareness that there is something more to be done. It would appear that awarenesses of meaning and tendency are, so to speak, forward-looking awarenesses, concerned in the one case with what we are going to think and in the other case with what we are going to do; while awarenesses of relation and determination are backward-looking awarenesses, concerned in the one case with what we originally resolved to think and in the other case with what we originally resolved to do.

Perhaps the most difficult and obscure discussion of imageless processes is that of Bühler (18). With the aid of two experts in introspection, Külpe and Dürr, as observers, Bühler carried out at the University of Würzburg some experiments on the nature of the process of thinking. In the first set of experiments, the observers were given questions to answer, such as, "Did the Middle Ages know the Pythagorean doctrine?" or aphorisms to understand: they then recalled and described all the processes which passed through consciousness in the interval between question and answer. In a later set of experiments the process of recalling thoughts was studied: the observers were given two related ideas and asked to establish in their own minds the connection: subsequently one idea was presented and the observers had to recall the other and to describe the process of recall. Or a sentence was given which required completion by another clause, which the observer had mentally to supply; later the completing clause was furnished and the original sentence called for; or two complete thoughts were presented, the observer having to find an analogy between them, and later, on the basis of this analogy, to supply one when the other was presented; or, finally, a series of thoughts was given in short sentences, and subsequently catchwords from the sentences were supplied, to recall the entire thoughts. On the basis of the introspective results, Bühler concludes that thought involves, first, ideas made up of sensations; secondly, feelings and conscious attitudes; and thirdly, thoughts. These last are simple, unanalyzable conscious processes, having no sense quality or intensity, but possessing clearness and vividness. Of these thought elements there are three types: first, "the consciousness of a rule," of a method of solving problems; second, consciousness of relation, either of the parts of a thought (intra-thought relations), or of whole thoughts to each other (inter-thought relations); thirdly, consciousness of meanings.

It is a discouraging field to survey, this of the non-sensational conscious processes. At least, one can hardly doubt, with such an array of authorities before one, that events do happen in our mental life which cannot be directly traced to any of the external senses; which are not made up of remembered sights, sounds, smells, touches, or tastes. The psychologists who still believe, however, that sensation qualities are the only raw material of our experience, have usually had recourse to one or both of two ways out of their difficulty. Some of the so-called imageless processes, they argue, are just *ordinary ideas*, that is, images, *in a state of indistinctness or vagueness.* Thus the conscious attitude of familiarity may be merely a vague, indistinct recall of the circumstances under which we last met the object recognized: awareness of the meaning of a word like 'city' may be a vague, unanalyzable jumble of the images which the word is capable of suggesting. So Müller (89) urges that some of Orth's conscious attitudes are nothing but indistinct ideas; as when he speaks of a conscious attitude representing "the memory of a similarly smelling substance used for toothache." Orth himself, as we have seen, does not deny that his conscious attitudes may be only ideas in a state of vagueness, but holds that they ought to have a name of their own. Further, Müller says of Ach's awarenesses that they are nothing but indistinct ideas. For instance, Ach calls the feeling that a name is just on the tip of our tongue, an awareness of tendency: it is simply, Müller argues, a very indistinct kinæsthetic image of the name. Or take the awareness that our task is not yet completed, that we have something yet to do, we know not what: here also there is simply an indistinct idea. Unless, Müller maintains, the presence of indistinct ideas can be excluded, it is unscientific to bring in anything new and mysterious like an awareness: it is also much too easy. Bühler himself considered and rejected the notion that his thought elements are indistinct ideas, under two aspects: one of these he calls the condensation theory, according to which thoughts are condensed, abbreviated series of images. This is untrue, he thinks, for surely such a condensation would not make the ideas lose all the characters of ideas, such as recognizable sensation qualities. (Precisely such an effect, as we shall see, might be expected in an abbreviated and condensed series of images.) The other form of the 'indistinct idea' theory Bühler rejects under the name of the 'possibility theory': thoughts are not subconscious images, for thoughts are perfectly clear and distinct. Evidently when Bühler says that imageless thoughts are distinct and Müller says that all imageless processes are indistinct images, they must each mean a different thing by 'distinct.'

Another promising opening for a sensational explanation of these imageless processes which so many psychologists discover, is to say that they are *made up of kinæsthetic and organic sensations*, either peripherally or centrally excited. An obvious, though fortunately not the only or the best, reason for choosing these modalities of sensation as the material for (apparently) non-sensational processes is that we are so little in the habit of attending to them and analyzing their combinations that they may really be the components of almost any experience not evidently derived from other sources. Titchener (137) is strongly inclined to the opinion that " the imageless thoughts, the awarenesses, the *Bewusstseinslagen* of meaning and the rest" are "attitudinal feels," describable "in the rough" without difficulty as visceral pressures, distributions of tonicity in the muscles of back and legs, difference in the sensed play of facial expression, and other kinæsthetic and organic sensations; and that "under experimental conditions, description would be possible in detail." Feelings of relation he is sure are in his own mind kinæsthetic, and moreover roughly localizable and analyzable.

There are still other ways of disposing of alleged non-sensational processes besides those of identifying them as obscure sensory images or as kinæsthetic and organic sensations. Münsterberg (95) classifies some of these processes as properties of sensations; that is, he includes the spatial and temporal orders of sensations under the head of 'form qualities' of sensation, while some, at least, of the conscious attitudes and relational elements fall in the class of 'value properties' of sensation:

thus, the difference between the idea of a past event and the idea of an expected event is a difference in 'value quality.' Wundt (160) has a convenient scheme for dealing with all non-sensational processes: he recognizes besides sensational elements simple feelings of many qualities, capable of entering into a great variety of combinations. This body of elementary feelings may be grouped into three classes, feelings of pleasantness or unpleasantness, feelings of strain and relaxation, and feelings of excitement or depression. It is an easy matter to explain any mysterious imageless process as due to the presence of a special feeling quality or combination of feeling qualities.

In attempting to deal with non-sensational or imageless processes on the basis of our general theory regarding the nervous substrate of conscious processes, we shall avail ourselves of both the 'kinæsthetic' theory and the 'condensed image' theory. To begin with, let us ask whether there is not some significance in the fact that certain of the imageless processes which have been enumerated by various writers can be *readily named*, while others cannot. Thus, some of them are clearly designated by being called 'likeness,' 'the feeling of *but*,' 'expectation,' 'louder than,' and so forth. On the other hand, Orth says of some of the conscious attitudes that they cannot be described or named; they can only be recognized; while Woodworth speaks of certain processes as being "nothing else than the particular feeling of the thought in question."

Now, the process of naming is a motor response; an experience is named when it calls forth a special reaction of the articulatory organs. When we get the experience that two ideas are opposed to each other the word 'but' springs to our lips without hesitation; when we recognize that one experience is like another, the word 'like' is instantly forth-coming; when we get a certain conscious attitude we describe it without delay as one of doubt. On the other hand, we do not adequately describe the inkling of a forgotten name that haunts us by calling it an 'inkling': it is not like any other inkling, and we have no word to express its differentiating character.

If two processes (in our terminology, two movement systems) are associated with the same motor response, the great probability is that they are so associated by virtue of being essentially alike. We call many individual animals by the name 'dog,' but we do so because of certain features that are identical in them all. It would therefore seem probable that if we promptly and unhesitatingly use the word 'but' when two conscious processes are in a relation of opposition, no matter what the nature of the processes thus related may be, whether they are two colors or two theories of the universe, the butness is due to a nervous process essentially the same in both cases.

Further, if to every word that readily occurs to us as a name for an 'imageless' process there corresponds a single characteristic nervous process; if all cases of 'ifness,' 'butness,' likeness, difference, 'greaterness,' 'lessness' (we have not always the proper abstract noun), and so on depend, each class, on a single and always similar nervous process, which accompanies the various sensory excitations, visual, auditory, and so on, then there is good antecedent probability that these common factors are kinæsthetic in character. There is no other kind of sensation that so regularly accompanies other kinds as do the sensations produced by our own movements. Colors are not regularly accompanied by sounds, nor do smell, taste, or temperature sensations constantly accompany all other modalities of sensation: but we continually make movements of the eyes, the organs of speech, the fingers, or other parts of the body in connection with sensations of sight, hearing, taste, and so on, and these movements give rise to kinæsthetic excitations. As Beaunis (9) has said: "Muscular sensations enter not only into our sensations, but into perceptions, ideas, sentiments, emotions, in a word, into the whole psychic life; and from this point of view it may be said with truth that the sense of movement is the simplest and the most universal of psychic elements." This fact, which is apparent to every one, is one of the bases of our theory, according to which the whole play of conscious processes depends on the interaction of movement systems, and the connections between ideas are based on the connections between kinæsthetic pathways and motor pathways.

Let us suppose, then, that the more readily namable an imageless process is, the more it tends to have a kinæsthetic basis: the less readily namable it is, the more it involves processes of other modalities, less constant factors in experience.

If, then, some of the imageless processes are kinæsthetic in their origin, why should they be thought of by so many psychologists as non-sensational? Just what does the term 'non-sensational' mean?

A kinæsthetic process is recognized and identified by introspection as a sensation when it is *referred to a definite point in the body;* this reference involving, of course, the excitation of certain motor responses appropriate to the particular locality concerned. Now, as we have seen, individuals differ a good deal in their habits of reacting to their own kinæsthetic excitations: some persons, Stricker and Titchener, for example, with skill in attending to the sensations from their own movements, might therefore be expected to call certain processes kinæsthetic sensations when other persons were unable to localize the processes in question. Further, many of the kinæsthetic processes which occur in the organism none of us have formed the habit of localizing, because we have not needed to do so. Whether we form the habit of attending to the location of an excitation or to some other characteristic of it depends on practical considerations. In the case of the large majority of kinæsthetic excitations, attention has been directed, not so much on the location of the muscles involved, as on other characteristics of the excitations: for instance, their duration, whether they involve a change from a previously existing attitude, whether they are mutually inhibitory, and so on. Since it is only when we localize a kinæsthetic process that we call it a sensation, and since we have seldom been interested in localizing our kinæsthetic processes, it is not surprising that many processes which are based on kinæsthetic excitations do not reveal themselves to consciousness as sensational (145).

Further, it would seem natural to suppose that two conditions notably influence the readiness with which a combination of kinæsthetic excitations can produce conscious effects that are analyzable by introspection. Or, to put the matter in simpler language, there are two conditions which, when a number of muscular contractions occur at the same time, make it harder for us to locate the exact muscles that are concerned. The first of these is the frequency with which the muscles in question have acted together in the past. If two motor responses invariably accompany each other, we naturally cannot attend to them separately. And if their invariable coöperation is secured by innate connections between their motor pathways, if, that is, their movements form an innate system, we cannot hope to discover by introspection the complexity of the system.

Secondly, since the analysis of a kinæsthetic fusion means the reference of the various kinæsthetic excitations that make it up to different points in space, the more varied the actual spatial position of the muscles involved, the more hope there is of such analysis. This means that a movement system which is widely diffused through the body will stand a better chance of being analyzed than one that is limited to a smaller local range.

Now, there are certain imageless or relational processes which seem, if sufficient time is allowed them to develop, to pass over naturally into processes that involve a rather wide and general bodily disturbance. It is concerning the analyzability of these processes that the introspective testimony of different authorities most diverges. Examples are the 'feeling of *but*,' which develops into the unpleasant 'conscious attitude' of confusion or contradiction; and the 'feeling of unexpectedness,' which passes over into the emotion of surprise. *Whether these experiences are regarded as simple and unanalyzable, or as the reverse, depends on whether one is thinking of them in their contracted or in their expanded form.* Thus, when Titchener says of the feeling of 'but,' "I do roughly localize it and I can roughly analyze it into constituents" (137, page 187), one may surmise that it

is not the momentary 'feeling of but' which he has in mind
so much as the conscious attitude of bafflement or confusion into
which the 'feeling of but' may develop. This is a diffused motor
attitude, and being diffused, stands a better chance of having
its component excitations localized.

There are other namable imageless processes, whose nam-
ability, if I may coin the word, strongly suggests the existence
of a kinæsthetic basis for them, which do not develop into
analyzable conscious attitudes. It is therefore not possible to
prove from introspection that they are kinæsthetic, but it is
equally impossible to prove from introspection that they are
not kinæsthetic. When we remember that only under certain
restricted conditions can we expect to analyze a kinæsthetic
fusion and, by localizing the various excitations which it involves, to realize introspectively their kinæsthetic character,
we are not justified in denying that a certain conscious experience has a kinæsthetic basis because introspection furnishes
no evidence of the fact.

We shall, therefore, assume that all the namable relational
or imageless processes are based on fusions of kinæsthetic excitations, proceeding from certain definite and characteristic
systems or attitudes. When, in the interplay of movement
systems which is constantly going on, certain emergencies
arise, certain characteristic motor attitudes are produced. Some
of these have a tendency to develop and diffuse themselves
until they produce in consciousness analyzable organic attitudes like the emotion of surprise or the conscious attitude of
doubt; others have not this expansive tendency. These latter
cannot be described, although they can be named. Our object
in what follows will be to investigate, for a number of namable
processes of both classes, the nature of the situations which
produce the characteristic motor attitudes; and for processes
of the first class, to point out the nature of the analyzable attitudes into which they may develop.

Perhaps the commonest and functionally the most fundamental of all these motor responses accompanying certain hap-

penings in the interaction of movement systems is that which, apparently, may accompany any *sudden shift* of motor excitation, provided that attention is directed to the relational or kinæsthetic aspect of the process; that is, provided that motor responses to this aspect are called forth either by the activity of the movement systems representing the 'context' (constellation) or by the influence of the activity attitude representing a problem idea. The consciousness accompanying a sudden shift of motor excitation is the feeling or awareness or consciousness of *difference*. Suppose that a certain tone is sounded, and after an interval the same tone is given again. The second occurrence of the tone finds its motor response in greater readiness than the first occurrence did, through that tendency to spontaneous recurrence on which the memory after-image is based. The memory after-image need not be actually present in consciousness: we can hear the second tone and judge it to be the same as the first without having a memory after-image of the first tone and consciously comparing it with the second tone. But the motor readiness on which the memory after-image is based must be in some degree present, or the judgment 'like' cannot be made. Suppose, now, that the second tone is not like the first. There then occurs a sudden shift of motor excitation from the recurrent response for the first tone to a different response for the second tone, and this shift is the cue for giving the verbal response 'different.' There is some reason for thinking that the judgment of likeness is made when there is absence of any ground for the judgment 'different,' and that the latter is the positive experience. Hayden (49), experimenting with lifted weights, reports this with certainty: the judgment 'like' occurs in the absence of any criterion for another judgment. Wolfe (155), working with tones, says that likeness is judged better than difference: this is a result that would occur if the observers, whenever they were in doubt, that is, not sure of a difference, said 'like.' Since such judgments would be correct when the tones were actually alike, the number of correct judgments of likeness would naturally be increased. Whipple (151) thus explains the greater number of correct 'like' judgments in his experiments with tones.

The attitude which corresponds to the feeling of difference has little tendency to develop into a more diffused and analyzable attitude. The case is otherwise when a more or less definite expectation exists; when the object attended to is not only different from the one attended to just previously, but *different from what was expected.* Expectation is even in its lesser degrees based on a bodily attitude that allows of considerable analysis. It very clearly involves for introspection a certain static attitude, giving rise to strain sensations; in fact, we commonly speak of strained expectation. This attitude is modified according as the expectation is wholly indefinite, wholly definite, or partially determined. We may be, that is, in a state of expectation of we know not what; or we may be expecting a particular something; or we may expect one of several definite possibilities. When expectation is wholly indefinite, it would not seem to differ from the attitude of strained attention, of being on the alert. When it is absolutely definite, along with the attitude of strain there are already excited the tentative movements which are the specific response to the stimulus awaited: thus, if we are watching for the waving of a white flag as a signal, we are already making responsive movements proper to that stimulus, such, for instance, as saying 'white' to ourselves. These tentative movements may or may not be accompanied by an image of the object looked for. If, in the third place, expectation is of several possibilities, there is infused into the attitude of strain an attitude of hesitation or doubt. This attitude occurs whenever a certain movement system suggests incompatible movements alternately; we waver between the different possibilities.

Now, the experiences of difference and of unexpectedness approach each other most closely when a person is told beforehand that he is to be given a stimulus that will either be like a particular one that he has had before, or be different from it. In this case he has set up a partially determined expectation attitude. He has the possibility that the coming stimulus may be like the former one, and the possibility that it may not: he makes the tentative movements adapted to the reception of the former stimulus, which perhaps call up an image of it; but these movements are not so marked and so uninterrupted as if the expectation were wholly definite, and the attitude of hesitation or doubt is present. When the expected stimulus comes, if it is unlike the former one, the shift of kinæsthetic excitation is not so marked as if the expectation of a repetition had been absolutely definite, and hence the experience of difference is not so marked. The more definite the expectation, the greater the tendency of an unexpected stimulus to give rise to a widespread bodily attitude, which may be the basis of the unpleasant affective experience of irritation at the 'incorrectness' of the unexpected stimulus. The general bodily attitude of 'surprise' occurs whenever there is a sudden and very marked shift of motor response, whether the preceding attitude has been one of expectation or not. I may be surprised at a knock on the door when I am sitting in idle revery. The attitude of *irritation at wrongness or incorrectness* gets its intensity, not from the degree of shift of motor attitude required, but from the steadiness and definiteness of the preceding expectation. A very slight mistake in some one's rendering of a familiar poem may give us the irritating feeling of incorrectness, an attitude which certainly does not owe its intensity to the fact that we have to disturb ourselves to attend to the new wording, but arises from the very definite way in which the movement system corresponding to the correct rendering was already in process of excitation.

The feeling of *but*, as has already been said, belongs to the class of imageless processes that naturally develop into analyzable attitudes. It resembles the 'feeling of difference' in not involving any expectation, and the experience of incorrectness in being capable of developing into a more marked and generalized organic disturbance than the experience of difference can evolve. It would seem to occur whenever two movement systems, developing simultaneously and on the basis of associative dispositions connecting them with each other, reach the point where dispositions of equal strength tend to excite incompatible movements. This occurrence appears to give rise to a definite and characteristic motor disturbance, in its lighter degrees reflected in consciousness as the 'feeling of but'; in its more developed and diffused state becoming the disagreeable conscious attitude of puzzle or confusion.

Nearly if not quite identical with the attitude of confusion is the attitude of *uncertainty*. Broadly speaking, we feel the attitude of certainty when an associative disposition works promptly and *without interference from other dispositions;* that is, when there is no inhibition from incompatible movements. Müller (89) has given an excellent discussion of certainty with regard to the recall of memory ideas: the chief criteria of certainty that the idea recalled is correct are, he says (1) the way in which the idea presents itself, whether alone or accompanied by other possibilities; (2) the promptness of the reproduction; (3) the distinctness and vividness of the idea; (4) the completeness of its detail; (5) whether it belongs to a modality in which we are accustomed to have accurate images. These bases for certainty in our judgments of the correctness of memory ideas are substantially the same as those of our certainty in regard to any kind of judgments: if the associative dispositions work quickly and without conflict from incompatible dispositions we are thrown into the kinæsthetic-organic attitude of certainty; if not, the attitude of uncertainty occurs. *If, although, unless,* are all words whose stimulus, so to speak, is an attitude produced by the occurrence of incompatible motor excitations.

The feeling of *knownness* or *familiarity* is another 'imageless' process which readily passes over into an analyzable attitude. It is closely related, of course, to the 'feeling of likeness,' and in many experiments on recognition the experience that is obtained is not 'knownness' but 'likeness.' The difference between the conditions for the two experiences is that, to make the judgment 'like,' one must refer to a particular past experience, while to judge that a thing is known, that it has been experienced before, requires no such definite reference. That is, a thing is known if it has been experienced somewhere, at some time, in the past; it is like if it has been experienced in a certain definite setting, either recently experienced or now recalled. When the material for recognition experiments is simple and of a sort that has often been experienced before, as, for instance, a musical tone, then the judgment made regarding it will be that of likeness or difference: the tone has often been heard before in many different settings, but the question is: Does it or does it not resemble one heard a few moments ago? When the material is more complex, like a photograph, or less frequently experienced, like a peculiar odor, the judgment is that of knownness or unknownness: since the face or the odor is not a common element in experience, the question is: Have I ever encountered it before?

Now, obviously we do not make the judgment 'known' every time we encounter a thing we have met before. In that case we should be making it at every moment of our lives: I should pause to recognize my typewriter and my chair on coming into my study, instead of instantly proceeding to make use of them. We recognize the known only in the midst of the unknown. Titchener (138) uses the example of a man's sitting in a street-car and glancing at the faces opposite until he sees one that 'looks familiar' to him. Now, such an experience as this can be described in terms of our theory somewhat as follows. There are successively active in the man's cortex certain rather large movement systems, each representing one of the faces opposite. These systems, so long as they act as wholes, fail to set any further systems into activity: they have no associative tendencies, they suggest nothing. This suspension of associative activity gives rise to a peculiar general motor response, which in its stronger and more diffused form may be described as a feeling or conscious attitude of strangeness, and in some individuals may become a highly unpleasant emotion. So far as it can be introspectively analyzed, it would seem to contain much muscular strain. When, however, the familiar face is attended to, the movement system which it involves begins to set into activity associative dispositions, although these may be too weak to produce actual recall. Nevertheless, the suspension of associative activity is relaxed, and with this the attitude of strangeness gives place to the attitude of familiarity, which Titchener has called 'a weakened emotion of relief,' although there must be something specific about it to distinguish it from other cases of relief. In any case, the familiarity or knownness feeling may be thought of as based on a peculiar attitude, tending, as it becomes stronger and more diffused, to pass over into a more or less analyzable experience into which bodily relaxation clearly enters. The natural course of events, when we recognize an object as known, is to proceed to the recall, in some kind of imagery, of the circumstances under which we have met it before. As the associative dispositions which it sets into activity become more numerous and more active, we begin to have imageless processes of the unnamable type, 'inklings' of the former setting of the recognized experience. Finally, these give place to definite imagery and the recognition process is complete.

Other attitudes which in their fully developed form are more or less analyzable are those connected with judgments of the intensity and duration of stimuli. We have already suggested that the intensity of a sensation is an experience based on the presence of a more or less diffused motor response, giving rise to organic and kinæsthetic excitations. The fact that intensity can be called, as it is by Ebbinghaus,[1] a 'common property' of sensations, implying that intensity is always the same kind of experience no matter what it is the intensity of, that the loudness of a sound is in some degree the same kind of experience as the hardness of a pressure, strongly indicates that it has a kinæsthetic basis.

Our absolute judgments of high degrees of intensity are

[1] *Grundzüge der Psychologie* (Leipzig, 1902).

probably based on the degree of diffusion of the stimulus energy through the motor pathways of the body. We can by introspection describe the attitude characteristic of high intensity as a kind of general muscular shrinking, which is at the same time a withdrawal and a summons of the muscular forces of the body to endurance, and we can more or less localize the kinæsthetic and organic excitations thus produced. In the case of absolute judgments of very slight intensity, another attitude is apt to be the basis of the judgment: a generalized muscular response, namely, which is not the result of the overflow of stimulus energy, but rather due to the strain that accompanies the effort to attend and to prevent distraction which will cause the stimulus to lose its effectiveness. The words used to express our judgments of absolute intensity are significant. The words for high intensities tend to vary according to the kind of sensation that is meant: thus we say 'loud' for a sound, 'bright' for a color, 'strong' for a pressure or a smell, to designate intense sensations; but for weak sensations the variety is less. Neither a color nor a smell nor a pressure can be 'loud'; but a sound and a touch can both be 'soft'; a sound, a color, a smell, can all be 'faint.' This is very likely due to the fact that in weak sensations the specific quality is poorly discriminated.

Judgments of relative or comparative intensity are, of course, a special kind of judgments of likeness or difference. If we lift two weights in succession, and judge the second to be heavier than the first, we are judging first of all that they are different, and secondly, that they differ in respect to intensity. We have in this case, then, first, the sudden shift of kinæsthetic excitation which is the basis of the judgment 'different'; this is modified into the judgments 'intenser' or 'weaker' according to the felt character of the general motor response. Of course practice in making such judgments of the relative intensity of stimuli might result in producing the verbal response 'stronger' or 'weaker' as the direct effect of the stronger or weaker excitation of the sensory centre immediately acted on by the stimulus. But in this case the judgment would be automatic, and there could be no question of the presence in consciousness of any special content representing the intensity. When the judgment is made with hesitation, the basis of consciousness of the 'relational element' 'stronger than,' 'weaker than,' which is recognized as an experience of the same quality, no matter what the sensations compared, is indicated by this very recognition of its uniform character to be kinæsthetic in its source.

Duration is another 'common' or 'generic' property of sensations: temporal 'long' and 'short' are felt to be the same kind of experience, no matter what kind of sensational content fills the duration. For a theory as to the kinæsthetic basis of temporal judgments we may refer to Wundt (160), since there are good reasons for thinking that what he calls 'feelings of strain and relaxation' are wholly kinæsthetic in their origin. A long-lasting stimulus produces a peculiar attitude of strain: its cessation an attitude of relaxation. Wundt distinguishes between the feelings of strain and relaxation on the one hand, and kinæsthetic sensations, which he says also enter into temporal judgments, on the other; but if one takes the ground that a process may be sensory in its physiological basis and yet not analyzable into localized sensations, it is easy to interpret Wundt's 'feelings' as unanalyzed kinæsthetic fusions, and his 'kinæsthetic sensations' as kinæsthetic processes which can be introspectively located.

To suppose a kinæsthetic basis for spatial judgments is in principle easy, whatever problems may arise in the working out of the details of such an hypothesis. So far as the judgments are quantitative, duration judgments play an important part in them.

There are, of course, three kinds of 'size,' corresponding to the three dimensions of space: there is the length of a line, the area of a surface, and the cubic size of a solid. The most obvious basis for judging a line as long or short consists in judging the duration of the hand and eye movements made in exploring it, whether these movements are fully performed or only tentatively performed. It must be remembered, though, that the movement systems involved in exploring objects that are extended in space have a peculiar characteristic: namely, that the movements they involve may be made equally well in either of two opposite time sequences: they form, as we have seen (pages 14–15) opposite, irreversible, successive movement systems. When the kinæsthetic sensations from such a system, whether the movements are fully or only tentatively performed, are of considerable duration, the judgment 'long' is suggested with regard to a line: when they are of brief duration, the judgment 'short' is suggested. The relative judgments 'longer than,' 'shorter than,' involve the experience of difference, plus the experience of long or brief duration of the kinæsthesis. The fact that the words 'long' and 'short' are used indifferently of lines and of durations points clearly to the common character of these experiences.

In the case of a surface whose area is judged large or small, a number of linear movement systems are linked together in a system of a higher order. A surface may be explored from right to left, or from left to right; from above downward or from below upward; and obliquely back and forth in any direction. The duration of the kinæsthetic excitations from these movements, whether of the eye or of the hand or both, is the basis of the judgments of the size of the surface. In like manner judgments of solid dimensions depend on sensations from the hand and eye positions needed to examine or explore the object: the amount of convergence and accommodation of the eyes; the extension of the fingers and arms needed to surround the object.

Nearly all of the 'relational' or 'imageless' processes we have thus far considered have been of the type which under certain circumstances develops into a more or less analyzable conscious attitude; and for this reason we have been able to indicate from introspection something as to the nature of the attitudes which underlie them. Thus, we have been able to suggest that the experiences of *but* and *if* involve strain and suspended movement; that familiarity involves relaxation; that high intensity involves a kind of shrinking; and so on. These descriptions have been extremely imperfect, but they have been perhaps sufficiently recognizable to make plausible the theory that there really are motor attitudes underlying the namable imageless processes. The so-called logical relational processes are less prone to develop into analyzable attitudes. The experience or feeling of *contradiction*, indeed, represents a fundamental logical relation, and it, as we have seen, quite readily develops into an attitude that can be analyzed with a fair degree of success. The experience of *causality* can best be conceived as dependent upon a peculiar attitude which may be called the 'why' attitude. I come into my sitting-room and see a tall vase lying on its side on the table. Instantly I fall into the attitude, 'Why?' 'How?' Now, this attitude on my part is not inevitable. The Kantian philosophers said that the principle that nothing happens without a cause is a fundamental, unescapable category or form of all thinking. They did not mean, of course, that thinking itself is unescapable. I may perfectly well, if my attention is occupied with something else, or even if it is relaxed and drowsy, gaze unthinkingly and uninquiringly at the overturned vase. Even if I attend to the vase and to its overturned position, the attitude 'Why?' is not inevitable: I may occupy myself rather with the future, the immediate practical consequences of the overturning, than with its cause. I need to be in a kind of backward-looking attitude to ask 'Why?'

We have assumed that our experience is based on the interplay of movement systems. Now, the relation of cause and effect concerns the sequence of two movements which not only form a successive system through having occurred in a certain time sequence on many occasions, the cause preceding the effect, but are linked into a closer unity through being associated with a simultaneous system, their meaning. In the chapter on "Simultaneous Movement Systems," it will be

remembered, we saw that when a successive movement system — a series of words in a sentence, for example — is connected with a simultaneous system,—for instance, the meaning expressed by the sentence, — the successive system gains
such unity that its latter parts, given alone, may through the
medium of the meaning recall the earlier parts. Such a unified
successive system is formed by a cause and an effect; on the
effort to complete it rests the tendency to seek for a cause.
Mere time sequence, the mere observation that B follows A,
is not a sufficient foundation for the causal relation: we need
to feel that the two phenomena are essentially one, the working out of a single meaning, that is, associated with a single
simultaneous movement system.

The weaving in and out of movement systems with their
attendant imagery is every now and then interrupted by the
incursion of an outside stimulus, a change in the outside world.
Many of these changes we have anticipated and expected;
that is, the movement systems to which their motor responses
belong are already in activity. Others are unexpected: the
motor responses to which they give rise are not a part of the
systems functioning at the time they occur. Now, the effect
which these unexpected stimuli produce depends on circumstances. If there are in action rapidly developing movement
systems that are actually incompatible with the motor response belonging to the unexpected stimulus, it may go unattended to. If it is attended to, since it and the systems already on the field have no connection, and cannot together
determine the following systems, there occurs a stoppage in
brain activity. What follows the stoppage depends largely
on the individual traits of the person. A weak or a lazy mind
will, after a moment or two of gaping wonder, leave the disconnected phenomenon unexplained. A person who has a
strong tendency to full rather than tentative movements,
what we call a man of action rather than reflection, will proceed to make movements appropriate to the new stimulus,
without any attempt to explain it; will, for instance, pick up

the vase and place it in its proper position. It takes a person of a naturally thoughtful and energetic mind to be seized by the problem of explaining the unexpected stimulus. To explain it means to reconstruct in thought the experience of a person to whom the phenomenon would not have been unexpected: in other words, to set in action the system of tentative movements that would lead naturally to the thought of just such a phenomenon, and hence must have been involved in the experience of one in a position to witness all the events which led up to it. To be thus thoughtful and energetic, one must be so constituted that a check in the systems of tentative movements is even more disturbing than the checking of a full instinctive movement; and so constituted that the activity attitude, on which prolonged intellectual work depends, alternates with relaxation at just the intervals most favorable to its long association with a given problem.

The idea of a cause is an idea that can put an end to the attitude 'Why?' or, in our terminology, it is an idea based on a movement system that is capable of putting an end to the attitude 'Why?' And such a movement system is one that forms the earlier section of a successive and irreversible movement system, whose later section is constituted by the effect, and which is held together by its association with a simultaneous system. The 'Why?' attitude is occasioned by the tendency of the latter half of a successive system to complete the whole system, and the temporary checking of this tendency. I see that the casement window behind the table on which the vase stands, though closed now, is not latched, and I immediately think of the probability that it blew open, and that the breeze thus admitted upset the vase. The ideas of the breeze and of the overturned vase, on the basis of frequent experience, form a successive movement system whose order is determined: wind and displaced objects have always occurred in just this sequence: never has a displaced object been followed, rather than preceded, by the blowing of the wind. In most cases, moreover, the system which is completed by the idea of the cause is a very large one, so that the order of events within it is determined, not merely by the observed sequence of the two phenomena called 'cause' and 'effect,' but by many other phenomena. I conclude that the breeze may have overturned the vase, not merely because I have often observed objects being blown over, but because this is a world in which an effect of this kind must have been produced by the application of a force in a certain direction and manner. It is absolutely essential to the conscious experience of the relation of causality that it shall be accompanied by the occurrence of a particular movement system which puts an end to the 'Why?' attitude; which attitude is occasioned whenever there is an obstacle in the way of the completion of a unified successive movement system whose latter half is given.

In the case of the logical relations of *subordination* and *supraordination* and of *whole* and *part*, we have attitudes that have apparently no tendency to develop into different and analyzable bodily disturbances. When we are aware, in considering two ideas, that the one is an idea of a whole and the other an idea of a part of that whole, as when we think of 'house' and 'roof,' we are in some way aware that we are passing from a smaller movement system to a larger one in which the smaller one is contained, or *vice versa*. Since it is usually simpler and easier to think in terms of wholes rather than parts, the passage from part to whole is, as it were, a release into free activity of certain associative dispositions that were held in check while the part only was being attended to. In the case of subordination and supraordination, that is, of the relation between a genus and a species, or between a general idea and a concrete example, the more general idea also represents a smaller movement system than the less general idea. There are not so many elements involved in the idea 'animal' as are involved in the idea 'horse.' How, then, does the relation of genus to species differ from the relation of part to whole: what is the difference between passing from the idea 'horse' to the idea 'animal' and passing from the idea 'horse' to the idea 'mane'? Clearly, to understand the relation of genus to species we must take into account, not only what the logicians termed the 'intension' of the concept, but also what they termed its 'extension.' By 'intension' is meant the qualities possessed in common by all the examples of the class which the general idea or concept represents. Thus, the intension of horse is composed of all the qualities belonging to all horses, and the intension of animal is composed of all the qualities belonging to all animals: evidently the intension is less, the more general the concept. The extension of a concept consists of all the individuals which belong to the class represented by the concept. Thus, the extension of horse is all the horses in existence, and the extension of animal is all the animals in existence. Evidently the extension is less, the less general the concept. Now, the extension of a concept would seem to constitute the type of movement combination which we have called a 'set of movements,' as contrasted with a 'system of movements.' We have a set of movements when a number of movements or movement systems are related only in that they all have a movement or small movement system in common. Thus, all the words which stand for opposites, like 'dark,' 'light,' 'large,' 'small,' 'high,' 'low,' belong to a set of movements connected simply by their common inclusion of the feeling of opposition and the word 'opposite.' Movement systems which belong to the same set of movements are commonly of about the same degree of complexity. Thus, when we pass from the idea of a whole to the idea of a part, while we go from a larger to a smaller movement system, in that the intension of the whole is greater than that of the part (there are more features belonging to a whole horse than to a mane), the two systems have about the same extension; that is, they put into readiness sets of movements, referring to individual horses and manes, of about the same size. On the other hand, when we pass from the idea of a species to that of a genus, while we again go from a larger and more complex to a smaller and less complex movement system, we at the same time pass from a movement system which tends to set in readiness a comparatively small set of movements (ideas of different kinds of horses) to one which tends to set in readiness a larger set of movements (ideas of different kinds of animals).

The study of the possible physiological basis of such processes as are involved in the 'feelings' or 'awarenesses' of the relations of subordination and superordination, whole and part, strongly suggests that they are attitudes which in some way depend on the number and complexity of the movement systems which a given system tends to set into action. What would be the difference between the activity of associative dispositions, that is, kinæsthetic processes, involved in the extension of a concept and the activity involved in its intension? The principal difference seems to be this: the movements which represent the intension are linked together in a true simultaneous movement system: each one of them is connected by associative dispositions with all the others. The characteristics which make up our idea of the meaning or intension of the word 'tree,' are all equally necessary to the system as a whole. But the movements which represent the extension are not so linked: an individual tree has features, which must be involved whenever it is thought of as an individual, that are actually incompatible with those of other individual trees. In the case of the simpler concepts we can think of the intension of the concept in a single generic image, so unified is the movement system involved in the intension. But the extension of a concept can never operate as a single whole or system to determine the direction of associative dispositions. In the extension, thought as it were scatters; in the intension, it grasps.

When we pass in thought from a concept of less intension to one of greater intension, as when we pass from the idea of 'tree' to the idea of 'elm tree,' the movement system is enlarged: an elm tree is a tree *plus* certain features that distinguish it as an elm. At the same time the unity of the effect is not disturbed: in other words, no mutually incompatible reactions tend to be excited. When the change is in the opposite direction, and we pass from the less general, from 'dog,' let us say, to 'animal,' the movement system is restricted in its scope: certain associative dispositions that were previously active are now inhibited. On the other hand, if we consider the processes underlying extension, when an idea of less extension, such as 'dog,' gives place to one of greater extension, such as 'animal,' there is an increase in the number of incompatible movements that are set up, alternately, of course: thoughts and images connected with a variety of individual dogs may give place to thoughts and images connected with the much greater variety of animals. That the 'feelings' of greater and less extension and of greater and less intension are due to peculiar motor reactions occasioned by these differences in the behavior of movement systems, but not further describable because they do not, like some of the other attitudes we have assumed as the basis of imageless processes, develop into more widespread bodily disturbances, would seem the most plausible explanation of them.

After this survey, all too hasty and superficial, of some of the imageless processes that can be named, and thus may be presumed to have a kinæsthetic basis which is for each process more or less uniform, let us turn to the other class, those which cannot be named. The inkling of a half-forgotten name is something individual; it is not like any other inkling, and yet it is not recognizably sensational. The meaning of a word, while it may often be an image, is quite as often something for the time being at least imageless; but it is something specific — as Woodworth says, "nothing else but the particular feeling of the thought in question." The physiological basis for imageless processes of this kind must be different in each case: it cannot be any form of general motor attitude.

Imageless thoughts of the non-namable kind seem to occur under two different conditions. On the one hand, as in the case of an 'inkling,' they occur *when something is blocking the associative processes*. I am inclined to think that they do not occur when associative processes are intrinsically weak, but rather when they are partially interfered with by incompatible processes. We can practically always distinguish introspectively between the case where we have wholly forgotten a name or a word and have no chance of recovering it, and the case when it is almost on the tip of our tongue and is worth trying for. In the former case the associative processes are weak and ineffective; in the latter case, when we have an inkling, they are fragmentary. The state of things in the latter case may be conceived somewhat as follows: a fairly complex movement system is set into activity, but some of its parts are wholly inhibited by certain incompatible innervations already on the field. The result is that the system is fragmentary, and the associative dispositions which depend on the system as a whole are prevented from being excited. The fragmentary character of an inkling is often revealed to introspection; we can be sure at times of the general rhythm of the word or phrase we are looking for, or of its first letter. I was once trying to recall a technical term in marine insurance, 'general average.' Something was wholly inhibiting the second word: the first word was active, apparently, just enough to set into action the associative dispositions connecting it with the word 'special'; thus, for a long time I could get no further inkling than a two-word rhythm and the word 'special,' which however was naturally unable to suggest 'average.'

On the other hand, imageless processes apparently occur *when thinking is especially rapid and easy.* We take a mental glance at a whole field of knowledge, and the glance occupies but an instant, yet we know what we have glanced at. Thus Külpe, observing in Bühler's thought experiments, says that he had momentarily the whole development of ancient skepticism, in three periods, before him in outline. In such cases the imageless character of the thought certainly seems most plausibly explained as due to the condensation of the imagery; to the fact that many image processes occur simultaneously and without the analysis which would require time to perform. Bühler, it is true, rejected what he termed the condensation theory of thoughts, that they are condensed and abbreviated sets of ideas, on the ground that such a condensation ought not to make them lose all the characters of images, such as intensity and quality. But if we remember that for a sensation or an image to possess quality and intensity for introspection requires attention to be directed to those aspects; that is, requires specific motor reactions to be made to them; and that this could not be done simultaneously for a great number of images, we must admit that a loss of the characteristics of images is precisely what we should expect of a condensed and telescoped train of images. When an extremely complex movement system, involving possibilities of a great variety of images, functions as a single whole in calling up other movement systems, as when Külpe thought about ancient skepticism in an instant of time, the consciousness produced by slight delay in its functioning will be a composite of elements each of which alone would be a recognizable image with the proper characters of an image; the whole mass of which, however, will certainly be imageless.

Besides condensation as a cause of the loss of the image characters in thoughts, we have the increasing prominence of the kinæsthetic elements in images as the movement systems on which they are based become more fully organized. It will be remembered that a movement system is formed when a number of movements, each of which has originally a stimulus of its own, come to be dependent for their excitation each on the kinæsthetic processes resulting from some other movement in the system. Thus, every motor pathway in a movement system has connections with two sensory pathways, one that of its original stimulus, which may have been visual, auditory, or of any other modality; the other, that of its kinæsthetic stimulus; and the consciousness that accompanies any delay in its functioning is a fusion of kinæsthetic sensation with the centrally excited sensation or image of its original stimulus.

Now the more thoroughly organized the system, the less delay is likely to occur, and the more consciousness tends to be restricted to the kinæsthetic processes, which are necessary, rather than to extend itself to the images of other modalities. Thus Book (13) found that in learning to typewrite processes of other modalities gradually gave way to kinæsthetic processes. As a movement system becomes thoroughly organized, then, its conscious accompaniment tends to become kinæsthetic, and kinæsthetic fusions are for reasons which we have sufficiently indicated, often unlocalized and hence often unrecognized for what they are. To express the truth that every idea has both an imaged (*anschaulich*) and an imageless (*unanschaulich*) content, we should say that every idea has a non-kinæsthetic and a kinæsthetic content. "Every idea," says Koffka (63), "has its *unanschaulich* content, and this may occur alone without the *anschaulich* foundation with which it was originally united." I am not sure that I understand Woodworth's (158) doctrine of imageless perception, but when he says of the 'mental reaction' which according to him constitutes 'perception': "It is something new, not present in the sensations, but theoretically as distinct from them as the motor reaction is. It adds new content which cannot be analyzed into elementary sensations; so that the sensory elements which are often held to supply, along with the feelings, all the substance of consciousness, in reality furnish but a fraction of it, and probably a small fraction. Each perceptual reaction is specific and contributes specific content," he seems to me to mean exactly what I mean by the kinæsthetic component of every idea. Certainly, when he goes on to identify the 'perceptual reaction' with form qualities, — that is, with the shape and size of spatial objects, the temporal form of rhythms, and the like, — he is ascribing to it precisely one of the functions of the kinæsthetic components of images. (It will be borne in mind that when I speak of the kinæsthetic or *unanschaulich* components of images, the kinæsthetic processes are themselves peripherally excited: the doctrine of tentative movements requires that all kinæsthetic processes shall result from actual muscular contraction.)

From our general point of view, finally, we can attack the problem of *meanings* and avoid McDougall's (73) conclusion that they form in themselves a refutation of the doctrine that association is fundamentally the association of movements.

McDougall seems to think that the existence of meanings as imageless processes disproves a motor theory of association. But we have seen that a process may be imageless to introspection, and yet have the same kind of physiological basis as ordinary sensations. The fact is that an idea and its meaning are based on systems that are equivalent for associative purposes. The practical value of a word is that it, a comparatively simple movement system, has the same tendencies to excite other movement systems that is possessed by what may be a much more complex movement system, its meaning. A meaning is not merely that which is suggested by a word: if this were so, then 'black' might be the meaning of 'white,' since the word 'white' almost instantly suggests the word 'black.' It is that which suggests nothing that the word itself does not suggest. When we express a thought, and some one else attempts to express it for us, we say, 'No; that is not what I mean,' the instant the speaker's words set up movement systems that are incompatible with those already active in our own minds, thus giving us the relational experience of contradiction. Obviously the same word may mean different things at different times, that is, in different contexts: obviously the context helps to determine the associations it will call up. Obviously the same image may stand for a particular object or for a general idea: the same drawing of a triangle may mean an isosceles triangle or triangle in general, according as its associative tendencies are limited and directed, by the constellating effect of the context or by a directing idea. To say that the triangle means an isosceles triangle is the same thing as saying that its associative tendencies are identical with those of an isosceles triangle, and any incompatibility between them will be felt as a contradiction: to say that it means triangle in general, is to say that its associative tendencies will be identical with those of triangle in general, and only incompatibilities between these two sets of associative tendencies will give rise to the attitude of contradiction.

CHAPTER XI

WHEN any two movement systems go on simultaneously, as they may if they do not contain incompatible movements, the natural tendency is for associative dispositions to be set up between them. When two systems are successively set into activity, the natural tendency is for them to form a single successive movement system. It is natural for us, in recalling an event, to recall its setting or surroundings, and to recollect the events which immediately followed and preceded it. But there are certain circumstances under which the normal and natural formation of associative dispositions fails to occur.

Let us consider some of these circumstances. (1) A person under great stress of emotion is interrupted by a call to the telephone on some trivial business: he answers the call intelligently and is then again overwhelmed by his emotional crisis. Later he has no recollection of the telephone call or of the appointment he made in reply to it. (2) A man is injured in a football game: he has later no recollection of the ten or fifteen minutes which preceded the injury. (3) A person is thrown into the hypnotic trance, and while in this condition he performs various actions at the suggestion of the operator: on coming out of the trance he cannot recall anything that occurred while he was in it. (4) A man finds himself unable to recall a perfectly familiar name. A careful introspective study proves that this name is associated with a disagreeable event, of which the man has been trying not to think. (5) A man is sitting with a pencil in his writing hand, and his attention centred on a book. In response to questions whispered in his ear, his hand writes a few appropriate words: on being recalled from his reading he has no recollection of the questions or of writing.

These are all cases where movement systems which should normally connect themselves by associative dispositions remain disconnected or dissociated. Four different conditions seem to be involved in them: in (1) and (2) the dissociation is apparently due to a general disturbance or shock to the organism; in (4) the disagreeableness of an experience seems to dissociate it from other experiences; in (5) concentrated attention appears to be responsible for the dissociation, and in (3) the conditions are those which produce the hypnotic trance.

Why should strong emotion of any kind, including shock, interfere with the normal formation of associative dispositions? An emotion is a movement system of the greatest possible complexity. When fully developed it involves practically every muscle in the body. Every bodily movement and every idea feel its effect, either in the way of excitation or inhibition. Now ordinarily, when one movement system intervenes upon another one, the interrupted system, while inhibited for the time, remains in a state of readiness to be resumed. In Poppelreuter's (112) suggested experiment,[1] where sentences from two different stories are read alternately, the interruption of one train of thought by another does not prevent the interrupted train from exerting its influence on its continuation. We do not hear the fourth or fifth sentence in story A as if we had never heard its predecessors: the two stories are both perfectly comprehended at the end. If, however, the place of the second story were taken by a violent emotion, story A's effect would be quite obliterated.

It seems most probable that when the two stories, read alternately, are thus connectedly understood; when the first sentence of story A forms associative connections with the second sentence of the same story, across the gap filled by the first sentence of story B, the reason is that the interruption has not been absolute. Some parts of the complicated movement system set going by the first sentence of story A continue in

[1] See page 136.

activity, even during the interruption: such parts, namely, as do not involve movements incompatible with those of the first sentence of the interrupting story B. Now the more far-reaching and complex the movement systems started by story B, the less possible will it be for any portion of A's movement systems to remain active over the interval. This would explain why a strong emotion makes so complete an interruption, and prevents the formation of associative dispositions between the events which preceded it and the events which followed it. The emotions and shocks which thus dissociate are always sudden in their onset, and not themselves the natural outcome of what has previously been going on. And they are movement systems so far-reaching and complicated that no portion of the previously active movement systems can last over during the interval filled by the emotion.

That an *unpleasant* emotion exerts a special dissociating effect apart from and unlike in its manifestations the dissociation produced by any sudden and violent emotion is one of the facts brought to our attention by Freud. We tend, he argues, to avoid recalling unpleasant experiences to consciousness. This tendency may make it impossible to recall anything that is associated even in the most casual way with the unpleasant set of ideas. Thus Freud (39) reports that he unaccountably failed to recall, in a conversation on Italian art, the name 'Signorelli,' and by careful introspection he unearthed the fact that the name was inhibited because its first two syllables, 'Signor,' are associated with the word 'Herr' through their meaning; 'Herr' has the sound of the first syllable of 'Herzegovina,' with which province Freud had at the time a very disagreeable association. To many of us this will seem far-fetched, but association with what is unpleasant and for that reason avoided in thought is very likely one of the actual causes of interference with the normal working of associative dispositions. To form an idea of how this effect is produced, we may first note that if a movement already belongs to a strongly formed movement system, it will enter with great difficulty into any system that contains incompatible movements with those of the first system. An example from my personal experience will make this clear. I once had occasion to see almost daily a person named 'Harkness,' who was a new acquaintance, a man of the intensely practical, traveling-salesman type, in the habit of declaring himself a self-made man, and implying suspicion of the value of a university education to one dealing with affairs, — in short, what would in the vernacular be called a 'hustler.' I found it almost impossible to recall this person's name, and after Freudian self-examination, I found an explanation undoubtedly far too simple to satisfy Freud. The name 'Harkness' was uniquely and firmly established in a classical setting in my mind. Not only had I in my youth used Harkness's Latin Grammar, but my Freshman Latin had been studied under the direction of a teacher of pronounced personality, named Harkness. The whole atmosphere of my new acquaintance was so incompatible with that of the classics that I simply could not implant so classical a name in so uncongenial an environment.

Now, if even a small and unimportant movement system, like the classical associations grouped around this name, could suffice, as I believe it could, to interfere with and weaken associative dispositions tending to connect one of its members with a new system incompatible with the old, how much more readily can a great and complicated system like what the Freudians term a 'complex,' a system of ideas bound together by being connected with a strong emotion, produce such interference. The suppression of a complex — that is, of the ideas connected with a disagreeable experience — takes place through the presence of a stronger emotional or affective state of the opposite character. The normal attitude of a healthy individual is an attitude of cheerfulness. Now, an attitude of cheerfulness is an actual static movement system, involving certain innervations, and while it is maintained it will inhibit all incompatible innervations. A person in the attitude of cheerfulness is incapable for the time being of a depressing

thought, for precisely the same reason that he cannot pronounce *t* and *g* at the same time: the movements involved are
incompatible. "How long, oh healthy reader," asks James,
"can you now continue thinking of your tomb?"

Complexes are suppressed, not simply in the case where
strongly unpleasant ones come into conflict with a dominant
attitude of cheerfulness, but whenever there is incompatibility
between their movement systems and those dominant at the
time. Thus, a complex may be interfered with because its
emotions conflict with all that carefully acquired system of
attitudes which we call 'propriety': or an emotion may be
suppressed because it is incompatible with the emotion which
we know we ought to feel, and which we therefore do often
feel, strongly enough at least to prevent the development of
incompatible emotions. It is not surprising if, as the Freudians
tell us, these cases of the interference of incompatible emotions
result in profound bodily disturbances and so-called 'hys-
terical' symptoms. When one movement system completely
inhibits another which involves antagonistic movements, if
the inhibited system is small, we may suppose that the
comparatively insignificant amount of energy which is thus
dammed up finds inconspicuous channels for its escape. But
an emotion, with energy enough to involve the whole muscular system, must when inhibited send its energy out with
more general disturbance: it cannot merely leak away.

The case of automatic writing (5) is a peculiar one. One of
the best examples recorded by a trained psychologist is that
furnished by Patrick's 'Henry W.,' reported in volume five of
The Psychological Review (104). Here, during many successive
sittings, the hand of the subject, whose attention was engrossed
in reading, wrote long series of answers, more or less coherent,
to questions asked in a low tone. The complete separation of
the systems of movement performed by the hand from the
systems concerned in the reading was indicated by the entire
failure of 'Henry W.,' on being diverted from his book, to
recognize anything that he had written. In other similar cases

it has been shown by the fact that the subject cannot feel pin-pricks on the hand. Sidis (128) reports a case where the patient, engrossed in reading, made no remonstrance on having the writing hand pricked, but the hand immediately wrote, "Don't you prick me any more."

Now, the first thing to be noted, I think, about automatic writing is that it involves the simultaneous operation of systems which need not contain any incompatible movements, although in an ordinary subject they would do so. The 'self' that does the writing involves hand-movement systems and systems connected with the ear: this self is talked to, and responds by writing. The 'self' that is reading involves eye-movement systems, and whatever systems are concerned with the ideas suggested by what he reads. It is conceivable that these two sets of systems, the eye-meaning systems, and the ear-hand systems, may go on side by side without interference, because they employ wholly different sets of muscles. The greatest chance for interference would come if articulatory movements were concerned in both sets, and they certainly would tend to be concerned in the case of the great majority of persons. Good subjects for automatic writing are rare. In most people, the movement systems set up by the reading and those involved in listening and writing would be so large that they would necessarily interfere with each other by containing incompatible movements. There is no way of explaining why this does not occur in such subjects as 'Henry W.,' except to say that *in certain individuals movement systems tend naturally to be restricted in their range,* and perhaps to add that in good subjects for automatic writing the articulatory movements are of less importance than in the majority of individuals.

We come now to the remarkable phenomena of dissociation as a result of the hypnotic trance. As with so many other subjects discussed in this book, our aim will be merely to indicate a few suggestions as to the direction in which an explanation for these phenomena may be sought consistently with our general motor theory.

What, in the first place, is normal sleep? Nobody knows. But the hypothesis as to its nature which best fits the general theory of this book is certainly that recently maintained by Shepard (125). "Sleep and sleeplessness," he says, "are mental processes." "Sleep is promoted by the situation in which we have really become accustomed to sleep." "Sleep is controlled by conditions similar to those which control attention generally." "As we go to sleep, then, we become absorbed in a mass or complex of fatigue sensations. These tend strongly to inhibit other processes, especially motor activity and consciousness of strain sensations in the muscles."

Translating these statements with little difficulty into terms of our own theory, we should say that sleep is a movement system. The apparent absurdity of this statement vanishes when we take the words 'movement system' in the broad sense, as including static as well as phasic systems. Sleep is a static movement system, an attitude. It is an attitude, as nearly as we can judge, of complete relaxation, the inhibition of any muscular contractions whatever. This attitude, like any other movement system, is brought about by the operation of associative dispositions. It is *suggested*. When all the surroundings are favorable, including the external surroundings, the quiet of the sleeping room, and the internal surroundings of fatigue stimuli, then the attitude of sleep is produced, just as a name is recalled when the associative dispositions leading to it are set into action. Now, if sleep as an attitude is complete muscular relaxation, perfect sleep will of course be unconscious, because consciousness is dependent on motor contractions. Imperfect sleep, however, is an attitude of incomplete relaxation. In imperfect sleep, various stimuli from outside and inside the organism, aided by perseverative tendencies, may set up movement systems, limited in scope, which are the basis of dreams. It is the limited and fragmentary character of these systems, liable as they are to inhibition at any point by the maintenance of the relaxed attitude of sleep, that is responsible for the fragmentary and incoherent character of dreams. There is reason for thinking that movement systems which have been initiated during the day, only to be inhibited by incompatible systems, have a special tendency to recur in dreams. Every one who is interested in recalling and studying his dreams must have noticed the fact, emphasized by Delage (28), that their material can be traced to impressions of the preceding day which were barely noticed at the time of their occurrence, because they did not fit into the train of thought at the time. Possibly the reason why these reappear in the dream content, rather than the movement systems which have been fully developed, the basis of those thoughts which have been our main occupation, is that having been set in readiness by the previous day's experience, they are yet unaffected by the fatigue processes which tend to substitute relaxation attitudes for all the more fully exercised systems.

In sleep that is not profound, certain thoroughly organized and long established systems may escape the influence of general relaxation and modify such recurrent and perseverating systems as occasion dreams. It is in this sense that we may understand Freud's (38) conception of a 'dream censor,' a representative of the waking self that will not permit certain dreams to occur, at least without modifying and transforming them. The most firmly rooted 'habits' and 'instincts' — that is, the best established movement systems — may thus repress and modify the fragmentary dream systems in so far as the latter contain movements incompatible with those of the habits and instincts. The Freudians, however, overlook the fact that precisely the same kind of transformation may result from purely temporary organic systems. A slight attack of indigestion may set into activity during sleep a movement system identical with that produced in terror, and in such a case a perfectly harmless object that is being dreamed of may become transformed into a frightful one: a small dog may grow into a lion with which one is desperately struggling. I have often experienced the sudden transformation of one person into another in the course of a dream, not by the action of a censor, but through the influence of the organic background. Thus I may dream of the illness of a member of my family: at the moment when the illness results in death the person is transformed into a stranger, simply because my organic attitude during sleep happens to be too comfortable to supply the strong emotion that would be called for by the death of some one near to me.

Sleep, then, may be plausibly thought of as a perfectly definite static movement system, a bodily attitude of complete muscular relaxation. This attitude, in going to sleep, is assumed first so far as full muscular movements are concerned: there is lethargy and an 'unwillingness' to move which amounts almost to incapacity. Every one is familiar with that state of extreme drowsiness in which, while one can still hear what is going on around, one's limbs feel leaden and paralyzed. Later, the relaxation attitude affects even tentative movements in all muscles, and when this occurs, of course associative activity is completely abolished. During various fluctuations in the depth of the sleep, that is, the extent of the relaxation, disconnected systems of tentative movements may be set into activity, either by outside stimuli or by their own perseverative tendencies, and they may interfere with one another and modify one another: they are the basis of dreams.

Now, if some such description as this fits the nature of sleep, how shall we conceive the nature of the hypnotic trance? Certainly, if normal sleep is an attitude that can be brought on by suggestion and the working of associative dispositions in the same fashion as an idea is recalled to the mind, hypnotic sleep is even more obviously the work of suggestion. The essential feature in all methods of hypnotizing is the suggestion of sleep: in certain subjects the mere command 'Sleep' is sufficient to send them off. But the essential difference in the suggestion which brings about normal sleep and the suggestion which brings about the hypnotic sleep is this: *the former is derived from what we may call a diffused source, the latter from a concentrated source.* A person who goes to sleep at night in his own bed gets the suggestion of doing so from all his surroundings, and especially from his own fatigue sensations. It is true that the hypnotizer generally arranges the surroundings to suggest relaxation, by darkening the room and keeping it quiet, but the main source of the suggestion lies in his words: 'You are relaxed all over; you cannot lift your arm; your whole body feels heavy; you cannot move at all.' There are no actual fatigue poisons acting on the patient in any quantity sufficient to bring about the relaxed attitude of sleep. The result of these artificial conditions is that the patient is not relaxed so far as the operator is concerned. To the operator's words he is all attention; to everything else he is relaxed. Every movement system that takes its origin in the operator's words has complete play, whether it is a full movement, as when the operator tells him to dance or sing, or a tentative movement, as when the operator suggests that he sees a rose before him.

Now, by no means every one makes a good subject for the deeper stages of hypnosis. Every normal person who does not set up in himself an active attitude of resistance will become sleepy and lethargic under the operator's suggestions to that effect, and is likely to find it hard or impossible to move a limb when its immobility is suggested. The 'lethargic' stage was thought by Charcot to be the initial stage of the hypnotic trance. But the 'somnambulic' stage, where negative suggestions such as 'You are relaxed,' or 'You cannot move,' give place to positive ones, such as, 'You are swimming,' or 'You see a glass of water on the table before you,' is not obtainable in nearly so many observers. The reason why some people enter it so much more readily than others is clearly related to the reason that makes some people display the phenomena of automatic writing so much more readily than others. The lighter stages of hypnosis demand an effect that is spread over all the organism, general relaxation, or even general rigidity. But the deeper stages demand that there shall be activity in certain restricted movement systems and relaxation elsewhere.

This means the possibility of smaller systems than are characteristic of the motor mechanism of the majority of persons. We cannot escape the conviction, since there exist such striking differences among individuals as regards their readiness to become hypnotized and to display the phenomena of automatic writing, that an important factor among others in bringing about dissociation, or the failure of associative dispositions to function normally, is an individual peculiarity of cortical organization, according to which there is a natural tendency to form small rather than more extended movement systems. The process of hypnotizing a person does not produce this characteristic; it merely gives it a chance to exhibit itself. The tendency to small movement systems would naturally be encouraged and developed by the frequent experiencing of conflicting emotions; that is, of large and complex movement systems having incompatible elements. The mutual interference thus generated would tend to prevent the occurrence of large movement systems in general, since any large system would be apt to call up the opposed emotions. Thus such conflicts between strong innate tendencies have a peculiar liability to produce dissociation, alternating personalities, and the more marked phenomena of hypnotism; the movement systems in such a case become small and restricted for much the same reason that two persons passing on a narrow footbridge make themselves as small as possible.

THE END

REFERENCES

REFERENCES

1. Abramowski, E.: L'image et la reconnaissance. Arch. de psych., t. 9, pp. 1–38. 1909.
2. Ach, N.: Ueber die Willenstätigkeit und das Denken. Göttingen, 1905.
3. Ach, N.: Ueber den Willensakt und das Temperament. Leipzig, 1910.
4. Alexander-Schaefer, G.: Zur Frage der Beeinflussung des Gedächtnisses durch Tuschreize. Zeit. f. Psych., Bd. 39, S. 206–215. 1905.
5. Angell, J. R.: Methods for the Determination of Mental Imagery. Psych. Mon., vol. 13, no. 1, pp. 61–107. 1910.
6. Arnold, F.: The Initial Tendency in Ideal Revival. Am. Jour. Psych., vol. 18, pp. 239–252. 1907.
7. Balaban, A.: Ueber den Unterschied des logischen und des mechanischen Gedächtnisses. Zeit. f. Psych., Bd. 56, S. 356–377. 1910.
8. Baldwin, B. T.: Associations under the Influence of Different Ideas. Harvard Psych. Studies, vol. 2, pp. 431–473. 1906.
9. Beaunis, E.: Les sensations internes. Paris, 1889.
10. Bentley, M.: The Memory Image and its Qualitative Fidelity. Am. Jour. Psych., vol. 11, pp. 1–48. 1899.
11. Betz, W.: Vorstellung und Einstellung. I. Ueber Wiedererkennen. Arch. f. d. ges. Psych., Bd. 17, S. 266–296. 1910.
12. Bigham, J.: Memory. Psych. Rev., vol. 1, pp. 453–461. 1894.
13. Book, W. F.: The Psychology of Skill. University of Montana Publications in Psychology. 1908.
14. Bourdon, B.: Influence de l'age sur la mémoire immédiate. Rev. phil., t. 38, pp. 148–167. 1894.
15. Brown, D. E., Browning, M., and Washburn, M. F.: The Effect of the Interval Between Repetitions on the Speed of Learning a Series of Movements. Am. Jour. Psych., vol. 24, pp. 580–582. 1913.
16. Brown, T. G.: On the Question of Fractional Activity ('All or None' Phenomenon) in Mammalian Reflex Phenomena. Proc. Roy. Soc., Series B, vol. 87, pp. 132–144. 1913.
17. Bryan, W. L., and Harter, N.: Studies in the Physiology and Psychology of the Telegraphic Language. Psych. Rev., vol. 4, pp. 27–53. 1897.

18. Bühler, K.: Tatsachen und Probleme zu einer Psychologie der Denkvorgänge. Arch. f. d. ges. Psych., Bd. 9, S. 297–365 (1907); Bd. 12, S. 1–92 (1908).

19. Calkins, M. W.: Association. Psych. Rev. Mon. Supp., no. 1. 1896.

20. Calkins, M. W.: Introduction to Psychology. New York, first edition, 1901.

21. Cattell, J. McK.: Psychometrische Untersuchungen, III. Phil. Stud., Bd. 4, S. 241–250. 1888.

22. Claparède, E.: L'association des idées. Paris, 1903.

23. Cordes, G.: Experimentelle Untersuchungen über Associationen. Phil. Stud., Bd. 17, S. 30–77. 1901.

24. Cornelius, H.: Ueber Verschmelzung und Analyse. Vierteljahr. f. wiss. Phil., Bd. 16, S. 404–446 (1892); Bd. 17, S. 30–75 (1893).

25. Creighton, J. E.: An Introductory Logic. New York, 1898.

26. Cumberland, Stuart: A Thought Reader's Experiences. Nineteenth Century, vol. 20, pp. 867–886. 1886.

27. Daniels, A. H.: The Memory After-Image and Attention. Am. Jour. Psych., vol. 6, pp. 558–564. 1905.

28. Delage, Y.: Essai sur la théorie de rêve. Rev. scient., t. 48, pp. 40–48. 1891.

29. Ebbinghaus, H.: Ueber das Gedächtniss. Leipzig, 1885.

30. Ebert, E., und Meumann, E.: Ueber einige Grundfragen der Psychologie der Uebungsphänomene im Bereiche des Gedächtnisses. Arch. f. d. ges. Psych., Bd. 4, S. 1–233. 1905.

31. Ehrenfels, C.: Ueber "Gestaltsqualitäten." Vierteljahr. f. wiss. Phil., Bd. 14, S. 249–292. 1890.

32. Ephrussi, P.: Experimentelle Beiträge zur Lehre vom Gedächtniss. Zeit. f. Psych., Bd. 37, S. 56–103, 161–234. 1904.

33. Exner, S.: Physiologie der Grosshirnrinde. Hermann's Handbuch der Physiologie, Bd. 2, Heft 2, S. 281. 1879.

34. Fechner, G.: Elemente der Psychophysik. Leipzig, 1ᵗᵉ Aufl. 1859, 3ᵗᵉ Aufl. 1907.

35. Fernald, M. R.: The Diagnosis of Mental Imagery. Psych. Mon., vol. 14, no. 1. 1912.

36. Finkenbinder, E. O.: The Curve of Forgetting. Am. Jour. Psych., vol. 24, pp. 8–32. 1913.

37. Fischer, A.: Ueber Reproduzieren und Wiedererkennen bei Gedichtsversuchen. Zeit. f. Psych., Bd. 50, S. 62–92. 1909.

38. Freud, S.: The Interpretation of Dreams. Translated by A. A. Brill. New York, 1913.

39. Freud, S.: The Psychopathology of Everyday Life. Translated by A. A. Brill. New York, 1914.

40. Galton, F.: Inquiries into Human Faculty and its Development. London, first edition, 1883.
41. Galton, F.: Supplementary Notes on Prehension in Idiots. Mind, O.S., vol. 12, pp. 79–82. 1887.
42. Gamble, E. A. M.: A Study in Memorizing by the Reconstruction Method. Psych. Rev. Mon., vol. 10, no. 4, whole no. 43. 1909.
43. Goldstein, K.: Merkfähigkeit, Gedächtniss, und Assoziation. Zeit. f. Psych., Bd. 41, S. 38–47, 117–144. 1906.
44. Gordon, K.: Meaning in Memory and Attention. Psych. Rev., vol. 10, pp. 267–283. 1903.
45. Groos, K.: Experimentelle Beiträge zur Psychologie des Erkennens. Zeit. f. Psych., Bd. 26, S. 145–168 (1901); Bd. 29, S. 358–371 (1902).
46. Grünbaum, A. A.: Ueber die Abstraktion der Gleichheit: ein Beitrag zur Psychologie der Relation. Arch. f. d. ges. Psych., Bd. 12, S. 340–378. 1908.
47. Hart, B., and Spearman, C.: General Ability, its Existence and Nature. Brit. Jour. Psych., vol. 5, pp. 51–84. 1912.
48. Hawkins, C. J.: Experiments on Memory Types. Psych. Rev., vol. 4., pp. 289–293. 1897.
49. Hayden, E. A.: Memory for Lifted Weights. Am. Jour. Psych., vol. 17, pp. 497–521. 1906.
50. Head, H.: Sensory Disturbances from Cerebral Lesions. Brain, vol. 34, pp. 102–254. 1911.
51. Hirszowicz, S.: Experimentelle Beiträge zur Analyse des Reproduktionsvorganges. Zürich, 1909.
52. Holmes, S. J.: The Reactions of Ranatra to Light. Jour. Comp. Neur. and Psych., vol. 15, pp. 305–349. 1905.
53. Howe, H. C.: Mediate Association. Am. Jour. Psych., vol. 6, pp. 239–241. 1894.
54. Hume, D.: A Treatise of Human Nature. London, 1739. Selby-Bigge's edition, 1888.
55. Jacobs, J.: Experiments on 'Prehension.' Mind, O.S., vol. 12, pp. 75–79. 1887.
56. Jacobs, W.: Ueber das Lernen mit äusserer Lokalization. Zeit. f. Psych., Bd. 45, S. 43–177, 161–187. 1907.
57. James, W.: Principles of Psychology. New York, 1890.
58. Johnson, W. S.: Experiments in Motor Education. Yale Psych. Studies, vol. 10, pp. 81–92. 1902.
59. Jost, A.: Die Assoziationsfestigkeit in ihrer Abhängigkeit der Verteilung der Wiederholungen. Zeit. f. Psych., Bd. 14, S. 436–472. 1897.

60. Judd, C. H.: Movement and Consciousness. Yale Psych. Studies, N.S., vol. 1, pp. 199–226. 1905.

61. Katzaroff, D.: Le rôle de la recitation comme facteur de la mémorisation. Arch. de psych., t. 7, pp. 225–258. 1908.

62. Knors, C.: Experimentelle Untersuchungen über den Lernprozess. Arch. f. d. ges. Psych., Bd. 17, S. 297–361. 1910.

63. Koffka, K.: Zur Analyse der Vorstellungen und ihrer Gesetze. Leipzig, 1912.

64. Kuhlmann, F.: On the Analysis of the Memory Consciousness. Psych. Rev., vol. 13, pp. 316–348. 1906.

65. Lay, W.: Mental Imagery. Psych. Rev. Mon. Supp., vol. 2, no. 3; whole no. 7, pp. 1–59. 1898.

66. Lange, N.: Beiträge zur Theorie der sinnlichen Aufmerksamkeit und der Aktiven Apperception. Phil. Stud., Bd. 4, S. 390–422.

67. Lankes, W.: Perseveration. Brit. Jour. Psych., vol. 7, pp. 387–420. 1915.

68. Lehmann, A.: Ueber Wiedererkennen. Phil. Stud., Bd. 5, S. 96–156. 1889.

69. Leuba, J. H.: A New Instrument for Weber's Law, with Indications of a Law of Sense Memory. Am. Jour. Psych., vol. 5, pp. 370–384. 1893.

70. Levy-Suhl, M.: Studien über die experimentelle Beeinflussung des Vorstellungsverlaufes. Zeit. f. Psych., Bd. 42, S. 128–161 (1906); Bd. 45, S. 321–340 (1907); Bd. 59, S. 1–90 (1911).

71. Lewis, T. A.: On the Transformation of Memory Content in the Comparison of Lights. Psych. Mon., vol. 10, no. 1, pp. 55–62. 1909.

72. Lipmann, O.: Die Wirkung der einzelnen Wiederholungen auf verschieden starke und verschieden alte Assoziationen. Zeit. f. Psych., Bd. 35, S. 195–234. 1904.

73. McDougall, W.: Body and Mind. London, 1st edition, 1911.

74. Mach, E.: Contributions to the Analysis of the Sensations. Translated by C. M. Williams. Chicago, 1897.

75. Martin, L. J.: Die Projektionsmethode und die Localisation visueller und anderer Vorstellungsbilder. Zeit. f. Psych., Bd. 61, S. 322–546. 1912.

76. Mayer, A., und Orth, J.: Zur qualitativen Untersuchung der Association. Zeit. f. Psych., Bd. 26, S. 1–13. 1901.

77. Meakin, F.: Mutual Inhibition of Memory Images. Harvard Psych. Studies, vol. 1, pp. 235–276. 1903.

78. Meinong, A.: Zur Psychologie der Complexe und Relationen.

79. Merkel, J.: Das psychophysische Grundgesetz in Bezug auf Schallstärken. Phil. Stud., Bd. 4, S. 117–160, 251–291. 1888.
80. Messer, A.: Experimentelle-psychologische Untersuchungen über das Denken. Arch. f. d. ges. Psych., Bd. 8, S. 1–224. 1906.
81. Meumann, E.: Oekonomik und Technik des Gedächtnisses. Leipzig, 1908.
82. Meumann, E.: Intelligenz und Wille. Leipzig, 2te Aufl., 1913.
83. Meyer, E.: Ueber die Gesetze der simultanen Assoziation und Wiedererkennen. Leipzig, 1910.
84. Michotte, A.: Gedächtnisversuche mit mehrfachen Assoziationsrichtungen. 3te Kongress f. exp. Psych., S. 259–263. 1909.
85. Milhaud, E.: La projection externe de nos images mentales. Rev. phil., t. 38, pp. 210–222. 1894.
86. Montague, W. P.: Consciousness a Form of Energy. Essays in Honor of William James, pp. 103–135. New York, 1908.
87. Moore, T. V.: The Process of Abstraction. Univ. Cal. Pub. Psych., vol. 1, pp. 73–197. 1910.
88. Müller, G. E.: Zur Analyze der Gedächtnistätigkeit und des Vorstellungsverlaufes. Zeit. f. Psych., Ergänzungsband 5, 1911.
89. Müller, G. E.: Zur Analyse der Gedächtnistätigkeit und des Vorstellungsverlaufes. Zeit. f. Psych., Ergänzungsband 8, 1913.
90. Müller, G. E., und Pilzecker, A.: Experimentelle Beiträge zur Lehre vom Gedächtniss. Zeit. f. Psych., Ergänzungsband 1, 1900.
91. Müller, G. E., und Schumann, F.: Experimentelle Beiträge zur Untersuchung des Gedächtnisses. Zeit. f. Psych., Bd. 6, S. 81–190, 257–339. 1894.
92. Müller-Freienfels, R.: Zur Begriffsbestimmung und Analyse der Gefühle. Zeit. f. Psych., Bd. 68, S. 237–280. 1914.
93. Münsterberg, H.: Beiträge zur experimentellen Psych., Bd. 1, Heft 1, S. 87–105. 1889.
94. Münsterberg, H.: Die Association successiver Vorstellungen. Zeit. f. Psych., Bd. 1, S. 99–107. 1890.
95. Münsterberg, H.: Grundzüge der Psychologie, Bd. I. Leipzig, 1900.
96. Murray, E.: Peripheral and Central Factors in Memory Images of Form and Color. Am. Jour. Psych., vol. 17, pp. 227–247. 1906.
97. Nagel, F.: Experimentelle Untersuchungen uber Grundfragen

der Assoziationstheorie. Arch. f. d. ges. Psych., Bd. 23, S. 156–254. 1912.

98. Offner, M.: Das Gedächtniss. Berlin, 1909.

99. Ogden, R. M.: Untersuchungen uber den Einfluss der Geschwindigkeit des lauten Lesens auf das Erlernen und Behalten von sinnlosen und sinnvollen Stoffen. Arch. f. d. ges. Psych., Bd. 2, S. 93–189. 1904.

100. Ohms, H.: Untersuchung unterwertiger Assoziationen mittels des Worterkennungsvorganges. Zeit. f. Psych., Bd. 56, S. 1–85. 1910.

101. Ordahl, L. E.: Consciousness in Relation to Learning. Am. Jour. Psych., vol. 22, pp. 158–213. 1911.

102. Orth, J.: Gefühl und Bewusstseinslage. Berlin, 1903.

103. Pappenheim, M.: Merkfähigkeit und Assoziationsversuche. Zeit. f. Psych., Bd. 46, S. 161–173. 1908.

104. Patrick, G. T. W.: Some Peculiarities of the Secondary Personality. Psych. Rev., vol. 5, pp. 555–578. 1898.

105. Pawlow, J. P.: The Scientific Investigation of the Psychical Faculties or Processes in the Higher Animals. Lancet, vol. 171, pp. 911–915. 1906.

106. Perky, C. W.: An Experimental Study of Imagination. Am. J. Psych., vol. 21, pp. 422–452. 1910.

107. Peterson, H. A.: On the Influence of Complexity and Dissimilarity on Memory. Psych. Mon., vol. 12, no. 2. 1909.

108. Pfungst, O.: Clever Hans. Translated by Carl Rahn. New York, 1911.

109. Phillippe, J.: Sur les transformations de nos images mentales. Rev. phil., t. 43, pp. 481–493. 1897.

110. Pillsbury, W. B.: Essentials of Psychology. New York, 1911.

111. Pohlmann, A.: Experimentelle Beiträge zur Lehre vom Gedächtniss. Berlin, 1906.

112. Poppelreuter, W.: Ueber die Ordnung des Vorstellungsverlaufes. Arch. f. d. ges. Psych., Bd. 25, S. 209–349. 1912.

113. Radossawljewitsch, P.: Das Behalten und Vergessen bei Kindern und Erwachsenen. Päd. Mon., I, 1907.

114. Ranschburg, P.: Ueber die Bedeutung der Aehnlichkeit beim Erlernen, Behalten, und bei der Reproduktion. Jour. f. Psych. und Neur., Bd. 5, S. 93–127. 1905.

115. Reuther, F.: Beiträge zur Gedächtnisforschung. Psych. Stud., Bd. 1, S. 4–101. 1906.

116. Ribot, T.: The Psychology of Attention. Translation. Chicago, 1898.

117. Ribot, T.: La vie inconsciente et les mouvements. Paris, 1914.

118. Rousmanière, F.: Certainty and Attention. Harvard Psych. Studies, vol. 2, pp. 277–291. 1906.

119. Russell, S. B.: The Functions of Incipient Motor Processes. Psych. Rev., vol. 22, pp. 163–166. 1915.

120. Schaefer, A. A.: Habit Formation in Frogs. Jour. Animal Behav., vol. 1, pp. 309–336. 1911.

121. Schaefer, W.: Ueber die Nachwirkung der Vorstellungen. Giessen, 1904.

122. Schaub, A. de V.: On the Intensity of Images. Am. Jour. Psych., vol. 22, pp. 346–368. 1911.

123. Scripture, E. W.: Ueber den assoziativen Verlauf der Vorstellungen. Phil. Stud., Bd. 7, S. 50–146. 1892.

124. Severance, E., and Washburn, M. F.: On the Loss of Associative Power in Words After Long Fixation. Am. Jour. Psych., vol. 18, pp. 182–186. 1907.

125. Shepard, J. F.: The Circulation and Sleep. Univ. of Michigan Studies, Scientific Series, vol. 1, 1914.

126. Sherrington, C. S.: The Integrative Action of the Nervous System. New York, 1906.

127. Sherrington, C. S.: Reflex Inhibition as a Factor in the Coördination of Movements and Postures. Quart. Jour. Exper. Physiol., vol. 6, pp. 251–310. 1913.

128. Sidis, B.: The Psychology of Suggestion. New York, 1898.

129. Smith, M. K.: On the Reading and Memorizing of Meaningless Syllables Presented at Irregular Time Intervals. Am. Jour. Psych., vol. 18, pp. 504–513. 1907.

130. Smith, G. W.: The Place of Repetition in Memory. Psych. Rev., vol. 3, pp. 21–31. 1896.

131. Spencer, H.: Principles of Psychology. London, 3rd ed., 1887.

132. Steffens, Lottie: Experimentelle Beiträge zur Lehre vom ökonomischen Lernen. Zeit. f. Psych., Bd. 22, S. 321–382. 1900.

133. Stout, G.: Analytic Psychology. London, 1896.

134. Stout, G.: Manual of Psychology. London, 1899.

135. Stricker, S.: Studien über die Sprachvorstellungen. Wien, 1880.

136. Stricker, S.: Studien über die Bewegungsvorstellungen. Wien, 1882.

136a. Sybel, A. von: Ueber das Zusammenwirken verschiedener Sinnesgebiete bei Gedächtnisleistungen. Zeit. f. Psych., Bd. 53, S. 257–360. 1909.

137. Titchener, E. B.: Lectures on the Experimental Psychology of the Thought Processes. New York, 1909.

138. Titchener, E. B.: A Textbook of Psychology. New York, 1910.

139. Toll, C. H.: Dissociation. Harvard Psych. Studies, vol. 2, pp. 475–482. 1906.

140. Trautscholdt, M.: Experimentelle Untersuchungen über die Assoziation der Vorstellungen. Phil. Stud., Bd. 1, S. 213–250. 1883.

141. Urbantschitsch, V.: Ueber subjektive-optische Anschauungsbilder. Leipzig und Wien, 1907.

142. Vaschide, N.: Sur la localisation des souvenirs. Ann. psych., t. 3, pp. 199–224. 1896.

143. Warren, H. C., and Shaw, W. J.: Further Experiments on Memory for Square Size. Psych. Rev., vol. 2, pp. 239–244. 1895.

144. Washburn, M. F.: A Factor in Mental Development. Phil. Rev., vol. 13, pp. 622–626. 1904.

145. Washburn, M. F.: The Physiological Basis of Relational Processes. Psych. Bull., vol. 6, pp. 369–378. 1909.

146. Washburn, M. F.: The Function of Incipient Motor Processes. Psych. Rev., vol. 21, pp. 376–390. 1914.

147. Watson, J. B.: Behavior: An Introduction to Comparative Psychology. New York, 1914.

148. Watt, H. J.: Experimentelle Beiträge zu einer Theorie des Denkens. Arch. f. d. ges. Psych., Bd. 4, S. 289–436. 1905.

149. Weber, J.: Untersuchungen zur Psychologie des Gedächtnisses. Zeit f. exp. Päd., Bd. 8, S. 1–81. 1905.

150. Wells, F. L.: Some Properties of the Free Association Time. Psych. Rev., vol. 18, pp. 1–24. 1911.

151. Whipple, G. M.: An Analytic Study of the Memory Image and Process of Judgment in the Discrimination of Clangs and Tones. Am. Jour. Psych., vol. 12, pp. 409–457 (1901); vol. 13, pp. 219–368 (1902).

152. Witasek, S.: Beiträge zur Psychologie der Komplexionen. Zeit. f. Psych., Bd. 14, S. 401–435. 1897.

153. Witasek, S.: Ueber Lesen und Rezitieren in ihren Beziehungen zum Gedächtnis. Zeit. f. Psych., Bd. 44, S. 161–185, 246–282. 1907.

154. Wohlgemuth, A.: Simultaneous and Successive Association. Brit. Jour. Psych., vol. 7, pp. 434–453. 1915.

155. Wolfe, K. H.: Untersuchungen über das Tongedächtnis. Phil. Stud., Bd. 3, S. 534–571. 1886.

156. Woods, E. L.: An Experimental Analysis of the Process of Recognizing. Am. Jour. Psych., vol. 26, pp. 313–387. 1915.

157. Woodworth, R. S.: Imageless Thought. Jour. Phil. Psych. and Sci. Meth., vol. 3, pp. 701–707. 1906.

158. Woodworth, R. S.: A Revision of Imageless Thought. Psych. Rev., vol. 22, pp. 1–27. 1915.
159. Wreschner, A.: Die Reproduktion und Assoziation von Vorstellungen. Zeit. f. Psych., Ergänzungsband 3, 1907–9.
160. Wundt, W.: Grundzüge der physiologischen Psychologie. 6te Auflage, 1911.
161. Ziehen, T.: Introduction to the Study of Physiological Psychology. Translated by C. C. van Lieu and O. Beyer. London, 1892.
162. Ziehen, T.: Die Ideenassoziation des Kindes. Sammlung von Abhandlungen aus dem Gebiete der pädogogischen Psychologie, Bd. 1, Heft 6 (1898); Bd. 3, Heft 4 (1900).

INDEXES

INDEX OF SUBJECTS

INDEX OF NAMES

CLASSICS IN PSYCHOLOGY

An Arno Press Collection

Angell, James Rowland. **Psychology:** On Introductory Study of the Structure and Function of Human Consciousness. 4th edition. 1908

Bain, Alexander. **Mental Science.** 1868

Baldwin, James Mark. **Social and Ethical Interpretations in Mental Development.** 2nd edition. 1899

Bechterev, Vladimir Michailovitch. **General Principles of Human Reflexology.** [1932]

Binet, Alfred and Th[éodore] Simon. **The Development of Intelligence in Children.** 1916

Bogardus, Emory S. **Fundamentals of Social Psychology.** 1924

Buytendijk, F. J. J. **The Mind of the Dog.** 1936

Ebbinghaus, Hermann. **Psychology: An Elementary Text-Book.** 1908

Goddard, Henry Herbert. **The Kallikak Family.** 1931

Hobhouse, L[eonard] T. **Mind in Evolution.** 1915

Holt, Edwin B. **The Concept of Consciousness.** 1914

Külpe, Oswald. **Outlines of Psychology.** 1895

Ladd-Franklin, Christine. **Colour and Colour Theories.** 1929

Lectures Delivered at the 20th Anniversary Celebration of Clark University. (Reprinted from *The American Journal of Psychology,* Vol. 21, Nos. 2 and 3). 1910

Lipps, Theodor. **Psychological Studies.** 2nd edition. 1926

Loeb, Jacques. **Comparative Physiology of the Brain and Comparative Psychology.** 1900

Lotze, Hermann. **Outlines of Psychology.** [1885]

McDougall, William. **The Group Mind.** 2nd edition. 1920

Meier, Norman C., editor. **Studies in the Psychology of Art: Volume III.** 1939

Morgan, C. Lloyd. **Habit and Instinct.** 1896

Münsterberg, Hugo. **Psychology and Industrial Efficiency.** 1913

Murchison, Carl, editor. **Psychologies of 1930.** 1930

Piéron, Henri. **Thought and the Brain.** 1927

Pillsbury, W[alter] B[owers]. **Attention.** 1908

[Poffenberger, A. T., editor]. **James McKeen Cattell:** Man of Science. 1947

Preyer, W[illiam] **The Mind of the Child:** Parts I and II. 1890/1889

The Psychology of Skill: Three Studies. 1973

Reymert, Martin L., editor. **Feelings and Emotions:** The Wittenberg Symposium. 1928

Ribot, Th[éodule Armand]. **Essay on the Creative Imagination.** 1906

Roback, A[braham] A[aron]. **The Psychology of Character.** 1927

I. M. Sechenov: Biographical Sketch and Essays. (Reprinted from *Selected Works* by I. Sechenov). 1935

Sherrington, Charles. **The Integrative Action of the Nervous System.** 2nd edition. 1947

Spearman, C[harles]. **The Nature of 'Intelligence' and the Principles of Cognition.** 1923

Thorndike, Edward L. **Education:** A First Book. 1912

Thorndike, Edward L., E. O. Bregman, M. V. Cobb, et al. **The Measurement of Intelligence.** [1927]

Titchener, Edward Bradford. **Lectures on the Elementary Psychology of Feeling and Attention.** 1908

Titchener, Edward Bradford. **Lectures on the Experimental Psychology of the Thought-Processes.** 1909

Washburn, Margaret Floy. **Movement and Mental Imagery.** 1916

Whipple, Guy Montrose. **Manual of Mental and Physical Tests:** Parts I and II. 2nd edition. 1914/1915

Woodworth, Robert Sessions. **Dynamic Psychology.** 1918

Wundt, Wilhelm. **An Introduction to Psychology.** 1912

Yerkes, Robert M. **The Dancing Mouse** and **The Mind of a Gorilla.** 1907/1926